The Battle

The Battle

PAUL O'CONNELL

with Alan English

PENGUIN

IRELAND

PENGUIN IRELAND

UK | USA | Canada | Ireland | Australia
India | New Zealand | South Africa

Penguin Ireland is part of the Penguin Random House group of companies
whose addresses can be found at global.penguinrandomhouse.com.

First published 2016
001

Copyright © Paul O'Connell, 2016

The moral right of the author has been asserted

Set in 13.5/16 pt Garamond MT Std
Typeset by Jouve (UK), Milton Keynes
Printed in Great Britain by Clays Ltd, St Ives plc

A CIP catalogue record for this book is available from the British Library

ISBN: 978–1–844–88223–6

www.greenpenguin.co.uk

To Emily, Paddy and Lola,
and my parents, Michael and Shelagh

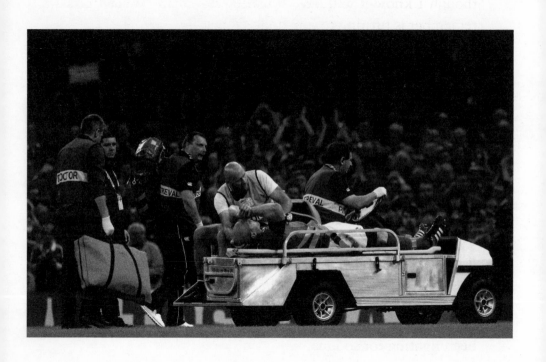

Prologue

With twenty minutes to go in the Heineken Cup semi-final in 2006, Jerry Flannery came up to me. I was twenty-six years old, injury-free and in my prime. I don't recall what he said, though I know it will have finished with 'man'. What I do remember is turning to him and saying:

'I'm so fit it's unbelievable!'

He walked away. He had no interest in listening to me praising myself.

For the rest of my career I never forgot how good I'd felt that day, the physical shape I was in, and I was always chasing that feeling. That game was like a reference point for me, and occasionally I got myself back there, but it didn't happen as often as I'd have liked.

In my thirties, when the injury toll mounted, I kept asking myself, *When is the moment going to happen when all this extra training that I'm doing pays off? Am I ever going to feel amazing on the pitch again?*

And then, in the middle of my fourth World Cup, I started thinking that maybe I'd finally won it – the battle that I'd been fighting for so long.

It was a mental battle as well as a physical one. It was always about trying to get the best out of myself, and my team. I found it tough, at times, but the challenges rugby threw at me were a big part of why I loved it.

Most of the success I had with Munster came in the first half of my career, when things seemed easier, but there was just as much satisfaction in the years when we weren't as strong and had to dig a lot deeper. What mattered was that we were trying as hard as we could to be our best.

During those latter years I suffered more than my share of injuries and they brought me some low moments, but I was able to see them as just another part of the battle. I was almost thirty-six when the 2015 World Cup came around, and I thought I was going to defy my age and the state my body was in after fourteen seasons as a professional. It even felt like I was going to defy my own mind, in a way, because there were times when I didn't think I could get there, no matter how hard I tried.

Nine months before that World Cup, I had felt like retiring. It was a thought I tried to chase away almost as quickly as it came into my head, but it wasn't the first time I'd had to overcome it. Munster had lost to Saracens in the Champions Cup, and we were poor, really poor. I was the player with all the international caps and the Lions tours. More than anyone, I needed to turn up – and I didn't.

On the plane home from London, Peter O'Mahony was asleep alongside me in the emergency exit row. I was trying to read my book, but the match kept flashing into my mind. I was putting the book down and leaning my head up against the seat in front. There was a sticker on the back of it – advice for an emergency landing. I'll never look at one of those stickers again without thinking of that journey home.

I just can't get there. I'm doing everything, but I just can't get back there.

Imagine if I play like that in the Six Nations!

Could I pull out of the tournament?

I can't pull out of the Six Nations – it would cause consternation!

I should have retired after the Lions tour.

Could I retire now?

I can't retire. People would think there's something wrong with me.

But how can I captain Ireland in this form?

Maybe I could get out of the captaincy. I could focus on my own job and row in behind whoever gets it.

No, I can't give up the captaincy now – the first game is three weeks away.

I could play the Six Nations, win it and then retire in May.

I could say the World Cup is a bridge too far – with my injury profile, people would understand.

I can't wait to spend the day with Emily and the kids tomorrow.

Where are Munster going?

Crazy internal conversations like that were nothing new for me after a loss. The longing to retire was something that hit me from time to time. But even in my demoralized state, I knew that quitting rugby, or even just giving up the Ireland captaincy, wasn't an option. It wasn't something I was ever going to do.

You know you're not gonna do this – so stop talking shit and go back to your book.

It took three or four days, but I got over the disappointment. I told myself I just needed a run of games. And then things started to turn.

Ireland won the Six Nations. I captained the team, played all the games and did well. Over the summer, in the World Cup training camp, I stayed injury-free and took part in every session.

On Saturdays, back in Limerick, I went training with Flannery. It was just the two of us, competing hard against each other on rowing machines and treadmills, and on the pitch. He was more than three years retired by then but still very fit. Taking him on, doing those extras, made me feel like I was doing what was required to get to where I wanted to be. The killer was that I never beat him once. He was ten kilos lighter than his playing weight, which was light at the best of times, but he was so fit he was a benchmark for me: to be where I wanted to be, I needed to be beating him. And I couldn't.

My big thing all year was that I wanted to arrive at the World Cup in the best shape of my life. That was first prize. If I couldn't manage that, second prize was getting there in the best shape I could be in, given all the injuries I'd had. I ended up with second prize, but I was OK with that. I came to terms with it, because I knew my fitness would be there when I needed it.

In my hotel room at the Hilton in Cardiff, on the night before we played France in the last game of the World Cup group stage, I allowed myself to think it was all going to come together for me: all the mental torture I'd put myself through, all the arguments, the discipline, the eating well, the early nights and the endless analysis.

I'd spoken to the players earlier about what was coming. Technically, we were miles ahead of anywhere we'd been before during my time playing international rugby, but I asked the question: from an emotion and passion point of view, where would we rank among the Irish teams that came before us?

'I don't think we'd rank highly at the moment,' I said. 'We need to combine the two.'

Our character needed to be on show for everyone to see – including the French players. I wanted my family to say to me, when it was over: 'You seemed to be in the zone. You looked like you were in a different place.'

Getting my mental preparation right was a big part of the journey I'd been on for most of my career. Being able to get through that week without too much stress made me feel like I was finally on top of it. As a captain, it's easier to focus on where the team needs to be when you're not full of anxiety yourself.

When I first started feeling nervous before games, I tried to banish the doubts, drive them out, insult myself for having them. If I didn't think I'd been playing well enough, I'd practically abuse myself before the next game. Sitting in the bus on the way to a Munster match once, I wrote in my notebook:

Axel has lost respect for you.

I went on to the pitch with a massive desire to be a stand-out player, so that Anthony Foley would think more of me. Later on, I was told by a sports psychologist that being so negative about myself was the exact opposite of what I should have been doing, and that successful people were all about positivity.

But it worked for me, at least for a while. I wasn't into positive thinking in 2006, the year I had probably the best season of my career, the only time I made the shortlist for IRB World Player of the Year. I had no time for sports psychology back then – I thought it was all nonsense. The way I saw it, either I had done the work or I hadn't; either I was good enough or I wasn't. In some ways I still believe that, but I came to accept that I could get more out of myself by embracing the psychology that goes into peak performance, because it put me in a better place.

I had to embrace something. I couldn't stay the way I was and keep playing. There were times when I hated the build-up to a big game so much, I couldn't get through the week without feeling like I wanted to retire, and the sooner the better. It was such a strange place to be in: to absolutely love what you're doing and enjoy the company of the people you're doing it with, to have a home life that brings you contentment, but then to get these feelings in the pit of your stomach around big games that made you want to get into a car, drive to the airport and leave the country.

I remember looking out the window of the team bus on the way to a game and seeing supporters knocking back beers on the street, already enjoying their day. And I thought: *I'd love to be out there with them, looking forward to the game and not dreading it.*

At the time, I thought the stress I put myself through made me perform better in games, and in some ways it did. That stress never really went away, but I worked hard at figuring it out, and it got easier.

Throughout my career I had spent most of my time in camp thinking about rugby, engulfed in the game, jumping in and out of the analysis room – twenty minutes here, ten minutes there, back in again whenever something else came into my head. There was no end to it. By the time we played France in the World Cup I was planning my preparation for the week, rather than leaving it open-ended. And when it came to the morning of the game, I was in a great place.

For nearly forty minutes against France, I was feeling really good. We were getting on top of them – we knew it and they must have felt it. My ball carrying was coming back. It came into my head that I'd be stronger in the second half.

And then, on 39.42, I got pulled out of the ring.

The clock was in red at the end of the first half when I went to poach. My foot got stuck in the ground. I could feel my hamstring tendon stretch to breaking point and pop. There was a searing pain as it ripped off the bone.

I hit the ground. Play moved on. For some reason I thought of Eoin Reddan. A few years ago, Redser broke his ankle in the last minute of a game against France and tried to get back into the defensive line. Then I got a flashback to Lawrence Dallaglio breaking his ankle in the first game of the 2005 Lions tour, against Bay of Plenty. It was just a memory from nowhere, and I don't know why things like that come into your head, but I started thinking: *This is just a hamstring injury. I haven't broken anything – I can surely get back up.*

So I tried, but it was too painful.

The medics came on. They were talking about bringing on a stretcher.

I said: 'I don't need a stretcher. Just get me up and help me off the pitch.'

I didn't want Emily, or my parents, to have to see me going off on a stretcher. I thought that Paddy, my son, would be watching it at home and maybe he'd get upset too.

They got me back on my feet, but I went straight down again. I'd ruptured my tendon, but it was the sciatic nerve that was causing the worst of the pain.

The stretcher came on and they gave me oxygen. I knew my Ireland career was over. I thought my move to Toulon, after the tournament, was gone too. I was sucking hard on the oxygen and I started getting emotional. I thought of Emily and the house we'd picked in Toulon, a really nice place by the sea, with a pool. I knew how much she was looking forward to a new experience, and I was sad for her. I put my arm over my eyes because I didn't want people to see I was upset.

Eanna Falvey, the Ireland doctor, was reassuring me all the time.

'You're going to be OK . . . Keep taking the gas.'

He was alongside me on the motorized stretcher as it started moving off the pitch. He said: 'You need to put your hand up in the air when the camera comes on you – so that Emily knows you're OK.'

I was lying flat on the stretcher and I couldn't see what was happening around me. After a few seconds, Eanna said: '*Now* – put your hand up.'

I gave the thumbs-up. Before I got off the pitch, he said the camera was back on me.

'Do it again.'

I didn't like doing it the first time, even though I knew he was right to suggest it.

'No.'

'I'm only saying this for Emily.'

'No.'

Under the stand I was shipped on to the bed, still in a lot of pain. They gave me two Co-codamol tablets. I was thinking, *Christ – you'd give a child that for a headache*.

They moved me into the medical room and after a few minutes Emily arrived. She was crying.

The first thing I said to her was, 'Sorry about Toulon – it doesn't look like it's going to happen now.'

'Don't be silly,' she said.

I asked her to ring Paddy. He was back at home with Emily's parents, and I was worried he'd be upset, but he was too young to really grasp it.

He came on the phone and I told him I had to go off because my hip was sore.

'How's your hip?' he asked me.

'My hip is fine,' I said.

My dad arrived ten minutes later and gave me a big hug. He called my brothers, Justin and Marcus, and when I spoke to them they were both in tears. We're a very close family and I suppose they were thinking, like I was myself, that this was how it had ended for me.

Soon, Peter O'Mahony arrived in the medical room, another casualty of the hard, attritional game we knew we'd get from the French. There was a TV on and we watched Ireland getting more and more on top. It was brilliant to see.

At full time I was brought into the changing room in a wheelchair. They lifted me off it and I was just about able to sit down at my place before the players came in. I was glad to be able to share that moment with them, because they are the moments you fight for and they're really what sport is all about. That feeling of being able to sit back and relax when you've produced the goods, knowing that it's done and the pressure is off, that's what makes sense of everything you put yourself through.

Later on, at Cardiff hospital, I was given morphine, and the texts were flooding through on my phone. I replied to some. I didn't know what the future held for me and there was nothing I could do about it anyway, so I just said: 'It's life.'

During the tournament, our defence coach, Les Kiss, talked about the Spartans. He said they were told before they went into battle to come back with their shield, or on it. And he said – joking, but still making his point: 'That's the attitude we need in our defenders – you finish the game with your shield, or on it.'

When I got back to the team hotel from Cardiff hospital the following afternoon, Les came over to me. He's a really deep thinker, and a good guy.

He said, 'Do you remember what I was saying about the Spartans?'

'Yeah, I do.'

'Well, it was never going to be any other way with you. It was going to be on your shield – or in your case, a stretcher.'

I know it was kind of cheesy, but twenty-four hours after the injury it gave me a little lift.

Three days later, I was at the Princess Grace Hospital in London for surgery. Lying on the operating table, I told the anaesthetist to let me know when he was giving me the stuff that knocks you out.

I've had a general anaesthetic for a lot of operations and I always like to fight against going to sleep. It's a nice feeling – battling it, knowing you don't stand a chance.

I knew the stuff was working when the guy started asking me stupid questions.

'How did you get down here?'

'How d'you mean?'

'Did you get down on a trolley?'

'Yeah, you know I did.'

Then I felt myself fading away.

PART ONE

I

I remember having no doubt, no stress, only certainty.

I was eight years old and waiting to be called on to the starting blocks for a gala swim final. Further up the pool deck I saw one of my rivals, Fergal Landy, sitting on his mother's knee. When he got up and wandered off somewhere I walked over to his mother. She didn't have a clue who I was.

I pointed at Fergal Landy.

'Excuse me, is that your son?'

'That's right, yes. Fergal.'

'He's racing me in my next final.'

'Is he?'

'He is, yah.'

'Is it under-nines front crawl?' she asked, gently.

'Yah.'

'Oh, he must be so.'

'Well, I'm going to beat him.'

I gave her this news like I was telling her the time. I suppose I just thought: she's his mother, she might as well know. Later in life, I would sometimes find that kind of self-belief hard to recapture. In professional sport, I saw what self-confidence did for the rare guys in rugby who had it in spades. And it pisses me off, just thinking about it.

In one way I was made for swimming, being taller and stronger than most of the boys I was up against. But being big and strong wasn't enough. Swimming was the sport that gave me the competitive instincts and the work ethic that came out in rugby, years later.

I loved the hard training that swimming demanded – more hours in the week than I was ever asked to put in as a professional rugby player. At twelve I was spending fifteen hours a week in the pool. I loved the fact that I could make myself good at something just by working at it. John Dempsey coached me, and later Gerry Ryan. If they'd told me to swim a thousand lengths without stopping, I'd have tried. When my mother worked that out, she found other uses for their influence on me.

'Paul, it's very important to put your towel on top of the radiator when you get home, OK?'

'OK, John.'

'Paul, I want you eating more vegetables to be big and strong for swimming, all right?'

'Yes, Gerry.'

I loved the racing and the competitiveness, the digging deep and the winning. I loved it that every training session was a race. You went off five seconds behind someone and five seconds ahead of someone, and every time you turned at the wall you could see if you were widening the gap on the boy behind you and gaining on the boy in front.

For every final in my own age group I was up on the block

in lane three, which meant I'd qualified with the fastest time. I looked left and right and I knew all the guys up against me – and I just knew they couldn't beat me. There were races when I gave myself way too much to do by hanging back and not giving it everything until it was nearly too late – but I always found a way to win.

At a gala in Dublin, after I'd won all my races, a nice man from a local radio station in Waterford who had a big interest in junior swimming came over to interview me. He asked me what I'd like to achieve in the future.

'I want to win seven gold medals at the Olympics,' I said.

'Seven gold medals! Why seven?'

'Because that's what Mark Spitz did.'

(I knew my stuff: I did a project on Mark Spitz at school.)

'Well now, Paul,' the interviewer said, 'we've a lovely swimmer coming up here called Gary Brennan. He's coming after you!'

I shook my head.

'He won't beat you?'

'Nah. He won't beat me.'

'He does thirty-three seconds for the fifty-metre front crawl.'

I shook my head again. My PB was thirty-one seconds.

'Nah,' I said. 'Nah.'

Whatever it took to keep me ahead of Gary Brennan, and anyone else coming after me, I was more than prepared to do. The kids who had dreams of making the Olympics all trained for three mornings during the week, before school started. This was on top of the seven sessions in the evenings and at weekends. The first time I asked if I could join them I was ten. The coaches said I was too young. So I begged them, and they gave in.

My dad promised he'd have me at the St Enda's pool for

ten to six, no problem. On the first morning, I set the alarm clock for 5.20 a.m. It felt like the middle of the night when it went off, but I dragged myself out of the bed and gave Dad a shake.

'Dad – it's twenty past.'

'OK – that's grand now.'

Straight away he headed for the bathroom to shave. Even if the birds haven't woken up outside, my father will not face the world without being clean-shaven.

I walked to my room to get dressed, but I felt exhausted. I headed back to the bathroom.

'Dad, I'm not going to go. I'm too tired.'

'That's fine, Paul,' he said. 'That's no problem.'

We went back to our beds, but straight away my head started churning.

You weren't tough enough to do it.

You're not a hard trainer.

I started imagining Dad at the dinner table with Mam later that night, telling her I wasn't able to get up for training, the two of them having a little laugh about it.

'I was up out of bed and all! Tells me he doesn't want to go – and I half shaved!'

And then I started to think: *What if I DO get up?*

Another scenario came into my head, the same as the first, only this time Dad had different lines.

'In fairness to him, he got up the first time and said he couldn't do it – but then he came back in to me.'

I got out of bed again and gave him another shake.

'Come on, Dad, we're going.'

After that, I began arriving at school in the mornings with the smell of chlorine off me, feeling good that I'd been swimming for two hours while everyone else was in bed. In my head, I was convinced that swimming had given me status in the school. I imagined the teachers thinking, *He's a serious swimmer, that young fella.*

Dad was never one of those obsessive fathers who put pressure on their children and mess up their heads. He never made me feel like I *had* to win – he just believed that I would. When you're young, that's a massive thing to have in your armoury.

When I was nine I entered an angling competition out in Foynes. It was a very cold day, miserable weather for fishing. I barely knew the first thing about it, but somehow – sheer fluke – a flounder jumped on to my line and I reeled it in.

It turned out nobody else caught a thing. After they handed me my prize – a fishing tackle box – I called Dad from a payphone in the village.

'Dad – I won!'

His first instinct was to tell the world, or at least the only other person in it who cared.

'Shelagh! He's after winning that fishing competition! Didn't I tell you?'

When he came out to collect me he kind of chuckled.

'It's funny, Paul – I just had a feeling you'd win it.'

And I remember sitting alongside him in the front seat of his car as we drove home, thinking: *I'm someone who wins things. If Dad thinks I'm good, then I must be.*

It's strange, the way things said decades ago stick in your head, the way a few words you hear as an impressionable child can stay with you for the rest of your life and maybe even make a difference to your character. Around the same time, on a day when I knew my mother would be a little late collecting me from school, I walked up to the principal, Mac Uí Ríain, and asked him if I could go back to the classroom, unsupervised, to do my homework. There was a rule at An Mhodhscoil which said that pupils weren't allowed back in the building after school was finished. But Mac Uí Ríain looked me straight in the eye and jabbed his index finger at my face.

'You can because I trust you,' he said. 'I trust you with my life.'

You can get lucky and spend your childhood trying to live up to a positive image that somebody has of you. And the kids who keep getting told they're good for nothing, maybe they go the other way.

Our house was a bungalow at the crest of a hill on a quiet country road, four miles from the city. If you go to the bottom left corner of the back garden now, you can see the Thomond Park stands in the distance, but when we were growing up we'd barely heard of the place.

The family moved out to Drombanna before I was born. It was a few weeks after Marcus came along to join my older

brother, Justin, who was five then. Mam and Dad wanted more space for their kids to play. In the summertime, out in the back garden, we played every game under the sun. I'm not sure I'd ever have made it in professional sport if we hadn't had those days. I remember being at birthday parties, and it seemed to us like every other kid in Limerick had a Super Nintendo or a Commodore 64. We were playing non-stop sport so we were never too bothered.

Throughout our childhood, Mam was always on the go, always busy with something. Every day she showed us the meaning of hard work. She could work a full day in her own bookkeeping service, run the house and feed us like kings without breaking a sweat. She brought us all over Limerick in her Renault 4, which looked like a postman's van, and Marcus made her drop us well away from school because he reckoned her car was a crock and he didn't want to be seen anywhere near it. He had a reputation to uphold.

Saturday morning was the only time of the week when she

wasn't there to put food on the table for us. Every week she drove to the market in the city and bought her potatoes and vegetables from the same guy, and her fruit from the same guy – always the same routine and the best of food. She wouldn't let the rest of us come with her because it was her morning and she knew we'd only drive her mad, especially Dad.

They had met in the summer of 1966 at the Seapoint Ballroom in Salthill, around the time when England's soccer team were winning the World Cup. Back then Mam was Shelagh Quilty, the oldest daughter of Johnjo and Moira from a farm in Donoman, Croom, County Limerick. Dad was from Ballinlough in Cork. He worked for Dunlops and played rugby for Sunday's Well.

That night he wound up in the Seapoint after a few pints with some lads up for the Galway Races. There were more than two thousand people in the dancehall – it was one of those ballrooms of romance where the fellas stood on one side and the girls on the other. My dad is such a good dresser he'd wear a shirt and tie pulling up weeds in the garden, so I'd say he was looking fierce when he walked across the floor and asked Mam if she'd dance.

It went on from there. The first chance he got, Dad moved up to Limerick. He made another good decision at the same time – he joined Young Munster. He played in the second row and they say he was a tough man.

At home, Justin invented games for us. He got Dad to move the car and we'd hit a tennis ball up on to our roof, running this way and that as it bounced back down off the ridged tiles at different angles. When my son Paddy is at the house now, he loves chasing after a tennis ball that Dad has thrown on to the roof.

Sometimes it was just the three of us playing – Justin, Marcus and me. Other times, the neighbours joined in: the Clancys and the O'Neills, the Shanahans and the Flynns. Me and Marcus were members of the Daredevils gang. Our clubhouse was in the back garden, beside the garage. The rival gang down the road was led by Dave Clancy and called Crait – which stood for something I can no longer remember.

We converted the attic to a bedroom for Justin when our family of five became six and I got a new sister, sort of. Mary, who has Down syndrome, is my dad's youngest sister. She slept in the single bed next to mine that Marcus vacated when he moved into Justin's old room. She used to love watching Gay Byrne on *The Late Late Show* and she'd be in front of the TV around nine o'clock, twenty minutes early, in her dressing gown and slippers, with her handbag by her side. Every week I used to put on my own dressing gown and slippers and watch it alongside her. In wintertime we'd pull the couch away from the wall and as close to the fire as we could, and I'd tell her Gay Byrne could see her through the TV screen.

Mary and I are still very tight. A week before our wedding in the south of France, Emily and I had a registry office ceremony in Limerick. There were only twelve people there, and Mary had her arms around us when we were putting the rings on each other. She had her own bouquet and she threw it over her head at the end.

Dad played golf once or twice a year. His black leather bag was shoved into the corner in the back kitchen, where we kept the washing machine and the wellies and the runners. He had Johnny Miller irons, a couple of battered woods and a Spalding Touring Pro putter.

Every time I looked at his bag I thought real golf would never happen for me because hanging from the side was a yellow tag which read 'Charleville Golf Club, Green Fee Paid, £7'. I couldn't believe it cost so much to play one round. But there was something exciting about it too, how expensive it was.

Our house was on a half-acre and I designed my own golf course in the back garden. I cut my green as tight as the lawnmower could make it and moved the guinea pigs' hutch around it so that, like miniature sheep, they chewed all around them until the grass couldn't get any shorter. For one hole, I teed off in the next-door neighbour's garden; for another, I had to hop over a five-foot wall and stamp down the high grass in the field behind us.

When Wimbledon was on we played tennis with wooden bats from the beach. We mowed the lawn so that the short grass was in and the long grass out. All me and Marcus wanted to do was dive across the court in our shorts and play a winner like Boris Becker, a little drop shot that just made it over the net. Or, in our case, over the timber pallets.

We played basketball in the front garden, football and hurling for South Liberties and, when Stephen Roche and Sean Kelly were racing in the Tour de France, we had our own bike circuit with a massive climb at the end. No matter what the sport was, I wanted to be better at it than Marcus.

He was a year and nine months older than me and was talented at every game he played. I had to try unbelievably hard to get near him. The way I competed was by doing the simple things right; the fancy stuff I left to him. I never had anything like his talent for basketball, but when he was always trying to shoot spectacular three-pointers, I concentrated on perfecting my lay-up. Marcus gave out that all my scores were boring, but for me it was all about finding a way to win and to beat someone better than me.

Justin used to run indoor golf tournaments – the Masters, the British Open, the Irish Open. He designed the courses and acted as referee. He put cups down for the holes, and pillows were our bunkers. Then he wrote down the scores at every hole and gave a running commentary.

The Irish Open was the first tournament I had a chance of winning. I was a shot clear of Marcus; all I needed was a par to close it out.

'And Paul O'Connell leads with one hole left to play!' Justin said, Peter Alliss style.

The eighteenth was a par five, from the dining room out through the kitchen, into the hall and straight down the corridor where our bedrooms were. The hardest part was trying to control your ball on the kitchen lino, which was bubbled and warped, or judging how hard to hit it through the doorway so that it didn't roll up the saddle, stop and roll back. To get back out to the hallway you had to whack it hard off the skirting board, and then it was straight down to the cup – but not too hard because if you missed you had to waste a shot by playing backwards, and not too easy because there were lumps and bumps all over the carpet and your ball could wobble off course if it was struck too gently.

My ball was two feet from the hole. According to the rules I was allowed to tilt the cup, move it sideways so that the ball was straight in front, and the shot almost unmissable. I can remember the moment so clearly that I know what I was wearing, as I stood there: a blue dressing gown over my pyjamas.

Maybe the pressure got to me: my ball hit the rim of the cup and rolled away to the side.

I didn't wait for Justin's commentary, or look across to see the joy on Marcus's face. I ran to the bathroom, locked the door behind me, threw myself on to the floor and burst into tears.

Now that I think about it, I should have been in a play-off.

*

Gary Brennan came after me all right. It took him three or four years, but after he beat me in a heat down in Tralee I was never the same swimmer again.

For most of the race I did what I'd been doing for years: I cruised along just behind the guy in front, thinking I could just zoom ahead in the last twenty-five metres. But when I upped the tempo, he didn't come back to me and I was beaten to the touch.

I was disgusted with myself. It was my first defeat by a boy in the same age bracket. At this stage my coach was Gerry Ryan. When I climbed out of the pool he was standing half-way down the deck, in front of our club flag, holding a stopwatch.

'Were you going a bit easy there?' he asked me.

'I was, yah.'

'You'll be OK for the final so?'

'I will – I'm kind of happy he beat me.'

I was a long way from being happy, but that's what came out. Maybe I was trying to convince Gerry – and myself – that nothing was wrong.

Up on the blocks next to Gary Brennan for the final, I felt my body tense with a new emotion: it was the fear of defeat, of failure. I gave it everything I had for every single stroke until I touched the wall. I won by three seconds – but things had changed, and it wasn't long before I knew it for definite.

At a gala in Galway, I made the final of the 100-metre backstroke in lane one, which made me the fourth fastest qualifier. Worse, not all of the big names from Dublin were competing – I knew, because I could list off every one of them and tell you what their best time was.

I sat on a wooden bench with the other swimmers in my final, waiting for the race, beating myself up.

Crikey, I'm really slipping.

I mustn't be training hard enough.

In the backstroke you launch yourself in an arc off the pool wall and land face up. In lane one, you've got waves of water coming back against you off the side of the pool. You're on the outside, expected to make up the numbers.

Even before we hit the water, I was a foot in front. With twenty-five metres left, I was leading by a metre and a half. I could see my clubmate, Paul Blake, walking down the pool beside my lane, just strolling along casually.

He started moving his right arm back and forth nonchalantly, as if he was saying: 'That's it, keep it going, you're getting there.' And I was looking up at Paul Blake and resenting how casual he was.

You don't understand how great a performance this is!

Don't you realize? I'm in lane one and I'm murdering them here!

I touched for the win and looked around me. Everyone was sitting down, like nothing had happened – and then I caught sight of Gerry Ryan and Corrie Ward and two other parents from our club. The four of them were on their feet, clapping and pumping their fists.

And I thought, *Yes! I'm still good.*

Turned out, it was only a temporary reprieve. Next came the ultimate humiliation: beaten by a boy from my own club.

For years I'd been better than Ronan De Hooge. First he passed me in the butterfly, next the front crawl. And then, on the day in Cork when I smashed my 100-metre back crawl PB by a second and a half, with my heart rate going through the roof, he beat me again. I had no excuses, nothing to fall back on. I'd given it everything – and he was still better.

I'm not sure that I ever loved swimming for itself. I was good and I was winning: that's what did it for me. All the medals I won are in a plastic bag in the attic at home and I saw them again recently, for the first time in twenty years.

When I went through them with Paddy and Dad, I recognized the big medals and remembered how they'd been won.

At fourteen or fifteen, other sports were beginning to turn my head, first golf and then rugby. I felt it was time to move on.

I broke the news to Dad, who had made thousands of journeys to swimming pools far and near, who had hung around from morning till night to support me at countless galas, who had risen from his bed without complaint early morning after early morning, and – who knows? – maybe dreamed a little himself too, of what I might achieve as a swimmer one day. I told him I wanted a break from it. I'm sure he knew full well that the break would almost certainly be permanent.

He said, 'That's no problem, Paul.'

He told me that, if my mind was made up, I had to let Gerry Ryan know myself – and tell him to his face. He drove me to St Enda's and when I saw Gerry my lips started quivering and I couldn't stop the tears.

'I just want to take a break for a while,' I told him.

He said it was fine, absolutely fine. He told me I could go back whenever I liked.

And I nodded, but I knew it was over.

2

A few years ago, I went to see Young Munster take on Shannon at Thomond Park in the All Ireland League. I was there with my dad and Dan Mooney, a friend of his from way back – they played together with the Cookies in the '70s. With around ten minutes to go, Munsters were 22–3 ahead. They had three tries scored. When they were awarded a kickable penalty, left of the posts, I thought the decision was easy.

'They should kick this to the corner and go for the bonus point,' I said.

Dan wasn't having any of it. 'They should not! They should kick it over the fucking bar!' he said.

'What about the bonus point?' I asked.

'Fuck the bonus point.'

The game was already won. I couldn't understand his reasoning.

'I don't think we're going to lose this one, Dan.'

'I know that, but I want the points on the scoreboard,' he said. 'You don't know about this fixture, youngfella! I want the points! I want to give them a hiding.'

It ended 36–3: a fair hiding. People started heading for the Shannon clubhouse, just inside the main gates.

'Are you going in for a pint?' Dad asked Dan.

'No way am I going in there,' he said.

There was silence for a few seconds, broken by Dan.

'Are you going in yourself?'

'I wouldn't mind a pint,' Dad said.

'I'll go in with you, so.'

In we went and Dan called a round.

When he came back with the drinks, he said: 'In forty years coming here, that's the first time I've ever been served straight away at that bar.'

He told us he was used to standing there forever in his Young Munster tie, at the front of the queue, watching the pints passing over his head to the Shannon members.

Later on, in town, we had a few more at the Still House. Miko Benson was in there and Dan started telling stories about the time Miko was playing for the Young Munster junior team.

'You knew when he'd been dropped,' he said. 'You'd arrive for the start of training and the stones under Miko's wheels were spinning as he pulled out of the car park.'

Miko put his pint down and pulled up the sleeves of his shirt, ready to have a go back. And I could have stayed there all night, listening to those guys.

A few months later, the club had a party to celebrate the twentieth anniversary of the greatest achievement in Young Munster's history, the winning of the All Ireland League at Lansdowne Road in 1993, before the biggest crowd ever to watch a club game in Ireland. Munsters had an unbelievable pack of forwards. I was thirteen then. In a lot of ways, I wish I could have been part of that team, even though their best days came before the game went professional and only one of them – Peter Clohessy – went on to make a living from rugby. You make the best out of the hand you're dealt, and that team will be remembered forever in our club.

I was invited to the reunion. It was a hilarious night, like something out of *Father Ted*, and that was the beauty of it. They presented a plaque to Dave McHugh, the referee who sent off the St Mary's College Number 8, Brent Pope, in the final. The plaque said 'Referee of the Century', but it was the kind of trophy you get when you've finished third in a go-karting race in Kilcornan.

There were a million stories told through the night, like the one about how their scrummaging machine was the biggest heap of crap ever built, with pads as thin as floor tiles. 'Imagine, like,' said Ray Ryan, with a totally straight face, 'eight of us, all eighteen or nineteen stone, hitting these pads and they're *that* fucking thick.'

The scrummaging machine had no wheels either, which meant they'd had to drive it through the training-ground mud while the backs stood on the other end of it, because after they'd kicked a few garryowens and run a few lines there wasn't a whole lot else for the backs to do. Or so Ray said, leading up to his punchline.

'We got off the bus at CIYMS, above in Belfast, and the first thing we saw was this brand new, top-of-the-range scrum-maging machine – the Rhinoceros. This fucking thing had massive pads, gears, wheels – the whole lot. When we saw that, we looked at each other. And we said, "We have 'em."'

I couldn't stop laughing that night, because the mentality was so different to what I was used to as a professional. The more stories I heard, the more I wished I'd been part of it all.

Back in 1993, a lot of people said the winning of the league was when Francis Brosnahan scored a try in the last few minutes away from home against the leaders, Cork Constitution.

'Lads,' I told some of the pack, 'I watched a video of that match against Con. Ye were pummelling their line with one-out runners, non-stop. And eventually – *eventually* – ye passed a bad ball out to the backs. Three loopy, brutal passes – and Brossy ran in under the posts.'

'I was the one who told Ger to flash it,' Declan Edwards said, claiming the credit twenty years later and deadly serious about it.

I told him they could have scored a try about ten phases earlier, if the ball had been let out. And Ray Ryan looked at me, the same way Dan Mooney had that day at Thomond Park – like I just didn't get it.

'You don't understand! You don't understand!' he said. 'We wanted to *kill* them!'

He was wrong about that, Ray. I did understand. Or at least, I had a fair idea.

Dad thought Ger Earls was something else. He scored an intercept try that day in Dublin, but he was better known for his ball-carrying and his tackling, and for being tough as nails. He was an openside flanker who laid carpets for a living. He scored two tries in a final Irish trial once but never got the call. For people like my father, that was an injustice and a disgrace.

Ger Earls and Peter Clohessy were considered legends by everyone in the club, and the admiration people had for them was mostly down to the physical nature of how they played the game.

Over our kitchen table at home, there were never any stories told about backs (except Serge Blanco) – it was always about forward play and the hard men. Away from rugby, Dad was as mild-mannered as they come, but there was something about the game that brought out a different side to him. He was always giving Justin advice over dinner, especially on the night before a big game. Justin was captain of his school rugby team, St Clement's, from the first day he put on the jersey until the day he left.

'You can't allow a fella to get away with stuff, Justin.'

'Drop the knee. Just let him know you're not going to be messed around.'

'Never take a backward step.'

'An eye for an eye.'

I took it all in, and it stayed with me. Years later, when I started making the Young Munster junior team, I lived by that advice. Dad never changed his mind about the way rugby should be played. He always said that if you went out on to the field and you weren't prepared to take the opposition on physically, it was game over. If they tried to impose themselves on you, and you didn't respond, you had no business being there.

I wasn't much good at the game when Dad first took me and Marcus to the Young Munster seven-a-sides, during the summers when I was seven and eight. I remember feeling distinctly average. It was all about swimming for me then, but during school holidays the following year I tried it again and I was better.

We played across the pitch, just amongst ourselves, kids whose fathers were Young Munster men. In Limerick, you played for your father's club – it was the unwritten rule. Our team was coached by Pat Micks, the father of my friend Trevor. We played with a Mitre ball in the first game I can remember that summer, a detail I can recall because I touched it down twice for tries in a 3–1 win.

I had a good fend, into the face. I was practically punching people. I just thought this was what you did in matches.

When that game was over, an old man walked over to me. His name was Mickey Cross and he was a legend in the club. It was almost the end of summer. The following week, the boys who were serious about the game would be back, wearing black and amber jerseys and playing for the Young Munster Under-10s.

I hadn't really thought about playing rugby into the winter, but Mickey Cross said: 'Well played, youngfella. Training is on Saturday at half-eleven.'

I played for the next two seasons, at out-half in my second year, because you couldn't push in the scrums and the coaches probably thought I could do a bit more damage in open play. I didn't have much of a passing game; mostly I just tried to run over people.

We were a tough team, maybe because plenty of our players came from tough areas in town – Southill, Moyross, Ballinacurra Weston. One of the lads was nicknamed Can O' Beans, after he turned up to training with one hanging out of his pocket. We all slagged him about it. It never occurred to any of us that the can of beans was probably his dinner and it was important that it made it home with him.

One of our best players was Ronan Connery, and one of the things we liked about him was that he had plenty to say for himself. He was great fun; small but incredibly fast and a brilliant tackler. He was always making out that the more fashionable clubs in town were after him. I saw him sitting on a wall one day, talking to the father of one of our players, John 'Bog' McNamara.

'Garryowen were trying to sign me during the week.'

'Go 'way! Were they, Ronan?'

'They had forms out an' all.'

'What did you tell 'em?'

'I told 'em to fuck off out of it!'

'Good man yourself. Fair play!'

At an Under-12s tournament in Bruff, I saw the team from Cork Constitution take off a set of all-black gear and change – for their next game – into all-white. We didn't even have matching shorts or socks – just jerseys that had seen better days. Our coaches, Kieran Kiely and Ollie Delaney, pointed over at them.

'Look at the Cons, lads. Who do they think they are? One set of gear isn't enough for 'em! They're trying to rub yeer noses in it! Are ye going to take that offa them, are ye?'

It was my first experience of the age-old rugby rivalry between Limerick and Cork. Limerick rugby men like Kieran and Ollie never called Cork Constitution by their full name: they were 'the Cons'. As a kid who had never come up against a Cork team, there would have been a part of me that thought the two sets of gear was class. But our coaches wanted us hating them, because Munsters hated the Cons – that's the way it was. Come to think of it, we seemed to hate everyone! And they wanted us to take those feelings on to the pitch.

As it turned out, we didn't get to play them because they qualified for the Cup and we only made it into the Plate. But by the end of the day we didn't care about that because we'd actually won the Plate and we celebrated like it was the World Cup. Kieran Kiely was first on to the minibus home, with the trophy under his arm. I can still remember the look of surprise on the driver's face when he saw it.

'Jaysus! A bit of silverware at last, Kieran!'

' 'Twas a long time coming, Liam!'

Kieran had played on the same Young Munster team as my dad. After training sometimes he'd go on about the state of Irish rugby. He reckoned the selectors were totally biased against the Limerick clubs, and Young Munster in particular. He used to talk to me like I knew loads about rugby.

'Can you believe they're still picking that fella for Ireland?'

Then he'd look at me, like he was expecting me to go, 'Yeah! What a joke!'

But I hardly knew anything about international rugby. I'd never been to Lansdowne Road, because the only games Dad took us to were Young Munster's. And by then I was already thinking I needed to devote myself completely to swimming, because I could feel the competition getting closer.

Before I packed in the rugby, we had a tournament up in Dundalk. We took the train to Heuston Station in Dublin, then went across town to get another train north. Outside Connolly Station, a black car with dark windows pulled up alongside us. Eoin O'Flynn wandered over to see who was inside.

He stared through the tinted back-seat window and shouted: 'It's George Best!'

Some of the lads started knocking on the window, but the chauffeur wouldn't wind it down, until George Best told him to. He signed a pile of autographs and Eoin O'Flynn said he'd never wash his hand again, because George Best shook it.

Up in Dundalk, all the teams in the blitz put sleeping bags down alongside one another in this big gym – except us. We were told to sleep on the floor up above. The coaches took turns to go to the pub, and when Mickey Cross had to look after us he just lay back against the wall and watched as we battered each other with shoes in the dark and sang the theme song to *Bouli the Snowman* for most of the night. In the morning, soldiers from the Irish army cooked us our breakfast and we all surrounded the coaches, full of excitement about representing Young Munster against teams from outside Limerick.

'Am I playing?'

'Am *I*?'

'Am *I*?'

Ollie got me to mark the biggest player on the Dublin team we were drawn against, De La Salle. 'I don't care how big he is!' he said. 'If you get him low, down he'll come!'

Every week we'd been coached to tackle low and hard, and told never to miss your man, but when the moment came the big guy ran right at me and I flinched. He went straight through me and kept going, until John Bog caught him with an unbelievable hand-trip. Back at Limerick railway station, Mickey Cross walked up to him and patted him on the back.

'Tell your mother, now,' he said. 'Tell her you brought down the biggest guy up there.'

I was alongside John Bog, feeling crap that I hadn't done it, because I was the man sent.

In my first year of secondary school at Ardscoil Rís, our geography teacher Des Harty would tell us to close the books and he'd start going on about the Munster Schools Junior Cup and the Senior Cup and the incredible rivalry. He'd coached the school team for years. He was obsessed with rugby and I was dying to let him know that my brother had been one of the best schools players around.

I stuck up my hand once.

'Sir, what's the rule about being cup-tied?'

He'd never seen me on a rugby pitch. He looked at me suspiciously.

'Why are you asking that question? How do you even *know* about that?'

'Oh, I just remember my brother used to always have

problems with being cup-tied when he wanted to play with his club.'

'Your *brother*? Who's your brother?'

'Justin O'Connell.'

'The Clement's guy? The back-row?'

'Yeah.'

'*Are you serious?* He's a fine player! He's a *fabulous* player!'

I knew what was coming next. I was waiting for it.

'Are *you* playing rugby?'

'No, sir. I'm a swimmer.'

He asked again when I was old enough to play in the Junior Cup. I told him I couldn't. Things had moved on. I wasn't swimming any more, but I had a new passion in my life.

'I'm a golfer now,' I said.

The previous summer, the professional at Limerick Golf Club, John Cassidy, had looked me up and down on the driving range.

'Hit a few for me there,' he'd said.

I'd learned my swing from copying the professionals on the TV. I gripped the club the way Dad showed me years before, in the back garden where I made my golf course. He'd told me it was the way Jack Nicklaus did it.

I swung hard and fast, but the ball scuttled along the ground. I made a mess of the next one too and John was straight over to me, grabbing the club out of my hands and making me change my grip. In my second lesson the first three shots I hit were absolute peaches.

John Cassidy nodded.

'Your handicap will tumble down now, it'll *tumble* down,' he said.

Everything I'd put into swimming, I transferred to golf. Everything and more, because it didn't come as easily. There were always guys who were better, who'd been playing for longer.

When the evenings drew in I practised my putting on the carpet at home. I scrunched up sheets of newspaper and wrapped Sellotape around them until they were the size of golf balls and hit them into the curtains. I hung bedsheets on the clothesline with about fifty pegs and put blocks on the bottom to keep them in place while I blasted balls for hours.

When we got multi-channel TV at home, the first thing I thought was, *This is unbelievable, I'm going to be able to watch golf all day!*

I read every article in every golf magazine every month. Every penny I got I spent on golf equipment. My driver was Dad's old wooden club, until I begged Mam to go halves with me on the new Howson Hippo. It was £60 in Gleeson's sports shop on William Street.

'I'll be able to hit the ball miles with this,' I told her, when I got my hands on it.

John Gleeson was head of the juniors. His favourite line was 'Nice guys don't win, lads'. He mentored us and kept on at us: practise, practise, practise. I was playing thirty-six holes a day in summertime. John gave me a book, *The Inner Game of Golf*, but I wasn't ready for sports psychology. All I wanted to read about was how to put backspin on a seven iron, or hone my short game.

Along with David Morris, Niall Gleeson and Paul Burke I was part of the Limerick Golf Club team that won the Munster Junior Foursomes in the summer of 1995. Me and the lads, we thought we were on our way, going places. We all had the same plan: win the South of Ireland, go professional, make the Ryder Cup team.

But not long after that I hit a wall: I couldn't get my

handicap any lower than four. I was never happy with what I was doing; I was always looking for something different in the magazines, something better. I could drive the ball 270 yards down the fairway into position A, but I was getting it there with a high, left-to-right fade and not the pure, low draw I was desperate to play, the kind of shot the pros hit.

Within twelve months of our big win, I knew the truth – I wasn't improving as quickly as I needed to. Not even close. I had hit a wall that I couldn't get over.

Maybe the day I realized I was never going to make it big was at a tournament up in Baltinglass. All the talk was about the hotshot who had just won the Ulster Boys champion-ship. Graeme McDowell was three months older than me, but his golf was on a different planet. I decided to follow him around after I'd missed the cut. As I watched his swing, the first thing that hit me was that I'd never heard that sound before: a golf ball being struck perfectly.

He split fairways with the kind of draw I fantasized about. And then there was the way he walked off the tee after his ball. There was a swagger in his stride, confidence, certainty. Maybe, back when I was ten years old, people could see that in me when I stood on the blocks in a gala swim final, posi-tive that I couldn't be beaten.

At Castletroy, in the Fred Daly Trophy, I was representing the club in singles matchplay when I got the shanks. I stood over the ball and it was like nothing I'd ever felt before on a golf course: the loss of all control.

Dad followed me around, feeling it just as hard as me, which was very hard. The embarrassment ended on the twelfth green: I was beaten 7&6. Dad tried to console me afterwards, but he didn't make out that it was just bad luck or tell me that the next day would be better.

I never made a conscious decision about it. I never said,

'I'm not playing golf any more.' I just started playing less and less, so there was always going to be space for something new.

Driving home that day, Dad spoke quietly and said something that had probably been on his mind for a while.

'Paul, maybe it's time to go back into team sport.'

I'm pretty sure he already had one in mind.

I don't remember telling Des Harty that I was finally interested in playing rugby for the school, or what he said in response, but I can't imagine he thought he was getting a serious player. I was sixteen and I hadn't played for four years.

We trained underneath the windows in the school library; they were our floodlights. I was five inches taller than David Brosnan but I was lifting him in the lineout because my jumping technique was all wrong. Slowly, though, I started finding my way: making tackles, looking for work, carrying a bit of ball. I was running straight at people, seeking out collisions. In my first year of Senior Cup we were knocked out by St Munchin's, our closest city rivals. We were by far the better team, but we had four tries disallowed. That suited their mouthy hooker, Jerry Flannery, who was already being tipped for big things.

In my second year we made the semi-final and I was jumping at two in the lineout, really making progress. Whatever indifference I'd once felt towards rugby during my swimming and golf days evaporated: I was loving it more and more every week. Just getting my gear ready gave me a buzz.

I was also getting into a few scrapes, throwing a few punches. I was trying to make my mark in the Senior Cup team and there were times when I took it a bit too far. One day, before a game, the referee came into our dressing room and headed straight for me.

'Have you calmed down now, since the last day?'

Dad was present at all my matches, and I don't remember him ever having much of a problem with my indiscipline. I was with him one day when we got talking to Dan Mooney, who'd heard I was getting on the wrong side of a few referees.

Dan looked me in the eye and shook his head.

'Don't worry about it, son – it's not your fault.'

Then he nodded at Dad.

'Apples don't fall far from their tree,' he said.

Our family went to Mass at the Dominicans, in town, just up the road from the corner shop on Catherine Street where John Gleeson, my golf mentor, gave me my first job. He trusted me with opening up on Sunday mornings, getting the newspapers ready for the early risers and keeping an eye out for the shoplifters. He was delighted the day I caught my first thief – an old man, immaculately dressed, with a cigarette dangling from his lips. He came in quite often, and I'd had my suspicions. I saw him slipping some rashers into his jacket and he was halfway across the road when I called out.

'Sorry there!'

He turned around. The cigarette was still in his mouth.

'You've a packet of rashers in your pocket that you didn't pay for!'

He stared at me for a while, and then he said, 'How dare you! I'm going to tell Mr Gleeson about this accusation you're making!'

'You're on the video, like!'

I thought about demanding the rashers off him, but he scarpered and never came back.

John liked to be there when his regulars arrived in from the Dominicans for their papers and milk, chatting about the latest goings-on around town, or whichever sport was throwing up a talking point.

I worked hard, because I wanted to show him his trust in me was well placed. On my first day I'd spent fourteen hours stocking shelves without a break, because no one had told me to take one and I didn't want to ask.

He was disappointed when I packed in golf, but he was always asking about my rugby, and it was good to be able to tell him I was getting on better than I'd thought was possible.

I don't know if anyone ever believes me, but I keep saying it, because it's true: if I hadn't been blessed with a lot of luck, nobody would ever have heard of me in rugby. I got called up for an Irish Schools final trial, up in Blackrock. I was in the Possibles XV, with Nicky O'Connor lifting me from the front and Rob McGrath from the back – both lineout technicians at a time when lifting had only recently been allowed. We stole three balls from the Probables because their jumper was being lifted by the shorts and he couldn't get near me. I became the first player from Ardscoil Rís to make the Ireland Schools team, and it went on from there.

With exams coming, I spent a week on my own in our mobile home at Liscannor, on the Clare coast, sticking rigidly to my study plan: fourteen hours a day, every day, in between rasher sandwiches. I was forever trying to keep up with the smartest guys in the class and get a good Leaving Cert, enough points to get me into a computer engineering degree course at the University of Limerick.

A letter came through the door in the summer calling me into the Munster Under-20s camp, where I met Scott Holden, a Kiwi coach who wore electrical tape around his ears when he played and turned in the collars of his short-sleeved jersey. Ted Mulcahy, a sub for Munster against the All Blacks in 1978, was one of our mentors. We called him Fucking Mul because in the dressing room he couldn't finish a sentence without saying 'fuck' a minimum of four times. Everyone loved him.

There were two second-rows ahead of me, both from Cork and both already in the senior Munster set-up: Donncha O'Callaghan and Mick O'Driscoll. But Scott rated me when I didn't really rate myself: he moved Micko to Number 8 and put me in alongside Donners.

I don't know what I would have thought if someone had said we'd be the Lions second-row Test partnership on the 2005 tour to New Zealand, a little over six years away. Whatever about Donners, nobody back then would have put me anywhere near a sentence with the Lions in it. We won the provincial Grand Slam, but I wasn't pulling up any trees and I didn't make the Ireland Under-21 squad.

Four second-rows were named ahead of me: Donners, Micko, Leo Cullen and Bob Casey. The next generation of Irish rugby was lining up.

Those four, unlike me, were also contracted to the IRFU academy. Among other things, they were getting specialist advice on muscle gain and nutrition – two subjects that were obsessing me as I tried to build myself up from the fourteen and a half stone I weighed on leaving school.

At the University of Limerick, I trawled the internet and the library in search of information about muscle mass and how to build it. I typed phrases like 'How to put on weight as a rugby player' into search engines. Everywhere there was caution about the need for a proper, balanced diet but I had my own methodology, which largely consisted of eating everything in sight, regardless of the fat content.

One protein supplement I took had a cartoon drawing of the Incredible Hulk on the front. I was eating a couple of packets of Jaffa Cakes every day because I'd read somewhere that they were a healthy source of sugar replenishment.

At the college gym I found a discarded weights programme used by a Munster rugby player – basic stuff, but
I hammered into it every day and all these efforts started
bearing fruit as my weight moved from 92 to 100 kilos. Along
with others involved in the Munster Under-20s I was
put through a fitness test, but I wasn't well on the day, and
performed poorly. Mark McDermott, the provincial development manager with the IRFU and captain of Shannon
into the bargain, wasn't impressed.

'Your fat is gone way up.'

'I know. I've put on a lot of weight.'

'Yah, I see that. You're obviously drinking loads of pints.'

Soon after that, I was sitting in our living room, reading
the *Irish Times* of 13 May 1999, when I saw that ten more players had been added to the IRFU Academy. I looked down
the list and saw that they'd picked another second-row, two
months younger than me: *Trevor Hogan (Dublin University)*.

And I was disappointed, no question, but the truth is that
I wasn't devastated, or anything like it.

I might have dreamed of the Olympics in swimming and
winning big tournaments in golf, but I'd never had that level
of ambition or self-belief in rugby. I was only three years
back playing and, while I'd given it everything, a big part of
me thought I was lucky to get that break for Ireland Schools.

I figured the guys my own age who were part of the professional set-up at Munster were there for a reason. So I turned
the page and mostly I thought, *Your man is probably better than me.*

But there was a part of me that thought I could catch
Trevor and the other guys who were ahead if I kept working
at my game, and kept improving. And definitely there was a
voice in my head that said:

I'm playing for Young Munster, we're in the First Division.
That has to count.

3

The Young Munster seconds were a team full of bitter men. Once a week we trained against the first team, full contact and often full-on digging matches. The story goes that when I was brought up from the Under-20s, I made an impression straight away and there was a conversation.

'Who's that lanky prick?'

'That's Justin's brother.'

'He'd want to calm down for himself.'

'He's Justin's brother though.'

'I don't give a fuck who he is.'

The guy who thought I needed to calm down was Declan Edwards, who would become a great friend. Not long after that, we were on the same team in a training match and my friend Eoin Hann was making a nuisance of himself in the other pack. Declan pulled the forwards into a huddle, started effing and blinding about Eoin and then looked at me.

'If he puts his hands on the ball one more fucking time, show him the silver!'

The first chance I got, I ran over to Eoin.

'Hann! You have to stop! They're going to kill you!'

Some of the junior team were bitter about not being in the first team, but that didn't fully cover it. There were a lot of chips on a lot of shoulders. It was a tough call to decide who was in the biggest hurry to make the first team, but my vote would have gone to our scrum-half, Mike Prendergast. Prendy, the son of a diehard Garryowen man, had left Garryowen to play first-team rugby at Young Munster. Now, here he was in the junior team, running out of patience.

Justin was annoyed, too. He'd spent the year stuck on the bench for the first team when he should have been playing. I had taken part in a three-week mutiny, refusing to take his place on the bench when he decided enough was enough. Back when he was a student in Cork, playing second-row for Dad's first club, Justin had played on the Sunday's Well team that won the Munster Senior Cup. On one of the craziest, happiest days in our father's life, they beat Young Munster in the final and Justin put Dad's Young Munster tie around his neck when we took a picture of them, together with the trophy.

He was a quality player and he was about to move on, but our coach Leonard Copley asked him to give the seconds a bit of leadership before he left. Which was how we ended up going to war together in the final of the 1999 Munster Junior Cup.

We were playing Kilfeacle – an older, more streetwise team. Maybe they thought they were up against boys, young-fellas who could easily be intimidated. If that was the case, they got that one wrong. Every step they took towards us, we took three back at them.

Prendy started the first fight and I was the next man in. I

was running along behind him when he was tackled late. By the time I arrived he had already punched the guy, and a thirty-man brawl ensued. We dug all around us and maybe Eddie Fraher did a bit more digging than the rest of us because he was the one singled out for a red card, along with one of their props.

The second fight happened in the second half, when we were well ahead on the scoreboard. After I kneed their Number 8 in the back on one side of the pitch, the play switched to the other side, where I carried the ball into a ruck and went to ground. The 8 saw me lying there, stamped on me and then fell over on to his knees. As he was kneeling, Justin wound up a huge punch and flattened him. Another thirty-man brawl followed.

This was my academy. Old school.

'Unfortunately,' it said in the *Irish Times*, 'the game was marred by two nasty outbreaks of fighting.'

It was Young Munster's first Junior Cup victory in fifteen years and we drank our loaves off, back in the clubhouse. As is the club tradition when a big trophy is won, the celebrations continued in town for the next couple of days, while I was doing my first-year exams at UL. Ian Ryan, our hooker, started a sing-song at eight o'clock in the morning in the early house next to Donkey Ford's fish and chip shop. He had his top off and held a mop in his hand which he pretended was a microphone. He told the handful of alcoholics dying for a cure to join in, or else.

Six years later, I was reminded of that final at a takeaway in Edinburgh, in the small hours of the morning after Ireland had beaten Scotland in one of my better games. I'd been out for a few drinks and I stopped off for a burger on my way back to the hotel. A guy with a Tipperary accent joined the queue and recognized me.

'How's it goin'?'

'Howrya. Grand, thanks.'

'Well done today.'

'Thanks.'

'You don't know me at all, do you?'

'Sorry, no, I don't think so.'

He told me his name.

'I played for Kilfeacle against ye that day. You said some bad things about us afterwards.'

A couple of years after the final, in my first interview for a big newspaper, I had mentioned that Junior Cup final to the *Sunday Times* in a fond sort of way. I talked about how tough games like that against tough teams were the making of me, at a time when other guys my own age were in the academy. Kilfeacle, though, weren't impressed.

'Yeah, sorry about that,' I said.

'We weren't one bit happy about it.'

'Look, I said it in jest – and out of respect.'

'You won't say it again, will you?'

Six years on, he was still standing up for his team, and as a Young Munster man I admired that. We picked up our burgers and went our separate ways.

After that Junior Cup final, Justin moved on, part of a mini exodus across town to UL Bohs.

'It's a fresh start for me, and if you want to come too it'd be great,' he said.

I got a call from John 'Paco' Fitzgerald, coach of the Young Munster senior team. He said he wanted to see me. When I turned up, my junior coach Leonard Copley was sitting next to him.

Leonard said, 'Look, Paul, we've heard a lot of chat about you going to Bohs.'

I wasn't going to deny that I was thinking about it, but I didn't get a chance to speak.

'We've five grand there for you if you'll stay for two years,' Paco said. I'd be starting for the seniors in the new season, he told me.

In Limerick club rugby then, there was no end of rumours about certain players being paid: *Your man is on three hundred quid a game, I swear to God.* It gave them a bit of status around town.

I thought it was great that anyone thought I was good enough to be offered money to play rugby. I talked it over with my family and decided to stay.

In the Young Munster first team, whatever few bob we were getting out of the club was mostly drinking money for us. Plenty of it ended up in the till at the Corner Flag pub, up on Henry Street at the top of the town, a couple of doors down from Mike and Katie's chipper. It was owned by Paco, who'd played prop for Ireland.

I'd starting hanging around with some buddies from the Under-20 team, usually Mark Quigley, Timmy Lane and Trevor Micks – friendships that have only strengthened over the years. Sooner or later, on a Saturday night after games, half of Young Munster would end up in the Flag – players, former players, coaches, committee men and their wives, all of them committed to the cause – and with the Cookies there was always a cause, a reason to remind ourselves of who we were representing.

At some point during the night, Paul Joyce would come in. He was a great clubman. We loved it when he was wearing his club tie and his Young Munster blazer with all the buttons done up. He was maybe forty, with red hair and the thickest jamjar glasses you've ever seen.

'Joycer,' we'd say, 'why are you in the blazer and the shirt and tie?'

He'd tell us he'd been filling in as manager of the Under-20s, or volunteering for some other thankless task.

And we'd go, 'But why the blazer?'

'Because,' he'd always say, 'I was a *rep-res-en-ta-tive* of Young Munster Rugby Football Club. So fuck off. Why wouldn't I be in a blazer?'

We'd tell ourselves we weren't staying too long in the Flag, that after three or four pints we'd be heading downtown to bars like Nancy Blake's and on to a nightclub. But there was something about those nights that kept us there long after the lock-in. We'd finally walk out the door after the karaoke and the sing-song and broad daylight would hit our faces.

There was plenty of new blood in the first team. Matt Te Pou, a New Zealander who had just played for Tonga in the 1999 World Cup at Number 8, came on board. Matt figured it was a good idea for me to sit down with him and talk, and we met one morning in a deli below his apartment on Mount Kennett Place.

Matt had a degree in sports science. He was into goal-setting. He took out a pen and paper and got me to write down some targets. Short-term first, then further into the future.

I thought about it for a couple of minutes and wrote down the first goal.

1. *To be a regular in the Young Munster team.*

He said the goals needed to be measurable, so I added:

. . . and start 12 matches.

I carried on. I liked the way it was forcing me to be ambitious.

2. *To make the Ireland Under-21s as a starting lock.*
3. *To get a Munster contract and start two matches by the end of 2001.*
4. *To get capped for Ireland by the end of 2003.*

Then Matt told me to put down a dream goal, my ultimate ambition – but not some wild fantasy. It had to be something I genuinely believed was attainable if I worked hard enough towards it.

I felt self-conscious because Matt had barely seen me play, and what I wrote was something I wouldn't have dreamed telling anyone else, even my own family.

5. *To be the Test incumbent second-row for the Lions in 2005.*

It was November 1999. I had five years and seven months to get there.

Matt took the sheet of paper and wrote his name at the bottom.

'Your turn now, bro,' he said. 'You're signing up to your goals.'

I signed my name and he folded the sheet of paper and handed it to me.

'That's as good as being written in blood,' he said.

The 1999–2000 All Ireland League season began three weeks before Christmas. In those days, guys would play for their clubs one week and the provinces the next, in the Heineken Cup. It took me a long time to get used to the fact that I was part of the same team as Peter Clohessy and Ger Earls. In one of my first games I only had one thing on my mind when the whistle blew – impressing the two of them with how hard I could be. Early in the first half I gave a guy an unmerciful boot when the referee wasn't looking. We were in a huddle a couple of minutes later when Peter nodded at me.

'I saw that, Paul. Fucking nice one. Beauty!'

I was so incredibly happy with Claw's compliment that I didn't go near the ball for the next ten minutes – I was too busy looking for more guys to shoe.

By February, I was a regular starter. I was on my way to ticking the first box in the list I'd drawn up with Matt Te Pou when the second one started looking good.

Donncha O'Callaghan was the standout second-row for the Ireland Under-21s: the only question was who'd be along-side him. I was called into the squad for the game against England. The senior team were playing them at Twicken-ham, and Bob Casey was picked to start. Leo Cullen, another of the guys ahead of me, was selected for the Ireland A team.

Donners was the most popular guy in the Under-21 squad – hilarious off the pitch and a class act on it. At that stage our friendship had barely got off the ground, but I remember chatting to him as we were walking to Booters-town Dart station, a few days before they picked the team.

'Me and you will be the second-rows – you're going too well not to be picked,' he said. It was the first compliment I'd ever had from him. I was delighted: that sentence and that moment meant so much to me at the time.

I was lucky to get in ahead of Trevor Hogan, and even though we were beaten I held my place for the rest of the campaign, starting with the Scotland match, a fortnight later. That was played the day before Warren Gatland, the Ireland coach, brought a raft of new players into the senior team, including the Munster half-backs, Peter Stringer and Ronan O'Gara, and a tighthead prop who, like me, had never seen the inside of an academy – John Hayes.

We beat Wales at Thomond Park in the final match and I had one of the best games of my life. When I got subbed near the end, people stood up in the stand and clapped me off. I'd never had anything like that before and it felt unbelievable.

Off the back of that game, I got a phone call from John Gallagher, the former All Black fullback, who was director of rugby with Harlequins. He asked if I'd like to go over to London for a chat, no pressure. He picked me and Dad up at the airport and he had another New Zealand legend along-side him in the front of his jeep – Zinzan Brooke, the head coach. They told us they were building a new team and showed us around the Stoop. After telling me I needed to be eating four meals a day to build myself up, they offered me twenty-five grand a year, sterling.

I called them a couple of days later and said thanks but no thanks. Maybe part of me was hoping that Munster would show an interest sometime, but mostly it was because I didn't want to leave university without my degree.

Out of the blue that summer I was called to an interview

for a place in the IRFU academy. It was nothing like the full-time academies of today, but it meant you were on the radar. I bought a copy of the *Sun* at Limerick railway station for the train up, to see if there were any rumours about Everton buying new players. As I waited outside the interview room, a young guy came out wearing his school blazer, shirt, tie and slacks, and accompanied by his parents. I was wearing jeans, a blue checked shirt and – for some ridiculous reason – still carrying the *Sun* under my arm as I walked in after him.

John Hussey of the IRFU started telling me that if I were to be offered an academy place I'd be starting on such and such a date.

Straight away I realized it was clashing with a holiday in Greece I'd booked with my best mate from Ardscoil Rís, Carl Bourke (aka Oola), and some other friends. It had taken me ages to save for it, working as a bouncer on the door at Nancy Blake's and Nevada Smyth's and getting a few quid here and there from Young Munster out of the five grand they'd promised me.

'I'd love to do it,' I said. 'The only thing is, I have a holiday booked for that week and I paid a lot of money for it.'

Eddie Wigglesworth, director of rugby development, peered at me from across the desk. He wasn't impressed.

'Do you not *want* to be a professional rugby player?' he said.

Maybe I was supposed to relent out of sheer gratitude at that point, but there was no way I was giving up my holiday.

'I do,' I said. 'I definitely do. But I had no idea I was in the running for this. No one ever said anything to me when I was with the Under-21 squad.'

I held my ground and they gave me my first IRFU contract, for four grand a year.

*

Maybe I came on the scene too late to fully get the Young Munster v. Shannon rivalry, because the best days of the Munster Senior Cup and the All Ireland League were over by the time I experienced it personally, but I do remember being psyched to the gills when I came on as a sub in a Senior Cup final against them in the autumn of 2000.

I'd been on the team beaten by Shannon in the final the previous year, and Munsters were sick and tired of being second best.

Ger Clohessy, captain of the 1993 team and our forwards coach, got into my head on the touchline. I'd had some knock the previous week, and I wasn't fit enough to start, but I knew I'd get game time.

Ger was Peter's older brother and for him it was personal. Munsters had been in eight finals in the previous ten years and lost every one, four of them to Shannon – or as Ger referred to them, 'fucking Shannon'.

We were five points down when I came on after thirty-six minutes. I was desperate to make a difference. Within three minutes I had shoed about four people. 'A five-point deficit at the break would have given Munsters hope,' the report in the following day's *Limerick Leader* said, 'but when Andrew Thompson floated a garryowen into their 22, Paul O'Connell was penalized in the resultant melee and the Shannon out-half does not miss chances like that.'

I was a yellow card waiting to happen, and it finally did midway through the second half. You'd think I'd have calmed down after ten minutes in the bin, but when Mick Galwey came off the bench for Shannon – after being out injured for a month – I kneed him in the back at a ruck and got away with it. As I was running over to a lineout, John Langford started shouting at me.

Langford was a superstar of a second-row – if it wasn't for

John Eales, he'd probably have won fifty caps for the Walla-bies. So he deserved respect, especially from a kid who had achieved nothing. I jerked my head in his direction and gave it to him: 'Go fuck yourself! Fuck off home to Australia!'

At the end I sat on the pitch and my eyes followed Langford as someone handed him a camcorder and he filmed the presentation of the trophy to Shannon, as their supporters sang 'There is an Isle'. It was easy to see what it meant to him. Looking at him follow the cup with his hand-held camera, I realized how much he had bought into Limerick and Munster rugby.

Over time I grew up and calmed down. I saw the bigger picture. I learned that indiscipline kills rugby teams, and that aggression must be controlled. I became a better player, tactically. But I'll always believe the reason I was offered the Munster contract that set me on my way was because they saw something in the guy who was mad enough to knee an Ireland captain in the back, and then abuse John Langford when he took exception. And I don't think I'd ever have gotten to be that way if I hadn't grown up in a Young Munster house.

Less than ten seconds into a game against Dungannon, after I'd chased the kick-off, their second-row, Paddy Johns, pinned me to the ground in a ruck, with his fist pressed hard into my face and then down on to my throat.

I'd never met him before in my life, never played against him. He had nearly sixty caps for Ireland and a reputation as a lovely northern gentleman, but on the field, I was finding out, he was a different animal.

For the next eighty minutes I fought with him and battled him, telling him to retire, telling him he was a has-been. Behaviour that would disgust me now.

Claw loved it.

The following season, with Matt Te Pou as player-coach, we came with a late run in the league, playing champagne rugby.

I was doing pretty well and Matt started marking me down as the latest victim of bias against the Cookies. He gave an interview to the *Irish Times* and talked me up, making out that I wasn't being given my chance as a professional in the big time with Munster because I played for the wrong club.

I scored three tries up at De La Salle Palmerston. Afterwards Matt and I were asked to talk to the Irish-language channel, TG4. I'd never been on TV before. The interviewer said I must be delighted, after scoring the hat-trick.

I said yeah, sure, but our performance wasn't all that good.

'As a team we have set ourselves standards – and not all of us reached them today.'

Years later, people told me that in virtually every interview I gave after a game, no matter how well things had gone, I said they could have been better. So maybe it was a case of start as you mean to go on.

'If we don't stop making basic errors, we won't make the top four and the playoffs,' I said.

I pointed out that Peter had knocked on a few balls – it was probably more like ten – which was disappointing for such an experienced international.

Matt nearly took the dressing-room door off its hinges on his way back in to where Claw was sitting. He couldn't wait to tell the rest of the team about my TV debut.

'What channel were you on?' Claw asked.

He gave a dismissive nod when I told him.

'It's all right, kid,' he said. 'Fucking nobody watches that.'

That night I was at a twenty-first birthday party in the Shannon clubhouse when Niall O'Donovan, the Munster forwards coach, shouted across to me. I was on his turf: he's a Shannon man to the core.

'I heard you scored a hat-trick.'

'I did, yeah!'

'Total of three yards, was it?'

'No, it wasn't, actually!'

A few weeks later I got a phone call from Declan Kidney, the Munster coach.

He said he wanted to meet up and talk.

In the space of just a year, Munster had become massive. Forty thousand supporters had followed them to Twickenham for the Heineken Cup final of 2000. I'd felt a million miles away from that kind of rugby then. When they beat Biarritz on another big European day at Thomond Park the following January, I watched the game after hopping over the wall.

The night before my meeting with Declan Kidney, I talked to Justin. He told me I needed to look the part, and that I should dress big.

'Whatever you do, don't wear stripes,' he said. 'They'll make you look long, and you need to look wide.'

The following day I was in the back seat of his green Honda Civic when he pulled into the car park at the South Court Hotel, well ahead of schedule. Dad was alongside him in the front. He'd come partly for moral support and partly because he was dying to know what Declan was going to say to me.

I'd taken Justin at his word. I was wearing a Canterbury top with green, yellow and red hoops under a Lowe Alpine fleece jacket, unzipped. Underneath I had two T-shirts, one long-sleeved, the other short.

Munster already had four second-rows in their senior

squad, so I was expecting to be offered a development contract on small money.

'Keep your powder dry,' Justin said in the car. 'You don't have to commit to anything today. You have other options.'

'OK,' I said, although that was a stretch. Option singular, maybe. Connacht had been on to me.

Dad nodded and Justin carried on, like an agent looking out for his client.

'Ask him how he sees your development going. You can't be cannon fodder in there for two or three years when you could be in the team somewhere else.'

'OK. I'll ask him.'

'He'll probably offer you about ten grand a year, but don't accept anything less than eighteen.'

Eighteen grand. My bottom line.

But then I thought, what if he offers me twelve or fifteen? It crossed my mind that maybe Declan Kidney didn't do haggling. From what I knew about him, which wasn't much, he didn't seem the type. Maybe he reckoned that no matter what kind of money he offered, I was going to take his hand off.

Declan was waiting in the hotel lobby when I walked in. He had a room booked and we walked upstairs.

I'd met him before. Earlier in the season, when I was out injured with a neck problem, he'd kindly invited me to travel with the Munster squad for a Heineken Cup game in Castres. Just being in the team room that weekend felt incredible. When they pulled off a brilliant win, I was alongside Declan when the players headed off to applaud the travelling supporters. He turned to me and said: 'Welcome to Munster rugby.'

When one of the supporters handed around a bodhran to be autographed by the players, I passed it straight on to Declan. He handed it back, along with the pen.

'Sign that now,' he said.

I was mortified to be signing the bodhran, putting my name down beside the guys who'd played that day, like Claw and Mick Galwey, David Wallace and Anthony Foley, and so many other class players who had put Munster on the European stage.

As Declan returned it to the supporter he nodded at me.

'We brought him over for the weekend,' he told the guy. 'The things we have to do to stop these fellas from going to Connacht.'

It was classic Deccie, I'd learn later.

Now, in the hotel room, he didn't cut to the chase straight away. He was bothered by Matt saying I wasn't being given a fair crack of the whip.

'I can't be influenced like that,' he said.

'But I never told Matt to say that,' I told him. 'He said it off his own bat.'

Once he'd made his point he smiled and said he wanted me to sign for Munster. He said he thought I had a good future ahead of me.

Then he offered me a full professional contract and £35,000 a year.

I stretched out my right hand.

'I'll take it,' I said.

The season moved into May. We went to Garryowen and won 42–0. We made the top four and brought 6,000 supporters down to Cork Constitution for the semi-final.

Their best player was Ronan O'Gara. In the first half I shoed him out on the touchline and when he started roaring at me I told him to shut the fuck up.

Later in the game, I knocked the ball out of his hands and made a fist-pump into his face.

'We were all competitive like that once,' he told the newspapers after he had kicked eighteen points and knocked us out.

Then he headed off to Australia with the Lions and I wondered if he'd still be thick with me the next time he saw me, when we were training together with Munster.

PART TWO

4

I played with a guy once who was fast, skilful and physically incredible. He had everything except one thing – he just didn't want it enough. Sometimes he'd let you know he wasn't giving it everything. Two days before a game, he might say something like, 'Jesus, I had a beautiful quarter-pounder last night in Burger King.' It was like he had decided to sabotage himself, maybe subconsciously. There was a part of him that didn't want to do everything right in preparing for a game, because somewhere in his psyche he thought that, if he did, he wouldn't have an excuse in his back pocket if things went badly for him. For a long time he was a conundrum to me: why wasn't he busting a gut to get the most out of his talent? And then, years later, I finally worked it out. It was because he wasn't living his dream, like the rest of us.

When I started out at Munster, all the guys who'd made it to the Heineken Cup final the previous year, or who'd even just been close to making the team, were like superstars to me. In just a few years, they had taken the team from being nowhere in Europe to within a point of winning the tournament. It was a monumental achievement and those players created the values for the ones who came next. They created a winning culture. The All Ireland League had produced a special group and a coaching staff who knew how to get the best out of them. By the time I got there, Munster were at a level where I expected never to lose a game.

David Wallace was one of the best players in the squad. After he got back from the Lions tour that summer there was competition between me and Donncha O'Callaghan over who was more in with him.

Me: 'Where were you?'

Donners: 'Down watching movies with Wally for the last two hours.'

Me: 'Bastard! Why didn't you text me?'

A few days later:

Donners: 'I couldn't find you earlier.'

Me: 'I was in the gym with Wally. An hour and a half. Just the two of us. Chatting.'

Donners: 'Ah, for fuck's sake!'

Me and Donners became zealots. For us, Munster was the be-all and the end-all, and the success of the team became the overriding driving force in our lives.

From day one the Munster camp was a friendly place to be. People like Wally, John Hayes and Mick Galwey were big names, but they were incredibly modest and decent. If you walked in at lunchtime and a table was full, you sat on your own at another table and the next guy in joined you. It didn't matter how big a star he was, or how much of an unknown you were: nobody looked around to find someone who was more familiar, more of a name. These guys were stars but they didn't have an ego between them. It was an example to me of how a Munster player carries himself.

There were times in the early weeks when I wondered if I was good enough to be there, but the biggest players on the team made me feel part of it, and pretty soon it was like I'd been there for years. I travelled a lot in Peter Clohessy's Range Rover, which gave me credibility. It meant he was vouching for me, and that counted for a lot, because anything Claw said was gospel in Munster. He and Mick Galwey ran the show.

Gaillimh was starting his fifteenth season and he was made captain again after Deccie presided over the election.

'Right, lads,' he said one day, 'I suppose we'll nominate a captain for the year.'

Tom Tierney's hand shot up.

'Ah, I'd like to propose Mick Galwey.'

'OK,' said Deccie. 'Have we a seconder?'

We had – any amount of them.

Alan Quinlan was great with all the young guys coming in: he slagged us, complimented us, advised us. He told me I could be judged on one game and I needed to be as fit as possible when that opportunity arose. I logged the advice and it made all the difference when my chance came.

During pre-season training at Thomond Park, I was in the Bs and we were mauled over our own line a couple of times by the As.

Dessie Clohessy, Peter's younger brother, pulled us in.

'We're not competing next time,' he said. 'We're just going to bring it down and then start fucking hitting them.'

We collapsed the maul and the digs were flying. I saw Quinny going after Denis Leamy, pinning him to the ground, so I rained five or six punches down on the back of Quinny's head. In the dressing room afterwards, he was laughing about it. He couldn't believe I'd belted him.

'You cheeky bollocks! After all I've done for you!'

We roomed together on my first trip away with Munster, over to Edinburgh for the opening game in the new Celtic League in August 2001. Back then it felt every bit as big as the Heineken Cup, with full-strength teams for every game. Once you're rooming with a guy, you hang around with him for the few days. So, because I was with Quinny, I was also spending time with Gaillimh, Claw and Anthony Foley, the most influential guys in the team.

There were more than five thousand Edinburgh supporters packed into the small ground. Me and Donners were on the bench, with Gaillimh and Mick O'Driscoll starting. Donners was brought on first and then, with a few minutes left, I got the call.

It was my competitive Munster debut, and my first involvement was a defensive lineout. I stole it and we went up the field. I got passed the ball off the bottom of a ruck and I stepped inside a guy, jumped over the side of the ruck and carried for seven or eight metres. They were caught offside and we got a penalty. The score was 22–22, there was a minute left, and as Jeremy Staunton lined up the kick the rest of us were in a huddle.

Quinny pointed at me. 'That's what it takes!' he shouted, poking me in the chest. 'We need more of that! That's what it fucking takes!'

I'll never forget that moment and how special it made me feel. I was standing there, listening to this, and my head was spinning.

Am I really in the middle of these guys?

Am I actually standing out as a player?

70

Is this a fluke or what?

Then Jeremy stuck the penalty between the posts.

In the dressing room Deccie gave a little sum-up speech. I'd already slipped my phone out of my bag and I had it in my hand while he was talking. I wasn't listening to what he was saying. I was just dying for him to finish so I could ring Dad. When I got through, I couldn't contain myself.

'It was unbelievable!'

'It couldn't have gone better!'

I told him about the poach and the carry, about what Quinny had said in the huddle.

He wanted to know every possible detail.

'And what did *you* say?'

'Well, I didn't really say anything – we were in a huddle.'

'Did Mick Galwey say anything?'

'No, it was only a couple of seconds, like. We were waiting for the penalty.'

'And did Declan Kidney say anything afterwards?'

Dad couldn't get enough of it. When it comes to cherished memories, that night is up there.

It was the greatest feeling. It felt like I was on my way.

The following January, in Paris, Declan pulled me aside. He said he had a bit of news. Malcolm O'Kelly, the first-choice Ireland lock forward, was struggling with an eye socket problem. The first Six Nations game of 2002, against Wales, was the following Sunday and it wasn't definite that he'd recover in time.

I was being called into the squad, Declan said, as cover for Malcolm.

He was doing his best to play it down. He didn't want me losing the run of myself, just as we were about to play Stade Français in the quarter-final of the Heineken Cup. And I was trying to play it cool, but my heart was jumping out of my chest.

'It's just a precaution.'

'OK.'

'I'm sure Mal's eye will be fine.'

'Yeah.'

'But it will be good experience for you.'

'Great, yeah.'

'They're going to announce it today.'

'Thanks for letting me know.'

I rushed off to tell Dad. Then I tried to put it out of my mind, but it wasn't easy. I reckoned that if Mal didn't make it, I'd probably be on the bench. If he did, it would still be incredible to be in an Ireland camp.

I walked back down to the lobby of our hotel. I knew I'd be starting the game and it felt amazing just being on the Munster team-sheet in a European quarter-final: Dominic Crotty; John Kelly, Rob Henderson, Jason Holland, Anthony Horgan; Ronan O'Gara, Peter Stringer; Peter Clohessy, Frankie Sheahan, John Hayes; Mick Galwey, Paul O'Connell; Jim Williams, Anthony Foley, David Wallace.

Gaillimh was milling around in the lobby. He said, 'Some of us are heading into town. Are you coming?'

The novelty of being out and about with the big names on the team hadn't worn off. We walked out on to the street and Gaillimh said, 'We've gotta find the Tube station, or whatever they call it.'

'The Metro,' I said. 'I'll sort that out.'

I had a small bit of French. I walked up to the first guy I saw, with the lads right behind me.

'Excusez-moi! Où est le Métro, s'il vous plaît?'

He looked at us and said, in the most obvious American

tourist accent I've ever heard: 'Are you guys looking for the subway?'

We headed for the Champs-Élysées, where we all bought a pair of boxers in Gap.

'Can I try them on?' Gaillimh asked the shop girl.

In the middle of McDonald's he and Quinny pulled down my tracksuit pants and Gaillimh stuck his foot in the middle. I had to hit the ground in the foetal position.

Thirteen seasons later, that kind of craic was still going on every day at Munster: the most childish stuff you could ever imagine, endless slagging of each other with almost nothing off limits. Girlfriends, wives, mothers, two-hour conversations without one remotely serious point being made – nothing was too personal or too embarrassing. You took the slag and you tried to give it back better.

It was vicious, but it wasn't.

It was like having the craic in a pub with eight pints on board, except you're stone cold sober.

If a guy broke up with his girlfriend and was really cut up about it, we'd play 'It'll be Lonely This Christmas' at full volume in the gym.

When Marcus Horan found out he had a heart condition, and was worried about his future in the game, we thought about the best song to play when he came back into the camp from surgery. We decided he needed to hear Feargal Sharkey singing 'A good heart these days is hard to find'.

When I got older, guys from the new breed, like David Kilcoyne, would say that every day after I left training I'd call into Milford Hospice, just nearby, so I could familiarize myself with the surroundings. Killer would offer to chew my food for me and blend my dinners, just to make it easier for an old man to get some nourishment. He'd say that, when the rest of the forwards were doing heavy weights, I'd go for a brisk walk.

At McDonald's on the Champs-Élysées, it never occurred to me that Gaillimh was a thirty-five-year-old man with a wife and children and that maybe acting like an adolescent in such a public place was a bit strange. We were too busy having fun to think about it, or question it. And that's the way it stayed for the rest of my Munster days.

Against Stade, in a dogfight of a game, we went 16–3 up before half-time, but they had an absolute gale behind them in the second half. We spent forty minutes making tackles, trucking it up, protecting the ball, doing exactly what Gaillimh and Axel Foley told us to do. Guys were picking me off the ground and slapping me on the back every time I made a tackle. Stade got it back to 16–14, but we hung on.

The Munster supporters invaded the pitch. People were jumping into one another's arms. My parents were there and I knew how much it meant to them, how happy they were. Young Munster guys like Ger Clohessy were hugging me. Coaches from my youth were coming up, choking with emotion.

Somebody told me I was man of the match. A while ago, I saw a clip of my twenty-two-year-old self giving a TV interview before they handed me the award. It was like watching another person. I had no idea how to deal with the media, no clue that there are things you should say and things you shouldn't.

I was in a complete daze and in the interview it all just poured out of me. When you're starting out, getting a man of the match award feels like a really big deal. I was living a dream and I couldn't believe that all this was happening for me, so maybe that's why the same word kept coming into my head.

'*It was just unreal coming off the pitch! I've never experienced any-thing like that before. Just like, people coming up to you that I've known since I was ten or eleven, you know? It was unreal – I've never experi-enced anything like it in my life!*'

'*The hits were just unreal out there, you know? But the guys in the team are unreal, like, you know?*'

'*Everyone is supporting you on the field and, you know, you're play-ing with great friends. It was unreal out there, like!*'

'*All these guys, you know – just carrying you along, like, and it was just – it was unreal, like!*'

'*We were able to pick out the people in the crowd you knew – and it was just unreal, like!*'

'*The money they spent to support us is unreal. I hope we gave a bit back to them today – you know?*'

Even though I cringed when I saw it back, in some ways I was jealous of that person. He didn't have anything going on in his head to make him doubt himself, or any leadership role to play.

Back in the dressing room, I apologized to Frankie Shea-han for letting a few lineout balls through my hands.

'It's OK,' he said. 'We'll leave you off this week.'

I joined the Ireland camp the next day at the Glenview Hotel in Wicklow, where my room-mate was Claw. We had a massive suite. It was going to be Claw's fiftieth cap for Ireland, but I got the impression that this had nothing to do with the size of the room: Claw was just used to getting special treatment.

Paddy O'Reilly – Rala, the team's bagman and all-round legend – came by every morning to smoke a fag with Claw and bring him breakfast in bed. One of the fringe benefits of being Claw's room-mate was that you got the same breakfast as him. There was porridge, orange juice, tea, toast, eggs, sausages and bacon.

Claw had already announced that he was retiring from rugby at the end of the season. That week he didn't bother telling me about what to expect in the international game, about the step up from what I was used to. He had no advice for me whatsoever: we just hung out together as friends, which helped me settle in more than anything.

I never knew it at the time, because he never let on, but after I'd been in the Young Munster first team for a while he started putting in a word for me in high places – and not just in the Munster camp. One day I met a Young Munster man, Tony Edwards, and he was bursting to give me his news.

'Listen, Paul. I said I'd tell you this now – because there's no harm telling you. I was in the car with Claw the other day, right . . . He was on the phone to Gatland – talking about *you*, like.'

Claw played every game for Warren Gatland. He had influence, plenty of it.

'He had Gatland on the loudspeaker. I could hear the whole lot. He says to Gatland, "Your man O'Connell will be starting for Munster soon." That's the truth now, Paul!'

I hadn't even been offered a Munster contract by then. It hadn't even been mentioned as a possibility. I wasn't dreaming every night of playing for Munster. It wasn't because I didn't want that for myself, or because I lacked ambition: I just didn't rate myself that highly. It just felt like it was progress enough to be making the first team for the Cookies. I knew that if ever I was going to be offered a professional contract, it was going to be down to what I'd learned in the old school.

Listening to Tony tell me his story, I just thought: *Jesus, what a thing for Claw to say for me.* And now here we were.

There was a system where everyone in the squad wrote their initials on the labels of their training gear and it got washed and brought to the team room. Except Claw didn't bother with initials; he just took whatever he wanted.

'I got your gear there,' he told me one morning, dropping it on my bed.

I looked for my initials and found other people's.

'Claw – none of this gear is mine!'

'It fits you, doesn't it?'

He told the concierge to bring us a video recorder and sent him off to rent movies for the week. Every night there was a card school in our room, only I didn't play cards. Claw, Hendo, Frankie Sheahan and a few more sat around at the far end of the suite, playing poker and ordering pizza, while I read a book or watched one of Claw's videos.

He'd turn on the TV when the card players had headed back to their rooms and I was trying to get some sleep. Once, in the early hours of the morning, I heard him pick up the room phone. He always used that, rather than his mobile, because all his hotel expenses were paid.

I could hear a TV ad in the background, plugging a CD box set of sixty-four classic love songs.

'Well,' he said on the phone, 'could I order *The Power of Love*, please?'

He called out his name and address and credit card details. Then he had a thought.

'D'you want one too, kid?'

'That'd be great, yeah!' I said.

It never arrived. Or maybe Claw still has my copy.

The Wales game was Eddie O'Sullivan's first as Ireland head coach. He'd been given the job after the IRFU sacked Warren Gatland. His assistants were Deccie and Niall O'Donovan, who were double-jobbing until the end of the season and then leaving Munster, with Mike Ford as defence coach.

I wasn't remotely expecting to make the team. If Malcolm O'Kelly wasn't going to make it, I was fully expecting Gary Longwell to start alongside Gaillimh.

On Wednesday morning, in the team room, Eddie called out his starting fifteen. He got to Gaillimh – who was captain in Keith Wood's absence – and then I heard my name. It was a complete shock.

Denis Hickie was the first man over to congratulate me. 'Enjoy the mayhem today,' he said.

Winning your first cap means you're in demand on media day and I was put up for interview, with Gaillimh alongside me at the top table and a load of tape recorders and microphones in front of us. I got peppered with questions about where I'd come from and how I'd got here. So I told them about the swimming and the golf, about giving up rugby as a boy and then coming back to it.

'I think I've found my niche now,' I said, and immediately I was cringing inside when I heard myself. *Oh God, what will Gaillimh think about that?*

When I headed back to the room, Claw was doing an interview with Gerry Thornley of the *Irish Times*. I pretended to watch TV while I listened to him go on about how much he disliked the French, how he loved playing rugby but hated running, hated the gym. And he talked about his first cap for Ireland, nine years before, and the pride he felt standing for the national anthem.

I looked up the words of 'Amhrán na bhFiann' on the internet, and our masseur, Willie Bennett, helped me to learn it off while he was giving me rubs. Then I was standing there at Lansdowne Road myself, with my family in the crowd, pumped up and proud. I didn't sing the anthem, or 'Ireland's Call', because I couldn't take my mind off what was coming.

*

The last thing I remember, before it all went blank, happened twelve minutes and thirty-eight seconds into the game. We were 10–0 ahead and playing well. I was running up behind Simon Easterby as he went to catch a kick-off. I recall it clearly, and then it's like someone zapped the TV screen then switched it back on seventeen minutes later.

I've seen the missing minutes back and it's the strangest feeling, remembering none of it when you're watching yourself scoring a try for your country on your debut. It's gone, wiped – permanently. Just over a minute after Simon caught that kick-off, Craig Quinnell carried the ball and I moved in to tackle him. I was too high: he smacked me on the forehead with his elbow near the halfway line. I was laid out on the pitch but I came round after fifteen seconds of treatment and got back into position. There was a lineout next and I was beaten in the middle by Ian Gough off Frankie Sheahan's throw. Well beaten.

The next thing I remember, fifteen minutes later, Gaillimh was calling a four-man lineout and Frankie was ready to fire when I stepped away.

I went down on one knee, and for the second time in the game I felt a wet towel on the back of my neck. When I got to my feet Simon Easterby was saying something I couldn't understand.

For half a second, I stepped back into the line but I felt totally disorientated.

Peter Stringer escorted me off the pitch and Mick Griffin, the team doctor, sprinted across from the far side.

He asked me what had happened.

'Strings took me off.'

He asked me why.

I couldn't think of a reason.

'OK, count backwards from five for me.'

'Five, four, three, two, one.'

'What's five times seven?'

'Thirty-five.'

'What's . . .'

'Mick, stop trying to make an eejit out of me! Stop trying to make it look like I'm concussed. I'm fine!'

He asked me my phone number. I couldn't remember it. A chink, but I recovered quickly.

'Stop bullshitting me! You're just trying to get me to come off!'

Maybe I was close enough to convincing him, until I started unravelling.

'Do me a favour, Mick. Teach me the lineout calls, will you?'

'Right, that's it! You're definitely coming off now!'

I looked up at the clock.

'I'm not coming off after two and a half minutes of my debut!'

He broke it to me gently. 'Paul, it's nearly half-time. You scored a try. There's two and a half minutes left of the first half.'

Then he walked behind me as we made our way around the perimeter of the pitch. By the time I threw myself down on a bench under the West Stand my eyes were red with tears.

In the medical room someone handed me a cup of tea. Chris Wyatt, the Welsh lock, was still in there after going over on his ankle, two minutes in.

'Fair fucks to you, mate – a try on your debut,' he said.

A television was showing the half-time analysis on RTÉ. I saw myself winning a lineout ball at four, off the top to Gaillimh. The boys got behind him and drove forward. Then I took the ball off Gaillimh five yards short and we mauled them over, with three Welsh players hanging out of

me as I grounded it. I celebrated like I'd never done before, or did again, pumping my right fist with the ball tucked under my other arm.

It didn't seem real, watching it.

Wales were brutal that day – we put fifty points on them. The best player on the pitch, with one of his greatest performances for Ireland, was Peter Clohessy.

Eight years later I got another bad bang on the head during a game. We were playing Italy. I was running around the pitch after the ball and I couldn't figure out where it was. I was taken off and I vomited that night, but I was fine the following day. I suppose I was lucky: they were the only two concussions I had in more than twenty years playing the game.

When I started out, there was nothing like the same awareness of the impact that repeated blows to the head can have on a player. After the 2015 World Cup, I heard about a TV programme on the subject of concussion in rugby, *Hidden Impact*. Conor O'Shea, the former Ireland fullback who's a coach now, asked a question at the end. It was based on a hypothetical scenario: Ireland make the World Cup final, and on the Tuesday before the game Paul O'Connell gets a knock on the head in training. Conor could have named any guy in the team, obviously. But his question was straight to the point: 'Does he play?'

There's no simple answer to that. It depends on the knock. You could argue that players need a decision like that taken out of their hands, and you'd be right. But it won't always reach the point where somebody gets to decide, one way or the other.

If – in Conor's scenario – I was rendered unconscious and had to be carried off the training pitch, I think the Ireland doctors would have ruled me out of the game. There was a time when very few sports doctors would have made that call, but ten or fifteen years ago we didn't know that scores of American football players were suffering from brain trauma, or that further down the line rugby players would be retiring early because of multiple concussions.

If I'd felt better on the Wednesday or Thursday, I know I'd have tried to change their minds. I wouldn't have expected to succeed.

If my head was spinning after the impact but it wasn't obvious to others that I'd taken a blow to the head, I'd have covered it up.

If I knew that owning up to being concussed would cost me a place in a World Cup final, I'd have said nothing. I know that's not right, but it's what would have happened.

I wouldn't have tried to play on until I'd got my bearings. I wouldn't have let anyone see me stagger around. I'd have gone down on one knee, taken my time, hoped nobody had noticed.

Because it's a World Cup final.

And because I didn't grow up with the safety-first approach we have today, no more than the hurlers who played without helmets for their whole careers. Or maybe age doesn't come into it, because the culture of the game is that when you get a bang you pick yourself up and play on. To change it will require the kind of cultural shift that made drink-driving socially unacceptable. Right now there isn't a coach in world rugby who would rule a player out of a World Cup final on the basis that he *might* have had a concussion in training, five days before the game. In twenty years' time, that might still be the case.

But if they *know*, it's different, because most coaches have got good values and concern for the well-being of their players.

It's a very serious issue for rugby, and there's no easy fix. But if a seven-year-old grows up knowing that some things are part of the game – like you don't give back-chat to the referee, or you don't play on after you've had a bang on the head – then it's going to be a lot easier to keep players safe. It's the way it has to be, but it's going to take time.

Claw's final international game was against France, back in Paris. There were worse places for him to go out. And that he was there at all said a lot about him.

I remember, when I was sixteen, coming out of half-seven Mass at the Dominicans with Dad one Sunday night and seeing some of his pals from Young Munster milling around on the pavement, talking about Peter.

Earlier that Sunday he'd been banned from rugby for twenty-six weeks. People were already saying he was finished with Ireland, and maybe with rugby. He had stamped on the head of the French lock forward Olivier Roumat, in Paris. It wasn't the only incident he was involved in either, just the one they punished him for.

Outside the church, Dad's friends were disgusted by how long they'd banned him for. They were having none of it.

'If it was a French fella done it, he wouldn't have got half that ban!'

'They're after hanging him out to dry!'

'Fucking more of it!'

Dad said that, to understand why Peter did what he did, you had to know what was done to him at Parc des Princes two years earlier. He'd needed stitches in three places that day, where the headbutts had hit him.

Not that he was complaining. He didn't say he'd be getting his own back either, but that's what he went out to do. French teams had destroyed Ireland for so long. They had all kinds of enforcers who roughed up our players early in the game, before their backs ran riot. And here was Peter – stewing on it for two years and then sowing it into them on his own in Paris. Trying to take out any guy he could. To this day I still admire that.

That afternoon, in his final game, some of the French supporters at Stade de France applauded him when he was taken off in the second half. Grudging or not, it was respect.

I was called off the bench with fifteen minutes left. The game was over: France were blitzing us. Three minutes from time I smashed into Imanol Harinordoquy, the new star of French rugby, while he was still in the air. Before they kicked the penalty awarded against me I could hear Claw shouting from the sideline.

'Aboy the kiiiiiiiid!!'

*

There always had to be a new thing. It was like flicking a switch, once I'd achieved something. Straight away, it was all about the next step I could take – except it always seemed so far away. I was delighted to be an international player, but then I was thinking, *Jeez, how cool must it be to be Keith Wood or Brian O'Driscoll or John Hayes? How great would it be to be first choice, when everyone's fit?* That seemed miles away to me then, something I'd never achieve. But still, something to aim for.

In the Munster gym, before my Ireland call-up, I'd look at the guys with the white Canterbury socks and think that my life would be so much better if I had those socks. We weren't given socks at Munster – we had to buy them. And you couldn't buy the Canterbury ones in Ireland, which was what gave them their mystique for guys who were on the outside looking in. If you were strolling around in Canterbury socks, you were playing for Ireland. It was the first thing Hayes said to me when I got in the squad, because he'd heard me go on about it often enough: 'You finally made it – your very own Canterbury socks.'

When I was negotiating my first Irish contract, I wasn't bothered if they didn't give me any extra money. I just wanted the Ford Mondeo that came with the contract, because it meant you were a proper Ireland player. It was another little step on the road to wherever I was going.

Three weeks after Claw's last Ireland game, we were both back in France and I was jogging around on a patch of grass outside a fabulous country house near Montpellier, watched by Declan Kidney. It was the day before the Heineken Cup semi-final against Castres and I was doubtful, with a shoulder injury.

Deccie decided to conduct the fitness test himself.

'Right – down,' he said. 'Two press-ups.'

He wasn't looking for much from me, but I couldn't even manage one press-up: the shoulder was still stiff and I felt it straight away.

Deccie wasn't too bothered.

'OK, you won't have to do those in the game. Have a go at the tackle bag.'

He held the bag himself. I launched myself at it and as my head came up it collided with his face and knocked out one of his front teeth.

He picked the tooth up, put it in his pocket and pronounced me fit to play.

We had the hotel to ourselves, and hundreds of emails and faxes from well-wishers were stuck up all over the walls. Eight thousand supporters had dug deep into their pockets to be there, arriving on chartered jets or making the long journey in cars and vans. We dug out the win, 25–17. Donners came off the bench for Axel after fifteen minutes and had a stormer at 6. It was a turning point for him with Munster.

In the final against Leicester, maybe we were beaten before we began; maybe the occasion got to us. We discovered that our ability to grind out a result didn't cut it against the very best. They had their work done on us and we were outclassed in the lineout. I played the game carrying an ankle injury, which didn't help, but we couldn't figure out how to defend their four-plus-one lineout. They were bringing one of their halfbacks in to lift, and it was like the game had suddenly moved on in a very short period of time and had caught us out. We were still calling lineouts from the front, going through a list of calls, rather than checking where they were defending and basing our decisions on that.

But mostly they were just better than us.

All the talk beforehand had been about us winning for

Claw on his last day as a rugby player, about winning it for Gaillimh and making up for losing the 2000 final. But in rugby you usually get what you deserve, and the bottom line was that we weren't good enough to be Heineken Cup champions – not over a class team like Leicester. We weren't ready.

If you'd asked us a couple of hours after the game, or even a few months later, we wouldn't have agreed that we weren't mentally strong enough. It was only when we moved to another level that we could see what we didn't have then.

5

A few years ago, the week after a loss in the Heineken Cup, we were reviewing the match before training at the University of Limerick. One of the younger players, very talented, had given a poor kick-chase. Axel was forwards coach. In the meeting, he stopped the video and said to the player: 'We chatted a lot about kick-chase before the game – what do you think of your kick-chase here?'

The player went, 'Yeah, sorry, sorry – I needed to go harder there.'

Later, I was looking at him out on the training pitch. I was really frustrated and annoyed with his answer. *Why wouldn't you kick-chase hard enough in a Heineken Cup game?*

I spoke to him afterwards.

'How many times did we talk about kick-chase and how important it would be in the game?'

'I know, I know.'

'What's the story?'

'Well,' he said, 'to be honest with you, the kick was too long and I actually slowed down to stay in connection with Rog.'

As soon as he said it, I knew he had a good point.

'Jeez, that makes sense. You know that everyone in the room thinks you didn't bother kick-chasing hard enough in a Heineken Cup game?'

'Well, that was kinda the answer the coach wanted.'

'You couldn't have just said that the kick was too long?'

'I didn't think he wanted to hear that.'

'All he wanted was your opinion. You think that's going to win us a Heineken Cup – doing that in a meeting?'

'I didn't think about it like that.'

I walked off then. I should have been more understanding of him, a young guy still making his way. Sometimes, though, I think about what it took to get over the line in the Heineken Cup, and it always comes back to the way the playing group took ownership of what we did.

In the Munster team that finally broke through, we had guys coming up with two or three things on their own and saying, 'This is the answer! If we do this right, there's no way we won't win!' It might not have been the right thing. It might only have been 75 per cent of the right thing. But once we were all hooked on something we believed was the answer, very often that was all we needed.

There was a group of players with a great attitude, which Deccie played a big part in developing. They felt the team was theirs. They didn't need Gaillimh or Axel or anyone else to drive them. They appreciated that the plaudits and the big wins only come with hard work, especially when you're up against teams with bigger budgets and bigger names. If they screwed up, they'd think, 'If I was fitter, I think I could have made those two tackles and saved the game for us.'

When a team doesn't have that level of initiative to solve problems, you see the lack of it in different ways, on and off the pitch. Sometimes it's obvious – a quiet group with no solutions after a loss – but often it's more subtle and it can take a while to put your finger on what's wrong.

I think most leaders are very competitive people. They can't stand by and accept what they see as a losing mentality, or a game plan that's failing the team. They'll be thinking: *Just do it my way and we'll win.*

That's how I was, once I became a senior player – so many things to say, so many solutions in my head all week for winning the game on Saturday.

Once players are thinking they've found the right way to do it – and feeling like they're running the show – then they're on the right road. I think they'll generally go out and be more focused, more disciplined. They'll do the simple things well because they have taken responsibility for the team's performance. At the end of the game, the only direction they'll point fingers is towards themselves.

The England team that won the World Cup in 2003 were unbelievably driven, with massive self-belief. There was Lawrence Dallaglio, who felt he should have been captain. Neil Back and Matt Dawson, probably the same. Richard Hill was a guy who led by example, captain of Saracens. Jonny Wilkinson had the respect to be captain. Martin Johnson had captained the winning Lions tour in South Africa. Most of the rest were leaders too, or they had plenty to say for themselves, or they had the kind of talent to turn matches in a flash, like Jason Robinson.

For a successful team you need the player who can speak up and take ownership of what's going to happen on the pitch, not because it's expected of him, but because he has self-belief and a drive to win that won't allow him to place his faith entirely in someone else. And we had plenty of people like that in our dressing room long before we started winning trophies. Axel, John Kelly, Frankie Sheahan, myself, Flannery, Marcus Horan, Quinny, O'Gara, Stringer – all leaders and potential captains.

We learned through experience, we got better as we went on. In the years before we made the breakthrough, there were times when we played not to lose. We learned that the mentality of champions is all about going out there to dominate. But it wasn't just about experience through matches, it was about talking rugby every day over our teas and coffees, discussing what we were going to do at the weekend.

People on the outside will never understand how much John Kelly brought to our team. He believed so passionately in Munster, and thought about our success so deeply, that whenever he spoke everyone listening had the same thought in their head: *This guy has it sussed here. I'm going with him.*

And when you get that level of belief in a team, you're not just playing with fourteen other guys, you're playing *for* them.

John Hayes gave me more through lineouts and kick-offs than I gave him in scrums, but when I was behind him he got everything I had to give.

Me and Donners, we went to the well so many times together there was always a nod and a hug before we left the changing room. We resolved to drive each other and compete with one another.

We had a nickname for guys who were injured a lot: Mr Glass. Back then I thought they were a bit soft, but it wasn't long before that attitude changed as my own injuries mounted up.

After carrying my ankle in the Heineken Cup final against Leicester, I got selected for Ireland's tour to New Zealand that summer and made the Test team in Dunedin.

We nearly won the first Test, should have won. I don't remember being devastated. I didn't have enough standing in the team, or enough perspective, to see it as that big of a chance missed. I went very well against their lineout and it was a good lift for my confidence after the Leicester game, but with twenty minutes left I got driven back on my shoulder and I was ruled out of the second Test.

I flew home, got off the plane and my back was at me. Six weeks later, it still was, so I decided to have an operation. They told me I'd be out for four months and they were right, to the day.

Before I got back on the pitch, I went on a supporters' trip to Gloucester with my buddies Timmy Lane, Trevor Micks and Mark 'Squiddy' Quigley. It was a week before my twenty-third birthday. I was so naïve – and so in love with the whole Munster thing – that I wore my training gear to the game. We booked into a B&B around the corner from Kingsholm and on the Saturday morning we walked down the road to a pub called the White Hart, owned by the former England and Lions backrow Mike Teague. At half-ten in the morning, as we ordered our first pints of Stella, the place was already full of Munster supporters. Not long after that, an English couple – Steve and Zoe Murray, huge Munster supporters from Leamington Spa – sat down beside us and we struck up a conversation. Three hours later we were still talking.

I had to leave the pub a little earlier than I'd have liked, because when I pulled out the match tickets I found I'd brought ones for the home game against Perpignan the following week. I had to wait outside the ground for the team bus to arrive, so that I could get more tickets from Jerry Holland, the Munster manager. As it pulled into the car park, I could see all the lads were deadly serious, staring straight ahead. They told me later on that, when they spotted me standing outside in my Munster gear, they thought I was crying. I wasn't; it was just that the drink had got the better of me.

Fourteen years later, I'm great friends with Steve and Zoe. They sent me lovely texts before every big game, and at the start of every season. That morning when we first met was a time before cameraphones. Facebook and Twitter didn't exist. You could go into a pub as a player and get to meet supporters properly. Back in the day, the supporters got to know guys like Quinny and Wally because they'd meet them in the clubhouse after a Shannon or Garryowen match. They were having conversations, not posing for photos.

Things changed at Munster while I'd been out injured. Jim Williams, a fantastic signing, had been elected our new captain, only a year after coming over from Australia. That said a lot about the respect people had for how he went about his job. With Deccie gone, we had a new head coach, Alan Gaffney, another Australian. Brian Hickey came in to replace Niallo as forwards coach.

Donners had forced his way into the team, ahead of Gaillimh and Mick O'Driscoll, and our second-row partnership was starting to come together. In April we beat Leicester in the Heineken Cup quarter-final. They had some big England players on the pitch – Johnson, Back, Martin Corry, Dorian West – and of course they'd beaten us in the previous year's final. But their systems capitulated and we did a job on their lineout.

We were thrilled with ourselves. It felt like big progress: a big win on the road and another semi-final.

Twelve thousand supporters came with us to Toulouse for the semi-final. They had players as good as Cédric Heymans, Jean-Baptiste Élissalde and William Servat on the bench. We came up short again, by a point. For some guys – Rog, Strings, Hayes, Axel – it was a fourth season in a row they'd made the semi-final or final and lost. I wasn't yet at the stage where I thought I'd retire unfulfilled and unhappy with my career if we didn't eventually win a Heineken Cup, but I was getting there.

Ireland's summer tour before the 2003 World Cup left me feeling I was making progress as an international player. It was also the first time I'd spent an extended period being coached by Eddie O'Sullivan.

Even in the short time I'd been involved, things had stepped up a lot. Eddie drove a massive improvement in our facilities, and on the training ground he demanded high standards. That summer he had us practising switches and loop plays in every session. I'd never done anything like it before and it made me and everyone else a better player. I learned the intricacies of running lines, continuity and so much more that was new and exciting. On gut instinct, Eddie had hired Mike Ford, a Rugby League man, as defence coach, and he was brilliant too.

Deccie was Eddie's assistant coach. They'd been brought together by the IRFU and it's well known now that as a partnership it didn't work. At the time I was still so new that I didn't see the signs until much closer to the end. Deccie was never going to have a bitch and a moan about it. If he was unhappy he was too professional to let it show in any way that might affect the team.

Our first match of the tour was against Australia in Perth. We trained at the facilities of the Fremantle Dockers Aussie rules club, and it was top-class, like nothing we'd ever seen. After the first session we were told to have a few beers and relax – and so we had a mad night. The following day the senior players arrived and I went out with them too. Bonds were being forged. Brian O'Brien, the team manager, was old school – a Shannon man. Guys could chat to Briano, and Eddie trusted him enough to cut us some slack on nights out.

With the Australia game a few days away, I dropped two balls in training. After the second one, Eddie went, 'Come on, Paul! That's two balls in a row!'

The criticism annoyed me, because no player tries to knock on a ball, and both passes had been really bad, but Eddie was going big on raising our standards and being ultra-self-critical. Not long after, I bought into that big-time, but at twenty-three I didn't think it served a purpose for a coach to be bawling me out.

Later on during Eddie's time as coach, when we were working on kicking strategies at training, I ended up having a few words with him after blocking a player from getting at Geordan Murphy. Geordan had come up out of nowhere and I thought I was doing the right thing in protecting him, but it wasn't by the book and so Eddie stopped the session.

'Paulie, what are you doing?'

'I was blocking for Geordan.'

'Geordan won't be there in the match.'

'Well, what do you want me to do now – pretend he isn't there?'

'Paulie, give me a break!'

I talked to him later on about it. I was apologetic.

'Look,' he said, 'I don't mind you making the point – but it's the way you make it. And the other thing is, I can't be seen to be having arguments with you in front of the players.'

He told me that if there was something I felt passionately about, I should say it to him privately so that we could have a proper discussion. That was fine with me, and I can appreciate now that you don't want to be arguing with a player on the pitch.

You could see the contrast in management styles between Eddie and Deccie in how they handled arguments. Eddie didn't want anyone else thinking that he wasn't running the show; Deccie *wanted* players running it. He didn't mind losing an argument in a public way, even if he thought he was right. If it meant the players thought they were deciding things, that suited him fine.

Eddie had a different style. He was very much the boss.

We didn't get anywhere close to Australia. Malcolm O'Kelly and Gary Longwell started, but I came off the bench and did quite well. Most of us flew on to Tonga, where we were

booked into the International Dateline Hotel, fifty yards from the Pacific Ocean. It sounded like the most fabulous hotel ever, but it didn't live up to its name. They gave us chicken wings and chips for dinner. There was a shack of a shop down the road selling M&Ms and we were going down there every night and buying five packs each.

On a roasting hot day, on a rock-hard pitch, we beat Tonga well but Eddie wasn't happy. In the dressing room he had a go at us over our standards. Back at the hotel, Rog had a go back, telling him the criticism was unfair. The next day Eddie said he'd looked at the video and found that we'd done a lot of things well. It wasn't exactly an apology, but in fairness he took on board what Rog and the other senior guys had said.

The Aggie Grey Hotel in Samoa was a major improvement. The Samoans were strong but we beat them well in thirty-five degrees of heat. For a redhead it was hard going, but I stuck it out to the end. The win gave us big belief, but Eddie always wanted more. He was working this system where the forwards were divided into two pods of four, and if you strayed from your other three guys you got absolutely minced in the video session.

If someone closed their eyes for half a second in a meeting, he'd ask them a question. He hit the pause button after a pick-and-go from me – for about a centimetre of go-forward – and said: 'Now, Paul – that's about as useful as a trap door in a canoe.'

He showed Stringer digging for the ball in the ruck and said: 'Lads, if you're going to ruck like that, Stringer may as well be looking for a Mars bar in a bucket of shit there.' He loved a one-liner, Eddie.

The tour did us a lot of good. You could feel the team spirit building – we got on with it, despite the bad pitches and the brutal food. For me, it was a big tour. By the end of it, I was a first-team starter. All these years later, I still have little scars on my hand and my knee, souvenirs from the powdered coral on the pitch in Tonga.

By the time we got to the World Cup in Australia, four months on, my confidence was growing. It was still an innocent time for me and I was a long way from being a leader, but I was fit and going well. I was carrying a lot of ball, partly because only some of us had the licence to do it – Eddie called us the designated ball carriers.

The memories of our camp in Terrigal, a beautiful place on the Pacific Ocean, have stayed with me. You can never underestimate the importance of a squad being in a happy place when you're a long way from home. We played Australia in our final pool match and lost by a point, but I mostly remember that game because it was the first time I really

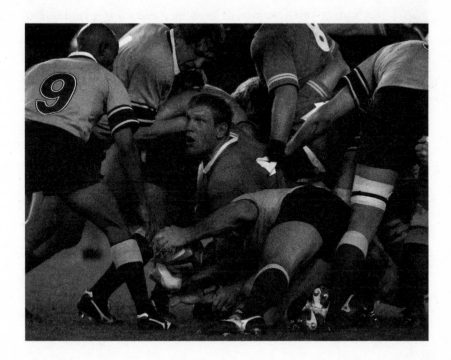

spoke in the dressing room. It was probably gibberish – something about them not being able to live with our pack – but the fact that I spoke at all was another step in the journey. There was nothing pre-planned about it, and I was a little bit worried after the game that I might have over-stepped the mark by speaking up, but nothing was said.

Everyone knew it was Woody's last tournament. He had patched himself up for one last stand and he'd needed anti-inflammatories to get through the games. France beat us out the gate in the quarter-final. Not for the first time, we had a completely new game plan. It was supposed to create massive overlaps, but it didn't work. It was only as I got older that I realized we weren't playing to our strengths by manu-facturing new game plans almost every week, instead of deciding on a way of playing and imposing it on other teams, with just a few tweaks here and there. We had world-class players who just needed to be given the ball. Brian O'Driscoll could get you a try from nowhere and Woody, even then, was one of the most dangerous players around. We needed to give them half-chances against players who weren't as good as them.

Back in Limerick, after the tournament, I was getting rec-ognized a lot more on nights out, but mostly I just carried on as before. Becoming better known never really felt like a big deal. Maybe I was deliberately playing it down in my own head, but I don't remember any moment where I thought to myself: *God, my life has changed.*

Brian was always going to be the man to follow Keith Wood as captain, after being given the job when Woody was out injured. I didn't really know him then. He was my room-mate one of the first times I was ever in the Ireland camp, but we barely spoke that week, because his life was really taking off and he was shooting back home to Dublin as often as he could. I'd never met him before that, although we'd had a moment in the Celtic League final a few months previously. When I saw him getting involved in something, I said the first thing that came into my head.

'Fuck off and stop trying to be a hard man!'

He just laughed. He was only nine months older than me, still twenty-two. But he had twenty caps for Ireland and three for the Lions. When he was playing in the 1999 World Cup, I was a bouncer at Nevada Smyth's bar in Limerick, hoping to break into the Young Munster first team.

He didn't need to try, he *was* a hard man.

I had fifteen caps to my name by the time the 2004 Six Nations came around. Brian was injured and Eddie asked me to captain the team in Paris. There was no big deal about it. Eddie pulled me aside at training on the Monday and asked me to call to his room that afternoon. When he asked, I told him I'd be thrilled to do it. At the press conference a couple of days later, I said the same thing. I was pretty naïve back then, and I hadn't given any thought to captaincy and what it called for. I was expecting only good things.

The only thing that really worried me that week was having to make a speech at the post-match dinner. Back then, public speaking made me very nervous. It hit me out of nowhere and I don't know why, because I did a bit of debating at school, and while I wasn't amazing I was comfortable speaking. But however it happened, there was a three-year period in my early twenties when my voice would start shaking and I'd go bright red whenever I spoke in public.

I was fine doing media, but if I had to make a speech off the top of my head I'd be a bag of nerves. I remember being asked to say a few words at a small charity event in the café at the UL Arena, and my voice was shaking so much I could barely get any words out.

When you're making the captain's speech at those dinners, you don't have to blow them away. You just thank everyone, say a few nice words about the opposition and sit down. I had my speech typed out and I was only going to be reading it. Fabien Pelous, the French captain, was sitting alongside me. He could see how jumpy I was. He was older and far more used to the kind of environment we were in. My speech was on the table, and before they called me to speak he leaned over and grabbed it.

I panicked. I was practically begging him to give it back. When he did, I read the whole thing out without looking up once. Rog said afterwards that it was like I was twelve again, reading a letter from St Paul to the Corinthians at a school Mass.

I was a decent international player at that stage – injury free and in good shape. I was offloading, playing on instinct. I was told there was interest in me from Toulouse and Leicester, which was very flattering, but I had no real interest in pursuing a move.

We lost that match in Paris, but we beat England at Twickenham three weeks later, playing one of Eddie's wide-wide game plans. The tactics worked, but the big factor was all the line breaks that Gordon D'Arcy made, which put them under savage pressure. When you can do what Darce did to England that day, any game plan works.

We finished with four wins out of five. It gave us a Triple Crown, which meant something then, seeing as how Ireland hadn't won it since I was five years old.

In the summer we went down to South Africa, believing we had the beating of them. We practised all kinds of running lines in training to beat their blitz defence, and some of them came off, but we weren't as far forward as we'd thought, and we didn't have the ball carriers to win down there.

We stuck to it, kept improving, and beat them in the autumn, comfortably. Eddie's stuff was coming out in us – we were becoming a really good side.

6

By 2004 there were more guys in Munster who were ready to make a step up. You could see it in the way they trained, strong characters like Denis Leamy, Stephen Keogh, Trevor Hogan and Jerry Flannery. Leamy was aggressive, athletic, hungry. He was only nineteen when I first joined Munster, and a couple of years later he was pushing hard for his place, exactly the kind of competitive young guy we needed coming through. Keogh and Hogan were excellent players too. They just happened to be there at a time when our pack was at its strongest, which meant they didn't start as many games as they might have done in later years. They ended up moving to Leinster, which was a reflection of where the two teams were back then.

What Flannery had came from a self-belief I had never seen before, and haven't seen since. It came from never giving up at anything he took on. At twenty-three, he was going nowhere. Munster didn't rate him. Nobody had a pro contract for him. He joined Galwegians in the All Ireland League, hoping that Connacht would notice him. After a year they saw enough to sign him and he stayed for two seasons, until Munster finally took him back. If you were in our set-up and you didn't see him as a coming man, you just weren't paying attention. He spent day after day making himself better and better, waiting for his chance.

With the younger guys looking to make their mark, our training sessions were no holds barred. Brian Hickey would referee the games between the team picked to start at the weekend and the rest, but he didn't use his whistle very often. He'd be pulling people out of rucks, shoving them away.

'You're offside! Get back! Get back!'

He always tried to get the tempo as close as he could to match day. When a maul was over he'd tear off down the pitch and he'd become the touch judge, raising his invisible flag in the air.

'Lineout for the Blues here!'

The team going forward would put all eight forwards into a maul, and the opposition would have eight guys defending, sometimes more. Everyone was effing and blinding and often the two teams had the same jerseys, or else some flimsy singlets, so half the time we weren't sure who was with who. There was no citing commissioner or TV cameras, so people were getting punched, pulled down, stamped, elbowed, everything.

Some of the younger guys weren't making the squad at the weekend, so they'd go and play All Ireland League rugby for their clubs. They must have felt frustration over that, and sometimes it came out if they drove the first-choice forwards back in a maul. There were fist-pumps into faces and choice words.

I could never let them have that moment. Even if it was

Stephen Keogh doing it, one of my best mates in the squad, I had to come back with something.

'Save it for the AIL, kid! Save it for the AIL!'

It used to kill him that I was so horrible, but for me it was like fighting with your brother in the back garden. You couldn't bear the idea of him beating you, at anything.

We knew Hickey might occasionally penalize us, but conceding a penalty wasn't the end of the world in training. One day I was at the front of a maul and Trevor had fallen out the back on the other side. He was six or seven metres away, lying on the ground, but he got up, ran straight at me and hit me with a shoulder straight into the side of my head.

I went for him. I had him pinned down. I said: 'Trevor, I could break your fucking jaw now if I wanted!'

He wasn't one to back off, Trevor.

'Go on so! Go on so!'

He threw a punch up at me from the ground and caught me on the face. At this stage Wally was on my back, trying to break it up, warning me not to retaliate.

For a long time in those training games, I had a switch. I'd start playing more on the edge of the law, or over it. I wasn't too bothered by somebody shoeing or stiff-arming me, but if they punched me I wouldn't stop digging until I was pulled off them. I think it came from growing up with Marcus, from hearing Dad talk about an eye for an eye, and from being coached at Young Munster never to back down from anyone. Even if the dig hadn't hurt much, I had to have the last word. There would always be a handshake after training and there was never any bad blood, but I used to go home feeling bad about losing it and throwing punches at friends and teammates. I loved it when there was a fight and I wasn't involved, because I could enjoy it and not have to come away feeling like I'd let myself down.

I remember trying to decide – for a couple of seconds – whether to hit Trevor back. As I was thinking about it, I had Wally in my ear. He knew what was going through my head – he'd seen it before.

'Paulie!'

'Paulie!'

'PAULIE!!'

But I was too far gone. So, bang – I headbutted Trevor.

Straight away I knew Wally was disgusted with me.

'PAAUUUL-IE!'

Hickey came over and said: 'That's a headbutt, for God's sake! You can't be doing that!' But he always wanted us aggressive in training games. Sometimes he'd throw a shoulder into a guy himself, just to get a reaction. He threw one into Donncha O'Callaghan one day. For about five seconds I genuinely feared for his life.

Literally straight after training we'd be slagging and joking about the stuff that had gone on, but a headbutt is really bad and I called Trevor that night to apologize.

He laughed it off. He didn't care.

Later on at Munster, incidents like that didn't happen so much. There were different reasons why. The training sessions became shorter and some of the most combative guys moved on, but the biggest factor was that the game itself changed in a big way. The kind of foul play that people used to get away with became unacceptable, and punishable by long suspensions.

Training also was where you grooved your habits for the weekend. 'You are what you repeatedly do' became a mantra I lived by. After a few years as captain I realized more and more the importance of discipline and winning the penalty count. You didn't do that by showing up on a Saturday suddenly with the right attitude. You did it by being conscious of it all week during training. You practised making the right decisions around the ruck, in the scrum, on the offside line. That made Saturdays easier and more natural. You weren't trying to get it right for just one day of the week.

Sometimes I'd meet rugby men from the old school and they'd be disgusted that the Munster pack hadn't unloaded on an opposition player when he was on the wrong side of a ruck, or offside all day. 'If he'd tried that against the Munster pack ten years ago,' they'd say, 'he'd have been walking off the pitch with his head split open.'

I'd tell them: 'That's not the way the game is any more. If a player did that today, he'd be serving six months of a suspension.'

And so, in my later years, the mauling in training wasn't as physical as it used to be and there weren't so many young psychos coming through the ranks, starting all these rows. The training sessions became calmer, which was maybe a bad thing. Every so often, when things got heated, it used to make me happy. I'd always feel we were mentally in better shape for the weekend when it happened.

There were times when I felt like I needed to rev things up. I remember, during a non-contact session, pulling Peter O'Mahony aside.

'The two of us will go full contact here now.'

'Are you serious?'

'Yes.'

I didn't think he would take me quite so literally. He went straight out and spear-tackled Simon Zebo. After that, we had a really sharp session.

Once I had got in the Munster team, I rarely threw punches during a game. I was able to control that side of myself and be calm, maybe even too calm sometimes.

Once, I remember beginning to panic when I got choked

in a ruck, because the player didn't let go for a long time. The way he had me, I couldn't punch him or try to elbow him to release myself. I couldn't breathe, I was about to pass out. I was already wrecked from the game, and when he eventually let go I wasn't able to get back up, or so I told myself.

I stayed on the ground and had a bit of treatment, but when I thought about it afterwards what really pissed me off was that I hadn't gotten up and jogged back. I shouldn't have allowed the medics to get near me.

Choking me was a little psychological win for that player, and I didn't do anything to level the score – I didn't come back at him. Some people would say that was good discipline out of me, but I had a nagging thought in my head for a long time afterwards.

Does he think he has it over me?

In training, I continued getting into scraps, until the day in 2007 when I realized that a lot of us had become so powerful through lifting weights that a single punch could hurt someone badly.

It happened at an Ireland camp before the World Cup, when Eddie was close to naming his squad for France. We were training at the University of Limerick and Ryan Caldwell, the Ulster second-row, was trying to make an impression. He'd been spoiling rucks all week, making a nuisance of himself. That was all fair enough – he was like me at the same age – but when he put me on the floor with a tackle in a non-contact session my switch went and I got up and threw a punch.

I didn't think I'd hit him too hard, but my right hand struck the side of his face and he went down, unconscious. What I didn't know then was that one of his teeth had burst his cheek and he was swallowing a lot of blood. The rest of us had to move away when the team doctor, Gary O'Driscoll, rushed over to him.

I kept looking over, from a distance, and the situation just kept getting worse and worse. Gary was trying to resuscitate him and he had blood all over his mouth. He was roaring for an ambulance. Then he started cutting the jersey off Ryan.

I was shaking by the time the ambulance came to take him away. I was starting to fear the worst, and I'm sure I wasn't the only one thinking that.

The ambulance drove off and Eddie came across the pitch towards us.

'What's the story?' I asked him.

'The story is, you nearly killed him.'

By then, the medics had stabilized the situation and Eddie told me he was going to be OK, but I was absolutely devastated that I'd put a fellow player in hospital with a punch, someone who was only trying to put down a marker in a training session.

The first guy to console me was Neil Best, one of Ryan's teammates at Ulster and a good friend of his. He said: 'You didn't mean for that to happen.'

It was very decent of him, and I remember John Hayes being supportive too when the horror of the situation was at its worst, but back in my room at the Castletroy Park Hotel I was disgusted with myself, embarrassed and in tears when I called Dad. Eddie came to the room, and talking about it helped. Other guys rang me and I felt bad that they had to make the calls, but I appreciated them too.

A few hours later I went to the hospital, and Ryan was unbelievably sound. He said: 'Don't worry about it – it was just bad luck, there's no problem.' They kept him in overnight as a precaution, but he was fine.

The following day, I apologized to the squad. I told them

we had great team morale but I had completely undermined it. Paddy Wallace, another Ulster player, was sitting in front of me. I could see him nodding his head as I was talking and it mattered so much to me that one of Ryan's friends was accepting my apology.

What happened to Ryan Caldwell changed me. It was the worst moment of my career. I never threw a punch in training again.

The following year, in a Heineken Cup game against Clermont Auvergne at Thomond Park, there was a skirmish near the touchline. I only went in to break it up, but then Jamie Cudmore, their second-row, hit me two digs. If you look at the video, you'll see me pointing at the touch judge after his first punch lands, as if I'm telling him: *He started this, he's leaving me no choice.*

After that I started lashing into Cudmore, which cost me a yellow card to his red. I never saw that as a loss of control on my part – it's a physical game we play and sometimes you have to defend yourself in a physical way when things get out of hand. There's a balance to be struck, a happy medium. You can never allow the opposition pack to dominate you, and I asked myself after that Cudmore incident if I should have got stuck into him the second he unloaded on me.

It wasn't about me and him. He was a player I liked and respected for years afterwards, and whatever problem there was between us in those few seconds was over by the time we reached the touchline. In throwing those punches, I was standing up for our pack, for the team. He was doing the same. He was taking the physical battle to us.

Me holding back for a second or two probably made the difference between a yellow card and a red. It meant we had an extra player for more than fifty minutes. We won that game, but for most of the second half Clermont dominated us, and I wondered how much of that was down to the physi-cal statement Cudmore made against me early on.

People talk about Munster's defeat to Wasps in the 2004 Heineken Cup semi-final as a turning point for us, but it isn't necessarily true. There was a short-term ripple, in terms of where Wasps were physically that day and how we compared. We brought in one or two new conditioning coaches, but our training didn't really change. We agreed it was far from ideal to have two training centres, one in Limerick and one in Cork, but we never did anything about it for another twelve years. Whatever change did happen was really only window dressing. The real change that came from that day was that a core group of players became more determined than ever before to make Munster successful. It wasn't that the organ-ization itself got better. It was that the hardest trainers in the group drew on the Wasps defeat. That was what really made the difference.

The word at Lansdowne Road that day was that Wasps were stronger and fitter than us. They probably were, but for a short time near the end we were down to thirteen men. We played great rugby, we should have won it. The game turned in their favour after Josh Lewsey stamped on one of our players and Nigel Owens put his flag out. He changed his mind and put the flag back down, and right at that moment Rob Henderson came in from the side at a ruck and got sinbinned. Donners was already off the pitch with a yellow card.

I once had a conversation about that game with someone who'd seen us on the train coming home. She told me she couldn't understand why we seemed to be in such good form, having just lost a Heineken Cup semi-final.

I tried to explain it to her. What sometimes happens, after

a defeat like that, is that when you're still with the playing group you can put off the reckoning. You know it isn't the time to address the defeat. For a short period you can ignore it, enjoy a drink together and have some fun. It isn't until the next day that you realize you've made it ten times worse. You've got a hangover and it's time to face up to what happened and the opportunity lost.

Sometimes I experienced a feeling of confusion immediately after I'd woken up on the morning after a game. For maybe a second and a half, I wasn't sure how it had gone the previous day. As I was coming to my senses, two questions came into my head.

Did we win?

Did we lose?

And when we'd won, especially a big game, it was one of the nicest feelings I ever got in rugby – that split second of sheer happiness when I realized that everything was all right. The aches and pains I felt in my body were there to remind me all day about the win and what I had put my body through to help achieve it. It was a lovely feeling. I had a day off ahead of me to spend with Emily and I knew everyone was going to be in good form.

When we'd lost, it was horrible. And when I got into my thirties, the same aches and pains were telling me it was time to retire, that I physically didn't have it any more. If I saw somebody in a Munster jersey around town later in the day and they were nice to me – which Limerick people always were, even when we'd been beaten – I'd feel embarrassed. I knew, too, that sometimes my family were going to have to spend the day on eggshells around me.

A big part of the reason I found it so hard to enjoy the build-up to the big games was because I was afraid of losing and of that feeling when I woke up on Sunday morning.

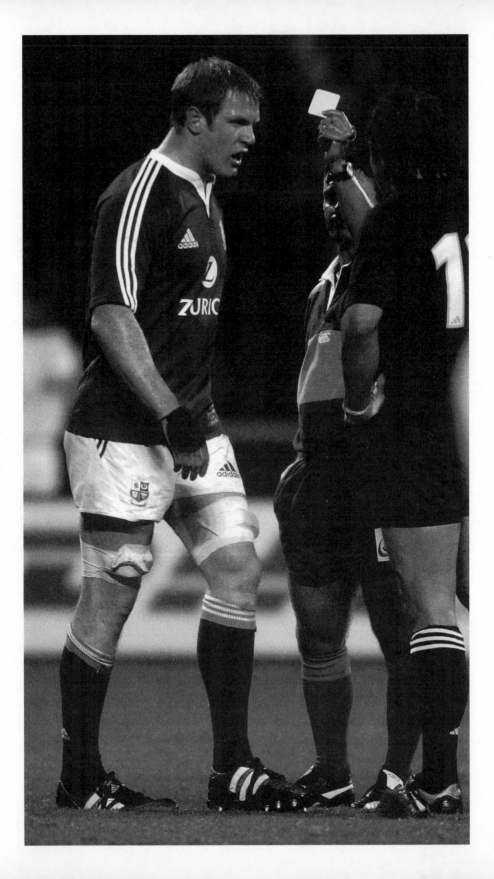

7

By 2005 I was being built up so much in the media that it was making me a little uncomfortable. I tried not to pay much attention, but it was hard to avoid hearing or reading some of it. I knew I was being mentioned in the same sentence as Martin Johnson, and I was named in most of the Lions teams selected by journalists six months out from the tour of New Zealand.

The 2004–5 season was mostly a disappointment, but I played a lot of games for Munster and Ireland and I was in good form. A few people mentioned me as a dark horse for the Lions captaincy, but I knew Brian was always likely to get it. I'm sure one of the reasons Clive Woodward chose him was because the Kiwis knew full well just how good he was. He had a talent that couldn't be denied, even in New Zealand.

You couldn't have said the same about me. I knew that, no

matter how many good things were being written in the northern hemisphere, I still had a lot to improve on, and a lot to prove.

When I thought about the Lions, I saw being part of a tour as something incredible. As an eighteen-year-old I had watched the *Living With Lions* video many times, the one from the 1997 tour in South Africa. The men in that video are legends of the game now. They were playing for the jersey and they were old-school in their approach, which was why their story resonated with me so much.

When you watched them getting psyched up in the dressing room, or bonding in the team room, it was like you were being sold a dream. The best scene showed the forwards coach, Jim Telfer, with his pack gathered around him on the day before the first Test. The camera closed in on Martin Johnson and Lawrence Dallaglio and it was obvious they were hanging on his every word.

'This is your fucking Everest, boys. Very few get the chance in rugby terms to get to the top of Everest. You have the chance today. Being picked is the easy bit. To win for the Lions in a Test match is the ultimate – but you'll not do it unless you put your bodies on the line.'

When I was selected for the 2005 tour, I imagined it was going to be all of that. New Zealand were playing unbelievable rugby and not many were giving us a chance before we went down there; but rather than listen to any of that negativity I used to think about what Telfer told the 1997 Lions, and I saw us rising to the same challenge.

At the Hilton in Auckland, on one of our first nights in the country, I was flicking through the TV channels in my room when a New Zealand journalist came on and started talking about playing his part in the Lions' downfall.

He said he saw it as his job to stick it to us as often as he could, to get under our skins. Apart from the fact that I'd been under the impression it was a journalist's job to report the news, it didn't bother me. It was just like what Telfer had said in the video.

'They don't rate us. They don't respect us. The only way to be rated is to stick one on them, to get right up in their faces and turn them back.'

A month later, after we'd lost the first Test badly, I was on a training pitch in Wellington. After five minutes of the session, it felt as though every emotion I'd experienced since the beginning of the tour – every ounce of pressure I'd been feeling – was being multiplied by ten.

Am I going mad here?

Can I not take the pressure any more?

I'd never been as worked up in training – not even remotely close. But then I'd never taken something called Focus before putting on my boots.

You could call it an energy drink, but that wouldn't cover it. It contained a massive hit of caffeine. Whatever you happened to be feeling at the time, whatever mood you were in, it exaggerated it.

The previous night, four days before the second Test, Clive had spoken to us in the team room at the Inter-Continental Hotel. Or rather, he had teed up someone else.

Alastair Campbell, Tony Blair's spin doctor, was with us because Clive had figured the Kiwi media would try to work us over. He wanted a big hitter to have our back.

After we were hammered in Christchurch, there was a press conference called to talk about the spear tackle – forty seconds into the game – that put Brian out of rugby for months. Clive kept asking why Keven Mealamu and Tana Umaga hadn't been cited for it. I understood the frustration, but I didn't think putting the incident up on a big screen in slow motion, in front of a roomful of journalists, was going to help our cause. You can maybe do that when you've won the game, but when you've been absolutely hockeyed it's a little more difficult. The New Zealanders were never going to roll over and apologize.

I liked Alastair. I know his intentions were good. But his big speech to the squad didn't go down well.

He said he knew next to nothing about rugby, but he did know what it felt like to be under serious pressure when everything was on the line. He talked about fighting elections for the Labour Party. When they were taking on the Conservatives, he said, it was like going to war and they'd do anything to win.

Then he upped it.

He told us that in every campaign and every crisis, there comes a moment when the people in the thick of it realize they need to dig deep – or they're in serious trouble. He talked about Northern Ireland, then Kosovo. He said he didn't get that feeling when he looked at us. He didn't have the sense that we were fighting back.

I was really insulted. I wasn't playing well, but I could not have been trying any harder. I was emptying myself in every training session and every match. I knew where I was and it annoyed me that anyone would question how much I wanted to win for the Lions when I was going to the depths of what I had in me.

On the training pitch the following morning, I was still thinking about Alastair's few words and getting more and more pissed off. I decided what I was going to do when the session was over: find Alastair Campbell and knock him out. There wouldn't be any need for questions or explanations. Everyone would know what it was for. But by the time training was over, the effect of the Focus had worn off, and I was back to normal. Or what passed for normal on that tour.

In the afternoon, once I'd done my analysis, I headed off into the city on my own. I didn't want to draw anyone on me, so I made sure nothing I was wearing had any Lions branding. I found an ancient-looking bookshop on the quieter end of the main drag with stock piled up all over the floor and a café upstairs with couches and tables. I remember sitting there drinking tea and reading *Atomised* by Michel Houellebecq, enjoying my own company and deciding I'd go back the next day and do the same.

I was finding the tour a lonely experience. The players had separate rooms. Looking back, that wasn't the greatest idea when you're trying to bring a team together for the first time. The dream I'd bought into was nothing like the reality. In trying to find the winning edge, Clive had broken with Lions tradition, and all these years later it's obvious that something important was lost. At the time, I couldn't really see that. All I knew then was that it was nothing like the 1997 video, and I felt as if I was contributing to the downfall of the Lions. There was very little perspective when you were in the middle of it.

After that first Test I started smoking the odd cigarette in my room. To this day I don't know why. When I was younger, most of my friends smoked. If I had a few drinks on a night out I might take a cigarette off them, but until that tour I hadn't smoked one in years.

I was brushing my teeth six or seven times a day: I wanted to brush away the smell of smoke. I wasn't getting a whole lot out of the tour and I remember thinking there might be one benefit before it was over.

At least I might have white teeth by the end of this fucking trip.

The world and his wife got stuck into Clive and blamed him for everything, but the players he had to choose from weren't in the best of form. He tried something different and split the squad into two groups – one for the Tests and the other for the midweek games – but none of us senior players were saying, 'This is wrong, it won't work' before it all unravelled.

There was a raft of changes for the second Test. Donners was named to start alongside me in the second row and I was really happy for him, but I felt bad for Ben Kay. Our lineout had gone to pot in Christchurch and he had suffered the consequences, along with Shane Byrne. A lot of the blame lay firmly at my feet and I felt like a bit of a fraud to get away with it. We were better in Wellington – and we lost by thirty points.

Looking back, we came across an excellent side and we never became the team we needed to be. There were so many of us on tour that it was hard to pull together and turn it around. Some of the coaching staff were unhappy – like the players, they were split into two groups. And some of the players were unhappy with the coaching staff – they didn't feel they'd had a fair crack at getting in the Test team.

Losing three of our biggest players – Lawrence Dallaglio in the first game of the tour, then Brian and Richard Hill in the first Test – really killed us. Any team is only as good as its leaders, and they were guys who gave the squad confidence and belief.

I took some more Focus before the second Test. I wasn't a coffee drinker, so it had a massive effect on me. Once the whistle went I was pumped to the gills. We started off really well and Gareth Thomas scored a try. Then Dwayne Peel made another big break that set up a ruck, and I could see Rodney So'ailalo coming over the top of it, so I ran at him from twenty metres away. I was lining him up to hit him as hard as I could. But he got out of the way just before impact and I went flying over the top.

Penalty to them, momentum gone from us. And it looked bad, it looked terrible.

'That,' said our hooker, Steve Thompson, afterwards, 'was a clear example of an Irishman on Focus.' I never touched the stuff again.

I knew I was getting slated and blamed, that all mistakes were being magnified. On the Thursday before the third Test, I sat on the balcony of my hotel bedroom in Auckland, overlooking the bay. I was brushing my teeth and watching the boats in the harbour, thinking how different it all was from what I'd been expecting. I was digging in and working as hard as I could, but I really struggled that week. I'd had plenty of setbacks since turning professional, a lot of defeats that hurt, but nothing like the humiliation we suffered on that tour.

And in the middle of it all, I split up with Emily over the phone. We'd met in Limerick on St Stephen's night in 1999 and had been together for more than five years. That season she'd been in Cardiff, studying interior architecture, and every time she came home I was engulfed in rugby. I didn't want to break up, but I could see it from her point of view. My focus at that time was rugby, rugby, rugby. I had so much of myself invested in it that I couldn't disconnect. I knew that wasn't fair on Emily, but I couldn't help myself then. I was living for the games and I was up or down, depending on how they went.

Thankfully we got back together the following year.

The performance in the third Test was better from us, and better from me. But nowhere near enough. After the game I spoke to a few of the reporters covering the tour. I had a bottle of Steinlager beer in my hand and I was already thinking about the plane home. One of them reminded me that the All Blacks would be at Lansdowne Road later in the year.

'Are you dreading it?'

I told him I was looking forward to it, actually. Which was true.

Even though the tour was a tough experience, it didn't kill the mystique of the Lions for me. I still badly wanted to be part of a winning tour and I was young enough to get another chance.

At Heathrow airport a couple of days later, on the journey home, I bumped into Ger Clohessy. It was around nine in the morning. We had a few beers in the bar at Terminal One and a few more on the plane home to Shannon. When it landed, we headed for Myles Breen's bar in the city centre, and then on to Austin Quinlivan's.

Somewhere along the line I told Ger about my fondest memory of the six weeks – watching the new Batman movie with Donners and a big bag of sweets at the cinema in Auckland. On a day when I'd felt particularly low, his friendship had lifted me.

Not long after that, I was stretched out on a chair, telling a dentist where my teeth were hurting.

'Here . . . here . . . and here.'

He took a good look and told me there wasn't a lot that could be done about the situation.

'You've brushed away your gums,' he said.

8

Even when Ireland were winning Triple Crowns under Eddie, we were incredibly inconsistent. I'd go down for breakfast on the morning we were playing England, or maybe France, and I'd look around the room. We had a very talented group and I'd be convinced that if everyone in the team turned up, we'd almost certainly win. But very rarely was I confident about what would come out on the pitch.

The inconsistency wasn't even a week-to-week thing. Sometimes, our performance was wildly different from half to half. In Paris in 2006, we went in at half-time 29–3 behind. Early in the second half, their lead stretched to 43–3. Then we proceeded to score twenty-eight unanswered points. The comeback proved how good we were capable of being, but the first half showed how susceptible we were to implosion.

What strikes me now is how two massively contrasting performances could live side by side in the same game, with the same players. Looking back, I can see there were a number of reasons for our inconsistency. The biggest of them was that we had too wide a focus on the skills of the game. We varied how we played so often it was hard to build confidence in any one way of playing. When I was involved in more consistent Irish teams, we had a much narrower focus. There were certain skills and ways of playing that we tried to be the best at. We built our game around those.

We were always better after a loss, which was another aspect of our inconsistency. We were still on a learning curve.

In our best years at Munster, I never had the same uncertainty. It wasn't that I didn't get nervous before the games. But I knew how hard people were training, and that created certainty in my mind when we were facing into the big games. There wasn't a lot of complication to how we played. Our heads were clear to deliver aggressively on our direct style of rugby.

People talk about a team's culture a lot these days. Our culture was all about training at a level that allowed us to deliver a level of intensity that teams couldn't live with.

When I started pre-season training after the Lions tour, Alan Gaffney had left for a job with the Australian national team and Declan was back as head coach after a season at Leinster. I'd matured a lot in the three years since he'd been in the job. By then I was one of the players trying to find answers every week. We never wanted a game plan served up to us – we thought we were better running things ourselves.

One of Deccie's biggest strengths was recognizing that quality in us and finding ways to make it powerful. In a way, his rugby philosophy was that having belief in what we were doing was almost more important than what we were actually doing.

A key part of his coaching was trying to get interaction out of people. Deccie figured out ways. Sometimes he explained things so vaguely that we were pumping him with questions.

'What exactly are we doing here?'

'Then what?'

'How about if we did this?'

That was his biggest strength.

If we lost a game, he'd have the decision-makers in for a meeting and he'd say, 'Make sure you look at it closely and have a think about it – because we're going to need answers.'

We'd have this big discussion – and generally an argument with Deccie. We'd half blame him for everything.

'We're doing the wrong things in training!'

'We're not preparing properly!'

Then we'd walk out, thinking: *Right, that's it, we've sorted it all out. From now on, we're doing things our way.*

And that, for Deccie, was probably the whole point of having the meeting in the first place.

Back then, a lot of us in the dressing room looked up to Roy Keane. The combative side of his personality was always about the upholding of standards. You've got to be the best – or if you're not, you've got to want to be, which means putting in the work and doing things right. And if you don't want to be part of the best team, then what are you doing here?

So if there was a problem, we ran straight at it, attacked it head on.

If we thought there was something that needed to be said, we said it.

Every single one of us was obsessed with winning the Heineken Cup. And we knew that people were beginning to think it would never happen for us, that we'd already had enough chances. I never paid any attention to that, because I knew how much the guys wanted it, but there was a limit to the amount of times the same players could keep coming back.

I completely switched off for the four-week break after the Lions tour. When I returned I felt I had a better sense of perspective and a clearer idea of what was required at the very top level. Eddie had secured a ten-week pre-season for the international players and I made the most of it.

My first game back was against Llanelli Scarlets in Cork. Near the end, I saw Simon Easterby giving Donners a dig, and when I punched him with my left hand I broke my thumb. That put me out for thirteen weeks, but it actually worked to my advantage. Because it was a hand injury, there was so much training I still could do. By the time I got back, I was the fittest I'd ever been, after three months of one-to-one training with our strength and conditioning coach, Fergal O'Callaghan.

A lot of it was old school. There was a run in the Cratloe hills, with the last two minutes on a massive gradient. Week after week I kept trying to beat my best time, with my heart rate rocketing. For the first time, I worked with a sprint coach, Tom Comyns, who made a huge difference to my training. We did a lot of circuit training too, weights with high reps, and I had to get my cast changed every week because it stank from the sweat. By the time I got back, against Connacht just after Christmas, I'd effectively had more than twenty weeks of pre-season training and only seventy-five minutes of game time. I couldn't have been fresher, or fitter.

Two weeks later, in Edinburgh, something clicked. We won by only a point, but we played great rugby and we felt a real buzz about our performance. We went down to Castres the following Friday night, full of confidence, and won 46–9.

We had a new midfield partnership in Barry Murphy and

Trevor Halstead, and they ripped Castres apart. Ian Dowling came in on the wing and played really well. Against Sale the following week, Barry scored one of the great Munster tries, a short walk from where he'd grown up. I don't think I ever played in a better atmosphere than there was that evening at Thomond Park. We chopped Sebastien Chabal low every time he got the ball. Instead of running over people, as he usually did, he was attempting chip-aheads.

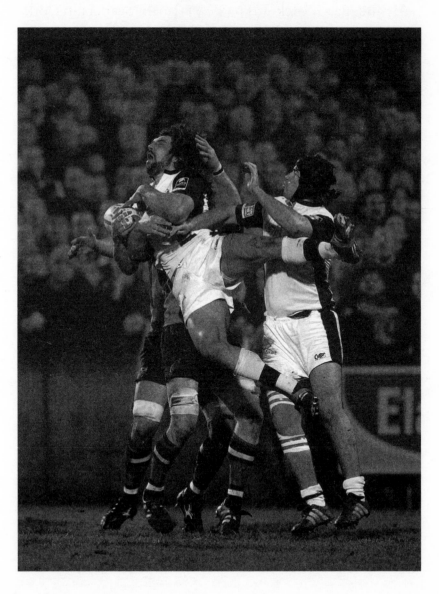

When Wally scored our bonus-point try right at the end, the Sale back-row Jason White was behind the goalposts, devastated. Later on he told a story that I loved. Sale were the best team in England then. They'd come to win. Jason said he was looking into the crowd, asking himself how it had all gone wrong for them. He made eye contact with a Munster supporter. They stared at one another for a couple of seconds, until the guy in the crowd shouted out, Limerick style: 'WHAT THE FUCK ARE *YOU* LOOKING AT?'

By then, we absolutely believed we were good enough to win the competition. The players who broke into the team that season, apart from being great talents, were workhorses. We were a youngish side and we weren't playing any particular style or brand of rugby. It was just work, work, work – take them on, run them into the ground. We could always rely then on Rog's intuition to do the right thing at the right time and put teams under pressure. We put our heads down and worked. He kept his up and surveyed what we should do next. He rarely got it wrong.

Flannery and Donners were fitness-obsessed, and it was infectious for the rest of the group. They were setting new standards in terms of diet, weights and conditioning. We piggybacked on their good work and learned from them.

There was a mindset in the squad: any problem could be ironed out through training and preparation. It was powerful, and our self-belief rocketed. When I looked around the pitch a few minutes before kick-off, I'd be thinking: *Whether we win or we lose here, we're going to absolutely give it everything, on the back of all the work we've been doing in training.*

Right or wrong, we felt all our problems could be solved through fitness.

In the week of a game we'd talk about the opposition and

their level of fitness and we never felt they could out-work us. There was no elaborate game plan. We'd go down blind alleys sometimes, and we'd have to figure out a way back, but that was always going to happen, the way we played. It was all about the intensity we were bringing, about taking ourselves to the point where we were gasping for breath – and seeing where that left the opposition. To break them, we had to nearly break ourselves. It's easier to draw on your store of fitness when your pack is on top and the scoreboard is going the right way. Sometimes, when you're behind, you can let yourself believe you're getting tired.

In a beast of a training game during the week before the quarter-final against Perpignan, Declan made sure we were physically ready. We dogged it out in Dublin that day, and on the train home we had a couple of lovely carriages to ourselves, with sofas and a bar at the end. We went on an unmerciful tear and I remember thinking how perfect it was on the train: for two hours it was just us, the players' partners, a handful of parents and the staff, knowing we had produced the goods and were in a good place.

There was never anything like the build-up to the semi-final against Leinster. I look at the two packs now and I don't see how the outcome could have been any different. They learned from that game and they changed, but in 2006 there were six or seven Munster players in the Ireland pack for every game, and all that week we kept hammering it into ourselves that we could take them up front.

They missed the first kick-off, we pounced on it and just pounded away at their line for an age. We kept going at them until it was over.

Come the week of the final, we were all under pressure. We trained on our own, without coaches, towards the end of the week. Another coach could have seen that as an attack on his authority, but Deccie knew we were a team with the leadership to deal with whatever needed to be sorted. It was something I brought with me throughout my career for big games. I always wanted the team to take ownership of everything we were doing as Saturday came closer.

I'd torn an ankle ligament in a Celtic League match fifteen days before the final. There were moments when I thought I wouldn't make it, and I'm not sure how I would have dealt with that disappointment. On the Tuesday, I convinced myself I was going to be OK, but I was so worried about my ankle that week I didn't get hit by the usual stress.

The night before, towards the end of Axel's team talk, I could hear his voice cracking with emotion and I saw his lips quivering. He was one of the original standard-setters. He'd started the first Heineken Cup game Munster ever played, eleven years before, and he was the final survivor of that team. He held himself together, but it didn't do any of us any harm to see what it meant to him.

On the morning of the game I tweaked my neck, and the pain got worse in the warm-up. I started thinking about the first scrum, with my head wedged in between Hayes and Flannery. A few minutes later, just before we went back into the dressing room, Rog was holding a tackle bag and I hit it with very little intensity. I was minding myself, ten minutes before a Heineken Cup final. And my head was all over the place.

I'm in trouble here.
I can't scrummage with my neck like this.
I could be gone after two minutes.
Maybe I should pull out now?
I'm not pulling out.
What if my ankle goes?
Stop panicking. Just go as hard as you can.

I had a picture of Padre Pio tucked into my sock, and a lot of my family had prayed to him that week, and put a few quid in the collection box at different churches in the hope that he'd get me through it.

I'm convinced we would have beaten Biarritz more easily if so many of us hadn't been off our feet with injuries in the run-up. It meant we didn't put up an eighty-minute performance, like we had against Leinster. We started well, but by the end we were hanging on. Rugby fitness is different to what's required in other team sports. Forty seconds on, fifteen seconds off is the zone a forward lives in. You need those fifteen seconds to recover and go again. But when the plays become longer, or your match fitness isn't fully there, the body experiences oxygen debt and lactate build-up. You start worrying that you won't have the legs to make the tackle that could win the game or lose it. With five minutes left, just as I caught the drop-off after the penalty from Rog that put us four points ahead, I knew I was becoming a liability. My leg was cramping and it was time to get off.

I was on the touchline when the whistle blew. When I ran on to the pitch, I hugged Donners and the emotion of the occasion got the better of me. The realization that we had done it was overwhelming. I hadn't allowed myself to think of what it would mean to me if we won. I hadn't imagined what victory would look like or feel like, and then suddenly it was real.

I don't have any medals or trophies or mementos lying around my house for people to see. But I do have one photograph from that game, taken after we'd won it, and what I like about it is that it captures just how unbridled it all was.

So many supporters came up to me and said: 'That was the best day of my life.' Not just a few. Loads and loads, for months afterwards, even years: 'The best day of our lives.'

Saturday night in Cardiff was tame for me. I relaxed and chatted and enjoyed the evening. Sunday and Monday were one long party, which started on an open-top bus through the streets of Limerick. On the Monday morning in Limerick, I was in town early with Timmy Lane and we ended up in Rasher's, a little pub on Gerald Griffin Street. There was nobody there, all the chairs were up on the tables, and me and Timmy had two pints in front of us.

By half-twelve, the place was packed. There was nothing arranged, but other guys from the team joined us, and then people just walked out of work when they heard that half the Munster team was there with the Heineken Cup. We were on it all day. I remember supporters drinking out of the cup and we were tipping it up as they were at it – guys with shirts and ties had beer spilt down their front and they had to go back into work like that. Some of them, anyway.

It was a great day – going from pub to pub, carrying the cup with us, seeing everybody in good form. It was like one of the Munster Senior Cup stories I'd heard about but never experienced.

Winning the tournament brought us a massive feeling of relief, at first, but it wasn't long before that turned to complete joy. For three or four days we felt things could not be any better.

9

The longer I played the game, the more sophisticated and nuanced coaching became, and it got increasingly difficult to break down defences. The coaches I played under all had different ways of trying to do it. Some wanted to isolate the weakest defenders and have powerful ball-carriers like Wally or Sean O'Brien running over them. For Eddie, it was about creating overlaps.

Before a game, he would draw a line on the board in the team meeting. He'd say: 'From the ruck to six men out, they're very good defensively – so we're just going to get beyond that sixth man.' He was like a general scheming his way across a battleground map: 'There's a hinge there. We get to the hinge – and we go down there.'

He used to plot these moves with Mervyn Murphy, our video analyst, and the two of them were purists. They never wanted to cut straight through a team; they wanted us to run them ragged and create a three-man overlap.

We didn't really play our rugby through the forwards then. We had a great backline, but I felt our forward pack could have been used more. We had to throw two long passes and go after the opposition out wide. They'd chase us to the touchline and then we'd throw two more massive passes and try to go around them again on the other wing. When it worked, it looked great, and we all became better all-round rugby players through practising Eddie's plays in training. But when it mattered most, in the games, it didn't work often enough.

I used to think that the try Girvan Dempsey scored for us against England in Twickenham back in 2004 was a mixed blessing. It was an incredible team score, and it was the try Eddie had been hoping to pull off for so long. But we spent years afterwards trying to do the same to other teams, and our strike rate wasn't good enough.

So much of rugby is an open book. You can analyse a game and come up with telling statistics: the number of times you got over the gain line and the metres made, the turnovers at the ruck and at the lineout. But what you won't see in the video review is the moment when your pack took over psychologically and their players knew it and felt it inside.

To the naked eye it may appear like it happened in an instant – an impact tackle, a maul to score, a big scrum – but it's an accumulation of dominant moments that really does it. It comes from an attitude that a pack takes on to the pitch, a conviction that they will be relentless in everything they do in every moment of the game. Sometimes you can get knocked back, but you have to stick with it until you've broken them. You can win a soccer match in one second with a piece of brilliance, but rugby is not like that. You need fifteen players who are ready to go further, psychologically, than the opposing fifteen.

The word on the street in November of 2005, after heavy losses to New Zealand and Australia, was that Eddie had lost the Ireland dressing room. To me, it didn't make any sense. For a start, I was never part of a team that motivated itself by playing for the coach. The way I saw it, you played for the team and not for any individual. I was injured for those autumn internationals, but I never had any sense that players had lost faith.

Eddie was an excellent coach. He gave the job everything. He was very strict, especially in the early years, and there wasn't a lot of banter about him – either within the set-up or outside of it. We bought into his coaching in a big way; we did everything we were told to and did it well. We were training on better pitches, eating better food, we had top-class analysis from Merve and everything ran like clockwork.

Once the team hit a bad run of form, some of the media went after him. I wouldn't say that kind of talk got to him, but maybe he felt the players could have been more comfortable in his company. In the camp before the 2006 Six Nations, he joined us for a meal and some drinks at a Chinese restaurant in Dalkey. For Eddie, that was a new departure.

There was a table for the non-drinkers, like Donners and Stringer, because they knew we were going out later and they were staying out of harm's way. Wally was sick and Rory Best wasn't having a drink either. They were a big loss to the drinkers' table. The rest of us didn't hold back.

We were singing songs, standing on chairs, throwing napkins at one other. When one of the napkins flew across the table and knocked over some glasses, the staff came running and we all pointed at the guys on the sober table.

'It was the nerds!'

Someone took it further and soaked his napkin in a glass of red wine, then started wearing it off the guy beside him. Next thing, Eddie was doing it. We were looking at each other, all thinking the same thing.

What's going on here?

What's gotten into him?

Eddie had decided to let his hair down too, and it was one of the greatest nights out I ever had with an Irish team.

We headed off on a bus to a nightclub in the city centre, Copper Face Jacks. The bus had a microphone and we were fighting each other to get hold of it and sing.

I got to bed at six that morning, knowing I had to be up at seven, so I stayed awake and played music on my laptop. By lunchtime I was down in Cork, at the Maryborough House Hotel. There was a Lions lunch on and Willie John McBride was the guest of honour. When he came over and joined me, he talked about the fitness of modern players – he thought it was really impressive. I wasn't saying a whole lot back, mostly because I had three of the free Milky Moo mints from the hotel reception in my mouth, hoping they'd stop Willie John from picking up the smell of alcohol on my breath.

We played quite well in that Six Nations, and we managed to convince Eddie that the night out had had something to do with it, so much so that it became a permanent fixture in our build-ups. We put the disappointing autumn behind us and there were some good performances. The best was at Twickenham in the final game, and it gave us a second Triple Crown in three years.

We went on a lap of honour, and I could see Mam and Dad behind the goal-line, ten metres to the right of the posts, right at the front after the England fans had gone home.

If I close my eyes I can still see Dad's face.

We had come from behind in the dying minutes and Shane Horgan's famous try had won it for us. Dad was trying to find words to say what he was feeling, but nothing was coming out. His only form of communication was to stretch out the fingers of both hands – chest high and straight in front, with his arms wide apart – and move them up and down. There were tears in his eyes and I remember thinking:

Could that man be any happier, any prouder than he is now?
Could he feel any better?

It's an image I will always have.

There were five or six people waiting for us at the airport when we landed in New Zealand for Ireland's two Tests that June. The previous summer, with the Lions, there had been hundreds. It felt like there wasn't a whole lot of interest in the games, which was a reflection of how we were seen down there.

Their opinion of us never changed during those years. They might have thrown a few compliments our way once in a while, but I don't think they ever felt threatened by us. Why should they, when Ireland have never beaten them? The only way to earn their respect is to beat them, and more than once.

We felt we were capable of winning that summer – and we were. We had so many players at the peak of their powers, and as a team we had come on so much under Eddie. There were seven Munster forwards in the pack and we'd never been fitter or more confident. From one to fifteen we played great rugby in both Tests, but came up short. I look back on the games now as lost opportunities, but for me it wasn't about making history. I never thought it would be something particularly special to be part of the first Ireland team to beat them. It would be such a modest boast – like being giant-killers, when really you want to be the giant.

Life was easier when I had blind faith in Munster and everything we did, when I just assumed it was all done brilliantly, even when it wasn't. We made some less than successful signings, but I never questioned them. Our squad was split into two centres – but for a long time I didn't see it as a problem, and it's only now that I realize I never had the same bond with some of the players based in Cork, especially the ones I didn't get to spend time with in Ireland camp. We also didn't get the time on the pitch that was required, particularly when the game moved on and more time was needed to develop skills, patterns and plays.

I can't remember exactly when I changed from being one of those players who just take things as they come to being someone who was always asking questions. I suppose it was a gradual process, but things moved to a different level when I took on the Munster captaincy, later in the summer of 2006.

For a couple of years before I took it on, I had seen myself as a future captain – but maybe it came a little bit too early for me. I didn't enjoy that first year doing it. We didn't play well either, so people said: 'Captaincy isn't suiting him.'

Perhaps there was always going to be a dip after we won our first Heineken Cup, but after I got the job I just thought: *When you're Munster captain you're successful – and that's it.*

We didn't know where we were that season, we didn't know ourselves. We no longer had that thought in our heads, driving us on: *If we don't win this before we retire, we're going to be so unfulfilled and so unhappy with our careers.*

All of a sudden we'd got it and we were trying to find a new source of motivation. So we floundered for a while and I found it a really difficult time. I underestimated what was involved in the role and how hard it would be. I never allowed myself to have an excuse when things didn't go well, even if there was a reasonable one available.

It was probably around then that some of the lads started calling me Keano.

As in Roy, giving people a hard time.

I think it was mostly meant as a compliment, given the respect that people in our group had for Roy Keane. But I'm sure some of them got tired of me giving out.

Once I was captain of Munster, I took an interest in everything we were doing as a club: the players we signed, our scouting structure, our academy. There were times when I held myself back, when I told myself: 'That's really nothing to do with you.' But then I reminded myself that anything to do with Munster had to do with me, and I needed to give everything to help make us successful.

Mostly, I got my views across without any problems. When I talked to Garrett Fitzgerald, the Munster CEO, I wasn't ranting and raving. I was always conscious of saying: 'Look, I know how hard your job is . . . but can we have a look at this? Can we see if we can do it better?'

I saw myself as being a really hard trainer and I was thinking: *Right – we're going to take our preparation to a whole new level here.*

Axel wasn't the hardest trainer, but he thought about rugby all week, and when he went on to the pitch he was a different animal. That was his way.

I wanted to do it differently. So from the beginning I was telling Deccie that if someone wasn't delivering, they'd have to be told straight out. I'd go through the squad with him and I wouldn't spare the ones I thought needed to work harder.

'This guy isn't fit.'

'That guy isn't putting it in.'

'We're not fit enough across the board.'

It was never as simple as that, but I saw things only in black and white then. As captain you have to be able to see the middle ground. Even when something is bugging you a

146

little bit, there are times when it's best to ignore it. And I wasn't able to do that during my first year in the job. I was a young guy and I was fixated on driving standards, relentlessly.

I had a thing about subs. If a player was on the bench on Saturday and he'd got very little time on the pitch, I felt he should be in training on Sunday. I never thought about him maybe having a family, or needing his time off. At the very least, I thought the extra session should be structured into his week. If I didn't see him doing it, or hear about him doing it, it used to drive me mad.

Sometimes I think you should be allowed to delete your old interview quotes, or burn them from everyone's memory. They're only a reflection of the logic that was getting you through at the time, but people think that because you said something five years ago, you still believe it. And sometimes you don't.

This is the kind of stuff I was coming out with that year: 'If you're good enough you can take criticism – you can take the most harsh, most vicious criticism from the people you're working with.'

I don't believe it now and I'd never think it now, let alone say it. Why would you *viciously* criticize anyone?

You move on, and you change. You learn that vicious criticism isn't everyone's idea of motivation and it certainly doesn't get the best out of people. But, for me, that change of attitude didn't happen straight away.

By Christmas, I was regretting taking the captaincy: I hadn't realized how big a job it was, and I was struggling with my form.

Sometimes, at a senior players' meeting in the first few months, Declan would ask me for my opinion on something or other, and I'd say: 'I don't mind, I'm easy on that one.'

Then he'd say: 'Well, you're captain now, you *have* to have a view on it.'

Axel would be alongside me. I'd look at him and say, joking but half meaning it: 'You can have it back any time you want!'

I probably had to go through that experience before I started learning. In those early days, Deccie was always on to me about looking after my own game and not worrying about everyone else. He was right. The first job of any captain is to make sure you're training and playing so well that your place is beyond doubt. Look after your own game first, so you can lead with actions. Then look at helping those around you.

Declan had a great way of developing people, but at times I was too stubborn. He was very patient with me. I remember him giving me a tiny newspaper cutting one day. It said: 'Let me be the best I can be at everything I can influence – and not worry about things I can't control.'

I just wasn't ready to take that kind of thinking on board. The way I looked at it, Axel and Mick Galwey were phenomenal guys and great captains, and I felt the success of Munster was down to them, in a lot of ways. And now the responsibility was on me.

Did I ever actually say that to myself? Probably not. But it was there in the back of my head. And so I took the losses incredibly badly.

In January 2007, we were beaten at home by Leicester.

To be captain of Munster the first time we lost at Thomond Park in the Heineken Cup, after twelve seasons – it was very, very tough to take. It was such a proud record. It motivated us. The thought of losing it churned our stomachs. The fear of being beaten was always far bigger in our heads than any thoughts about what winning might mean. Sometimes, if things weren't going well, someone would look around the dressing room at half-time and say: 'Lads, do we want to be remembered as the Munster team that lost the home record?'

Worse, I knew I'd made a really bad decision when the game was in the balance. With twenty minutes left, we were awarded a penalty close to the posts. If we'd kicked it, we'd have been 9–8 in front. We should have banged it over the bar, but I went against my own instincts.

Rog came up to me. He said: 'If we get this out of the scrum – we've a try here. We've a three-on-two on the short side.'

Our scrum had been in trouble for most of the day. We'd just driven them back and won the penalty, but they had Julian White in their front row and he was on fire. We probably caught him on the hop, once. I should have realized that winning that one scrum wasn't a reflection of where we were up front.

I went for the scrum. We got turned over. It was a big moment in the game for them, and for us. My decision-making and judgement in the moment were poor.

I rarely got criticized in my home town, but in Limerick that night a guy came up to me and said: 'I thought you were better than that.' I just turned and walked away.

Some of the diehard supporters tried to make me feel better by saying: 'That record meant nothing to anyone!' I remember appreciating what they were trying to do, but not really believing them.

I don't know how people can say they have no regrets at the end of their careers, or their lives. That game will always be a regret for me, but it taught me a lesson as well.

Losing cost us a home quarter-final. I was missing with a broken thumb when we were knocked out by Llanelli

Scarlets. I remember saying, after we had become champions the previous year, that we had to keep our foot on the pedal and drive on as if we'd never won it.

We tried hard to do that, but we got lost along the way.

In the November after the Heineken Cup win I made it on to the shortlist for IRB World Player of the Year. Richie McCaw won it.

Getting voted Player of the Year by my fellow professionals in Ireland was another big honour. The time wasn't long coming when recognition like that would have given me a lot of satisfaction, but it wasn't a big deal to me then, probably because I was always more fixated by the next challenge. Seven years after I won the Irish Rugby Union Players Association award, an employee at the IRUPA office came across it: a piece of cut glass, with my name engraved on it. She'd found it lying around the office somewhere: I'd forgotten to take it home. Nine years later, when I won that award again at the age of thirty-five, I was absolutely delighted. It meant a lot to receive it in a season when we'd won the championship and at a time when I'd been battling to beat injuries and find form. But at twenty-six it was all about moving on to the next thing.

We played well again that autumn and beat two of the big three – Australia and South Africa. It was my first win over Australia in five games, and another sign that we were a coming team. We'd come from a culture where we once enjoyed being seen as underdogs, but we were moving on from that and it felt natural and right.

Brian, as our captain and one of the best players in the world, was at the forefront of leading that change in our mindset. We were favourites for the 2007 Six Nations and he didn't have any problem with saying we deserved to be front-runners. Neither did I. We wanted to win champion-ships and Grand Slams and we found it frustrating having to listen to people from a different generation who didn't have the same ambition. We used to hear it from the big commit-tee guys, the sixty-year-olds who told us that with two Triple Crowns to our name, we were part of a golden era.

When we got beaten and they came up to us with a few consoling words, it was as if we were still back in the old days when Ireland were picking up wooden spoons.

'Don't worry about it – nobody can live with the French in that mood.'

'Listen – you ran into them on one of their special days.'

They meant well, but it used to make my blood boil.

There was a caricature of me: that psycho guy, over-competitive bordering on insane, every hour of the day. And there were stories to back up the impression that some people had – or maybe still have – about my personality: like nobody will play me at Monopoly because I ruin everything by being too desperate to win.

Maybe, like a lot of things, it was partly true. But I heard it so often that sometimes, when I just wanted to knock a bit of craic out of some game, I started questioning myself.

Am I losing my competitive instinct?

Am I not being myself here?

I know a lot of people's impressions of my character came from what they saw of me in the dressing room at Croke Park in 2007, just before we played France in the Six Nations – the clip from the documentary where I was going on about 'manic aggression', about putting 'the fear of God' into someone. It was a good documentary, and people loved it, but it bugged me that I was never asked about the use of that clip, because it's not something I would have agreed to. It's just too intimate for people to be sitting down with a cup of tea and a biscuit watching it. It shouldn't be for that kind of consumption.

That was me for half an hour before a rugby match, nearly ten years ago. It's very different to how I was – and how we all were – in my later years with Ireland, but it's probably what some people thought I was like all the time.

I *am* quite driven, but it doesn't apply to everything in my life. I'm sure that my personality is just the same as a guy working nine to five in a stationery office somewhere, who feels passionate about his job and wants his organization to be the best.

Even though it was only the second game of the tournament, it felt like we'd lost a Grand Slam that day in Croke Park. Brian had picked up a knock in the win over Wales and I was captain. It was our first time to play in the home of the Gaelic Athletic Association, the first time it was opened up to another sport. Most of us had played some hurling or Gaelic football as kids and we were desperate to do the occasion justice.

With five minutes left, we were a point in front. Wally took a lineout from Flannery's throw well inside our half and we mauled them twenty-five metres.

They collapsed it. Penalty. Rog. Over the bar.

We were four points clear with two and a half minutes on the clock. We needed to get hold of the ball after the restart and kill the game, but I lost the kick-off.

The plan had been for me to be further back on the kick-off receipts. I stuck to the plan and they kicked it short. I had to run for the ball and got taken out as I arrived.

Back at Munster the following month, Declan called me out on it: 'You should have been flatter.'

It was still such a sore point with me that I argued with

him: 'We'd done our analysis – that was exactly where I was supposed to be.'

He didn't back off. 'That was their last chance,' he said. 'They had to go short and try and win it back – you should have been standing further up the pitch.'

I wouldn't concede the point then, but when I went away and thought about it I realized he was right. The pre-match analysis was irrelevant to that particular situation and I should have adapted, but it never even crossed my mind. If I'd been flatter under the ball I'd have had a better chance of catching it, or at least when I was taken out it would have looked a lot more like a penalty.

The ball came back on their side. Thirty seconds later, I had the best view in the stadium of Vincent Clerc diving over our line. By the time I got a hand on his jersey he had already put the ball down.

My biggest memory of the England game, two weeks later, was saying to myself during the anthems: 'I haven't been part of anything like this before. This is amazing.'

I never experienced emotion on a rugby pitch that came anywhere close to what we felt that day. I was never more determined not to let people down. If we'd lost that game, I can't begin to imagine how terrible it would have made us feel.

I didn't believe for an instant that there would be a problem with 'God Save the Queen' being played at Croke Park, that people might respond badly to it. But I'd say they were very wary, the English players. That week they probably got a kind of *Michael Collins* movie version of our history. It must have been a little intimidating for them to think they were going to a place where British soldiers had gone in and just opened up, back in 1920. I can only guess that at least some of them thought: *This place that we're going to – it's going to mean so much to them.* They must have known, too, how much that kind of motivation works in rugby. We felt lucky and grateful to be there.

England were missing some leaders from the team that day, and as a group we thought we were better, more intelligent players than them. None of us expected anything like a thirty-point win, but it was hard to see how there could have been any other outcome than an Ireland victory.

The truth is that playing England probably stirs something in every Irish person, but it was only 2007 that stands apart in my memory as a game that felt different. It's true: we were more up for it, we believed it was bigger than any other game we'd played throughout our careers. A World Cup knock-out match would have been bigger in a rugby sense, but we were aware that England at Croke Park meant more to the country.

We were very good that day. It was probably the afternoon when everything we'd been working towards under Eddie for five years came together in a performance that wasn't far off perfect. One of the reasons they never really put it up to us was because they didn't have a Martin Johnson or a Will Carling in their team, someone who wouldn't have been intimidated by the history, a guy who would have revelled in spoiling our day.

Then we went to the World Cup in France and we were appalling.

Nobody needs me to rehash everything that's been said about that tournament. The bottom line is that when the pressure came on we had no way of fixing our problems.

Against Namibia we turned the ball over thirty-eight times. Afterwards, I stayed up until 3.30 a.m., trying to come up with answers. I kicked it around in the team room with Wally and Strings for an hour, while eating Nutella sandwiches, and none of us could figure it out. People said we didn't have enough rugby played, and while that's true it's also too simplistic an explanation.

Under Joe Schmidt, I learned that when you've had a bad day, you go back to your foundations – your big rocks – and put things right. The problem in 2007, I think, was that we didn't have the right foundations in place. That was the only possible explanation for five or six poor performances, one after the other; but the realization only came over time and after a lot more experience.

Towards the end of my career I was able to look back at that tournament and remember how I felt tired, walking on to the pitch at the beginning of games. We trained for an hour and forty minutes on Monday and Tuesday, ninety minutes on Thursday and forty-five on Friday, and a big part of the reason for that was because we had a brand-new game plan almost every week.

One involved the forwards being divided into two pods of four, who had to stick together always. In another, we had our front five in the middle, doing little plays off the 10. Left and right of us we had two back-rows with a couple of backs in one pod and the third back-row with a few more backs in the other. It was all designed to bust a defence and allow us to spread the ball wide. But it took a lot of time for guys to figure out where they were supposed to be and how it was all going to work.

Even at the time, I thought we were training too much, but it was hard to drive the point home as forcefully as I probably should have done, when we had been playing great rugby. It wasn't like we were in a slump, looking for solutions. For more than a year before the World Cup, what we were doing had been working really well. Eddie was the most successful coach Ireland had ever had and there was no reason for anyone to think we were going to unravel in the tournament.

We were younger then. We became better thinkers as the seasons went by, more confident about our own opinions on how best to prepare. Whenever we were given downtime in 2007, I always trained. Then I'd hear that Donners and Flannery were doing even more – and I'd train harder again. Some of us never allowed ourselves to take a break. I learned, eventually, that taking time off during hard periods of training was just as important as the training itself.

Eight years later, I saw guys who I thought had it in them to make the same mistakes I'd made by overtraining, and I told them about what happened in 2007. 'Make sure you take your time off and make sure you relax,' I said. 'You've trained hard for the last few months – you need the downtime as well.' We needed to let the fitness accumulate, to let our bodies catch up with the work we'd already done.

Back then, by the time we realized something needed to be fixed with one of Eddie's strategies, we'd already moved on to the next one. Sometimes, like the quarter-final against France in the 2003 World Cup, we didn't even have the time to figure out that the game plan was never going to work.

These days, no team tries to reinvent the wheel before every game. They're adding different wrinkles to their plays, but they're sticking to core principles. It's all about trying to figure out ways of imposing a game plan on the opposition. This allows you to dial up or dial down the amount of time you're spending on the training pitch, because you're not learning a whole new plan each week. You can get away with training less if you need bodies to be fresh. Some weeks you can do as little as your set-piece and a few power plays. The fresher you can keep people's bodies and minds, the better they'll play on Saturday.

The IRFU gave Eddie until the following Six Nations to turn things around. But we didn't get it done.

He wasn't around when we finally got there in 2009, but in many ways the making of that team went a long way back. So much of our rugby intelligence was picked up on the training grounds where Eddie was always demanding more.

10

Before we took the field at the Millennium Stadium for the 2008 Heineken Cup final, we believed we were better than Toulouse. Very often with us then, just having that belief was enough. Looking back, I'm struck by our confidence, because they were a crack side – but we were a serious team ourselves. Doug Howlett, a world-class winger, had come from New Zealand at the beginning of the year. Without ever saying a word, his values and behaviour made everyone around him better. Trevor Halstead had retired, but we had put together what was probably the best Munster midfield partnership of all time in Rua Tipoki and Lifeimi Mafi.

I missed all the pool matches after my back came at me again at the end of the World Cup. It didn't seem serious at the time, but it ended up costing me four months out of the game. A lot of that time was spent lying flat on my back, hoping it would come right without another operation. Even though I was captain, the longer I was out, the less I felt part of it. Anytime I spoke, I felt there was no conviction in my words. Mick O'Driscoll came in for me and was excellent. Going to those pool games in a suit was killing me. In the end it came right after an epidural injection and I was grateful to Steve Eustace, the consultant radiologist, for saving me from a second surgery in five years.

That final was a tight game, with only three points in it at the end, but from the moment Rog kicked us ahead with fifteen minutes to play we felt we were in control. I said afterwards that we made it a war, and that was what it felt like. Some people said we killed the game in the process, but that never bothered us. Closing it down when we were in front took massive work rate and heart.

The fact that we were capable of dominating a team as good as Toulouse when it was all on the line gave us great

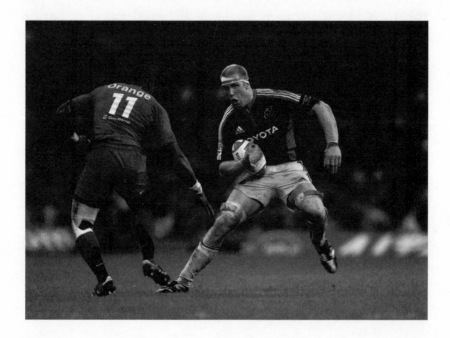

confidence. I can't remember having that feeling of control in any other game when there was only a kick of a ball between the teams on the scoreboard. For us, it was a new high.

The following night I was alongside Wally in Nancy Blake's, watching it back on Sky Sports. At the end there was a sequence of clips from the game, some in slow motion. The backing music was 'Everybody Wants to Rule the World' by Tears for Fears, and just as it finished they showed me and Rog lifting the trophy together. Every time I hear the song on the radio now I think of that evening with Wally, reliving what we'd done in front of more than sixty thousand Munster supporters, and it makes me happy.

Earlier in the day, for the second time in three years, a huge crowd had come out in Limerick to welcome us home. That was a great feeling too. If you'd asked us that afternoon, I know we'd have backed ourselves to be back in the final the following year. I don't think any of us saw then that there was a time limit on our success.

The second European title was huge for us, but it also meant we had to find a different motivation, after all the emotion of the first one and the disappointment of the season after it. We knew a third win would put us level with Toulouse and ahead of Wasps and Leicester. We felt like we deserved to be where we were, but we knew we were going to have to up it again to get the third.

In August, I wrote down my goals for the new season. There were four:

1. Retain the Heineken Cup.
2. Win a Grand Slam with Ireland.
3. Make the Lions Test team and win the series.
4. Make the World Player of the Year shortlist.

Looking at those goals eight years later, I laugh. The first three were team goals, and the fourth was up to a jury. I had no real control over any of them. I still had so much left to learn about preparation and high performance. I can understand now why finishing a season without a trophy was so tough for me. My definition of success was about finishing the season with silverware on the podium, irrespective of the circumstances, or of my own performance.

Once, at Munster, we were introduced to a concept called Bin Day. You texted your bad thoughts to the sports psychologist, the stuff preying on your mind and holding you back. So if you were a hooker, you might text:

My lineout throwing isn't where it needs to be

After that, you had to send a positive affirmation. Something that addressed the bad thought and turned it into a positive.

I've done a lot of work on my throwing this week. I'm going to be OK

Straight away, a text would come back.

That's it. Those bad thoughts are gone now. They're in the bin

Three weeks after Barry Murphy suffered a serious injury, just when he'd been playing the rugby of his life, Jerry Flannery sent a text:

I worry that since Barry broke his ankle we've become very one-dimensional in our play

He followed that up with his positive affirmation.

Everything is fine. Barry's leg is fixed

I never took it seriously either. I couldn't bring myself to send any texts.

Eanna Falvey was the Munster doctor then. He once sent an email to Declan Kidney about the team and how we motivated ourselves. I remember Deccie reading it out to us. It said our biggest strength was that we were able to make each game bigger than the last, no matter the opposition. That was true, but as a player who traded so much on passion and emotion, the effort to get myself mentally right was taking its toll. Having to be emotionally high for every game was very difficult. I was relying too much on external factors I thought might increase my intensity. Instead of focusing on my own preparation, and on the team's, I kept looking for reasons to resent the opposition, or the people I thought weren't giving us respect for what we'd achieved – anything at all to fuel our desire on the day. The responsibility of captaincy only made the knot in my stomach worse as the games drew closer.

Around the time when I wrote out my goals for the 2008–9 season, I was contacted by a sports performance coach, Caroline Currid. She was doing some research into peak performance, talking to people in different sports about the psychology behind sporting achievement. It was for her own purposes, not something she was planning on publishing anywhere, so I spoke freely when we met at the Castletroy Park Hotel.

She told me she didn't know much about rugby – Gaelic football was her sport. She was working with the Tyrone senior team coached by Mickey Harte and she'd played the game to a good standard herself. She had a list of questions, a tape recorder and a nice, easy manner.

Q: I'd like to get an idea of your mental preparation. How do you get yourself in the right frame of mind before a game?

A: Well, I don't do anything special really.

Q: You must have something driving you?

A: I suppose a bit of fear.

Q: Fear of failure?

A: Yeah. A fear of losing. Actually, a fear of not performing to our potential. There's a difference.

Q: How does that fear come out in you?

A: It's funny now – sometimes my heart will be racing and I'll be thinking to myself, 'Fucking hell, my legs feel like jelly! Am I not fit? Have I not done enough training? Do I just need to rest?' The reality is that there's nothing wrong with my legs – it's just nerves.
Other times I'll be telling myself I've either done too much weights during the week, or I haven't done enough. I'll be going around thinking, 'I dunno, am I right at all.' It's like I'm having a little battle with myself.

Q: It sounds very stressful. So it starts getting worse, the closer you get to playing?

A: Yeah, it does. It definitely does. A lot of the time around a big game I'd be happy to get on a plane, leave the country and hide, rather than deal with the stress over us losing or me not performing.

Q: It's nervous energy?

A: I suppose it is. Anything at all, I'll start questioning. I'll keep going back to the laptop, checking and then double-checking my lineouts. Early on in the warm-up before a game, my heart rate might rocket and I'll be there thinking, 'What's wrong with me? Have I a virus or something?' It's weird, I start fearing the worst or something. And I probably couldn't be in better shape.

Q: You're OK mentally, once the game starts?

A: Usually. Not always. Sometimes it will come into my head that I'm not fit enough, which is really annoying because your body begins to believe it eventually. Sometimes it's hard to fight the demons during a game, especially when you're coming back from an injury. But usually you just keep playing and doing what you're doing. You don't have time to think. You're on autopilot. The battle is the morning of the game and the two days before it. Well, for me anyway. I'm fighting my mind.

Q: What difference does being captain make to your preparation?

A: I feel a lot more responsibility for the team to perform. I take it very badly if we don't. And it makes me feel more pressure to play well myself, because my credibility as captain depends on me playing well.

Q: Apart from feeling that pressure, is leadership something you get enjoyment out of?

A: Well, there's no 'apart from'. It's like asking, 'What's wrong with your house – apart from the fact that there's no roof on it?' When you're captain you need to feel confident, you know? I've started to enjoy it a bit more than I did. I don't know if I was a natural captain, like Anthony Foley, but I was definitely a natural leader. It doesn't mean it's enjoyable, though.

Q: How do you know when you're ready for a game?

A: Sometimes my body reacts in the build-up, especially if it's a big game. If I throw up before we go out, I know I'm ready.

Q: But don't you know that has a really bad effect on your body? You're losing a huge amount of energy by getting sick. It saps your red blood cells. Even your eyes dilate when you throw up.

A: Jesus. I don't really know why I do it, really.

Q: You've got to stop doing that! How else do you motivate yourself?

A: How do I motivate myself? I suppose in a way I do it by being hard on myself.

Q: You're very self-critical?

A: I'll write down a load of things I want to do in a game and tell myself that if I don't do them, I'll have let the team down.

Q: You're unbelievable. Really?

A: I presume that's not the recommended way to go about it.

Q: No. It's the complete opposite. Most successful people are very positive in their thinking. Do you ever read about high performance, how people get the best out of themselves?

A: I read a lot of sports books.

Q: Biographies?

A: Yeah, mostly.

Q: But nothing about mental preparation?

A: Not really.

Q: Do you ever use visualization?

A. No.

Q: A lot of successful people in sport run pictures in their head, so that they're seeing themselves doing things well before they go out and play. You've never even tried it?

A: No. I know it's not really the same thing, but the odd time I might I visualize myself in the dressing room.

Q: OK. What are you doing?

A: I'm just sitting there, absolutely devastated. Everyone around me is the same.

Q: The team has lost?

A: Yeah, it's a horrible feeling.

Q: Why would you want to see yourself like that?

A: To motivate me to do everything I possibly can to make sure I don't have that feeling after the game that's coming up.

Q: More negatives, so?

A: More negatives.

Q: You spend a lot of time in the gym?

A: Yeah, I do.

Q: Your brain is a muscle too, you know. How come you're not exercising that?

A: I don't know. I suppose I never felt like I needed to.

She told me that every sports psychologist on the planet would say I was doing things completely wrong and that I had to change. She said successful people make a habit of replacing negative thoughts with positive ones. She started talking about motor neurons in the brain, creating habits, visualizing a line-out jump so that the body builds connections to the brain and it triggers a reaction that's a split second faster.

As much as I love new information, I wasn't convinced that this was something that was going to benefit me. I'd already had success as a player, far more than I could have imagined the day I was offered my first Munster contract. I told Caroline that my approach worked for me, even if the experts disagreed with it. I said there wasn't any good reason for me to change. She disagreed.

Q: In your career so far, when were you happiest with your performances on the pitch?

A: Two years ago. When I was at my fittest.

Q: Do you think you were getting the absolute best out of yourself?

A: I was incredibly fit. And I was playing really well.

Q: Explain what 'well' means.

A: We were winning and I was performing. Munster won the Heineken Cup and I made the shortlist for IRB World Player of the Year.

Q: You made the shortlist, but you didn't win it?

A: No. Richie McCaw won it.

Q: So why do you think you didn't?

A: Well, obviously Richie McCaw is a world-class player. And obviously the judges decided I didn't perform well enough to get picked ahead of him.

Q: So?

A: So what?

Q: So how do you know you wouldn't have got Player of the Year if you'd had a more positive mindset, or if you'd prepared differently?

I didn't have an answer to that.

A few weeks later, I was on the sofa at home watching Tyrone coming from behind to beat Kerry in the All-Ireland football final. It was their third title in six years and much of the team had been there in 2003 and 2005 when they won their first and second. They were slagged off and then written off, but they hung in and found a way to win again.

Watching them win, I wondered if performance psychology had made a difference to their players. I'd been thinking about my conversation with Caroline and asking myself if a different mental approach might work for me. I was worried about heading down a new road when things were already going well, but the idea that I could maybe get more out of myself by being open to new things was a more powerful thought.

I got in touch with Caroline the following day to ask if she'd work with me. We started with visualization.

Once I'd opened my mind to the idea of motivational psychology, I began reading books about it and underlining passages.

> The winner's edge is not in a gifted birth, a high IQ, or in talent. The winner's edge is all in the attitude, not aptitude. Attitude is the criterion for success – *Denis Waitley*

> The fixed mindset stands in the way of change. The growth mindset is a starting point for change, but people need to decide for themselves where their efforts toward change would be most valuable – *Carol Dweck*

It was all new to me, and it was fascinating. Just before Christmas, Pádraig Harrington came into the Ireland camp and talked for hours about psychology and how much it counted in his golf game. The talk he gave was coming from a guy who had just won his second and third majors, and I took it as absolute confirmation that this was something which could help me to be a better player.

I liked it most when I could relate something that I'd read directly back to what I was experiencing in my own career. When I came across some gems while reading in bed, I'd turn out the light, dying for the morning to come so that I could figure out how they might make a difference to me or to the team.

There was a line that struck me in a book by John Wooden, the legendary basketball coach. He argued that emotion is your enemy in sport, because it leads to inconsistent performances. I'd never looked at it that way before, but I could see his point. What I took out of it was that as a team we needed to find a different way of achieving consistency. We needed to get ourselves into the frame of mind that Eanna had written about in his email to Declan, without the stress of having to build a cause.

The difference that performance psychology made in the second half of my career was that I got much better at working on the process that went into winning, rather than being distracted by thoughts of what winning or losing might feel like. For me, the process became the key to high performance and, just as importantly, the key to enjoying the journey.

11

Declan was the obvious choice to replace Eddie as Ireland coach. He had two Heineken Cups to his name, and four finals. We were a forwards-orientated team under him at Munster and we'd had success, so I felt his appointment might give the Ireland pack more ownership of the way we played. I found I had a lot of the same ideas about rugby as Ireland's new forwards coach, Gert Smal, and he brought more precision to our set-piece. I felt these things, combined with what was obviously a great backline, could lead to winning a championship or a Grand Slam.

Four or five months after Deccie started, there was a meeting at a hotel in Enfield and afterwards a lot was made of it. Rob Kearney, who was relatively new to the set-up, spoke about trying to recreate with Ireland what Munster had at Thomond Park. As a Leinster man, he meant it in an admiring way. Afterwards, it created quite a stir. It wasn't as

big a deal as people made it out to be, but no one had brought up that subject before Rob did.

Back then, in Munster, we saw passion on a rugby pitch as a form of intimidation, and most of it came through the forwards. If a ruck or a maul put us on the front foot, if a big decision went our way, we celebrated with back-slaps and fist-pumps. It was pure, raw emotion. Maybe it looked over the top, but it was genuine.

With Ireland, we played very differently. We tried to go around teams. If people thought they didn't see passion from the Munster guys when they were playing with Ireland, it was only because we avoided so many of the confrontations that the whole Munster game plan was built on. Just because there weren't as many of those back-slapping moments when we had Ireland jerseys on didn't mean the Munster players were holding something back.

What I remember most from that meeting in Enfield was Deccie's intuition – the way he could pick up on somebody saying something and then pounce on it, make an issue of it, get a debate going and leave it in the air for people to think about.

After he was announced as the new coach, there was speculation in the papers about the captaincy – rumours that maybe he might be thinking about a change. I was interested in doing the job – I'm sure Rog would have put his hand up too – but only if Brian wanted to give it up. I never wanted the captaincy under circumstances in which it had been taken off him – it would have been a poisoned chalice straight away – and I was in no rush. The dynamic of a team has to be right, and Brian was our best and most important player.

Throughout our time together in the Irish team, Brian and I had a very good relationship. We weren't especially close, but we had big respect for one another. I wasn't sure what he was thinking then, or what he'd heard, but if he had any sense that I'd been lobbying for the job I felt I needed to put him straight. I didn't want him thinking that I was after it regardless of his feelings, in some kind of power grab.

At a camp in Limerick before the 2009 Six Nations, I knocked on his bedroom door at the Strand Hotel.

'In case you think I'm looking for the job,' I said, 'it's important you know that I'm not.'

It turned out there had been a question mark in his mind during the summer tour, but he said his head was all over the place at the time. His best friend, Barry Twomey, had taken his own life just before we flew out. I told him I was starting to enjoy the Munster captaincy for the first time and I was happy with the role I had for Ireland, which was true. As a captain, sometimes you don't want to talk, but you have to. Even if you feel a bit full of shit as you're coming out with something, you have to create an atmosphere. As vice-captain to Brian, I could talk or not talk, depending on how I felt. Usually I had something to say, and so I said it. I don't know if that ever annoyed Brian, but he never gave any indication that it did.

In his room that day he told me he didn't want to be captain of Ireland forever, but that he enjoyed doing it.

'Fair fucks to you for coming up,' he said.

It was only years later, when I had the captaincy myself, that I realized our conversation probably helped him, and it made me wish I'd had more of those little chats with him. I should have reassured him more that I was happy with my role as pack leader.

When I captained Munster, I always knew that Rog felt I was the right man to be doing it. He was a really good ally for me over the years, and I tried to be the same for Peter O'Mahony, when his time came. He was a young player and he was taking it on at a time when we weren't the force we once were. I knew from my own experience that it was a hard thing for him to do and I wanted to make it easier. Sometimes I asked Peter if there was anything he wanted me to say before or after he spoke to the team. I hope my attitude was always, 'You're the man for this job – and I'm the man to sweep everything up after you and help you.' I probably didn't communicate that to Brian as often as I should have – it never occurred to me that he might have found it helpful in doing his job. He always seemed so confident and in control. He never showed vulnerability.

It only struck me that he might have welcomed some affirmation of how he was leading us after I'd made another speech after another defeat to New Zealand, the game at the Aviva in 2013 when we were seconds away from beating them. It was a simple speech – I cracked one joke and I was gone in four minutes – but later on he complimented me on what I'd said. I'd been respectful about their achievement in going unbeaten for the full year – but probably not over the top. At the end of the night, as we were going down in the elevator, Brian said: 'You did that well. You said exactly what needed to be said – in the right way.' It's such a shit job to make that speech after you've lost, so getting a few generous words from someone who had done it so many times before made me feel like I'd hit the right note for us going forward.

I remember thinking that I'd never once complimented him on a speech he'd made. I suppose I never really felt that he needed it. But looking back, I'm sure it would have been appreciated.

You hear it a lot from retired sports people, when they're asked about their careers.

'Any regrets?'

'I wish I'd enjoyed it more.'

I look back on our Grand Slam in 2009, and it's true I could have enjoyed it more, but it's not really a regret because I was in a different place then. There's a big part of me that's happy I played as long as I did, because I developed a good sense of perspective later in my career. You can't expect to have a proper appreciation of different stages of the journey when you're in the middle of living them. It's like asking a six-year-old to enjoy an episode of *The Office* – he's just not ready for it yet.

Coming into the tournament, the Munster players were very confident. Under Tony McGahan, we were playing some unbelievable rugby. Tony had joined us as defence coach during the season we first won the Heineken Cup and a lot of guys raved about him, especially Rog. He was from the new breed of coaches. He was young, ambitious and direct. He confronted things head on.

We still had the good things Deccie had given us, and Tony had brought more structure to our play. We were enjoying a very good period. In the final two pool games of the Heineken Cup, we'd walloped Sale at home and Montauban away. Leinster, meanwhile, had barely scraped into the knock-out stages. As Munster players, that first week in the Six Nations camp, we were thinking we needed to drive it on.

Throughout the tournament the team played a very practical style of rugby, but we scored some very good tries as well, especially against France in the first game, through Brian and Jamie Heaslip. When it was on, we tried to play.

After beating France we felt we had a real chance of a Grand Slam. We knew we were good enough. People said we didn't play any rugby against England, but they came to Dublin with a strong pack and that game was all about taking them on physically.

No Irish player has scored more tries than Brian O'Driscoll, or better ones – but I'll remember him most for the tries he scored for us from a yard out in that tournament.

Two metres from the England line in Croke Park, after four or five of us had tried and failed to get past their defence, a second centre got the job done, somehow. He had figured out it was the only way we were going to score.

A few weeks later, when I came up a foot short in Cardiff, he was there again to get the ball down on the Welsh line, somehow, for a split second. It was a great spot by the referee, Wayne Barnes.

When the final whistle went in that game, after the Stephen Jones penalty that fell short, I completely lost it. Something came over me and I ran off around the pitch. I'm just glad I was never picked up by the TV cameras, because I'd hate to see it back.

Throughout the tournament, there was a confrontational aspect to our game that served us well. Maybe it was the difference. In those five games, a lot of the things we'd been working on came off for us. Before that Six Nations, I'd been at so many team meetings where we were reviewing games we'd lost, and I'd been sitting there thinking: *We did some seriously good stuff out there. Surely it's all going to come together soon.*

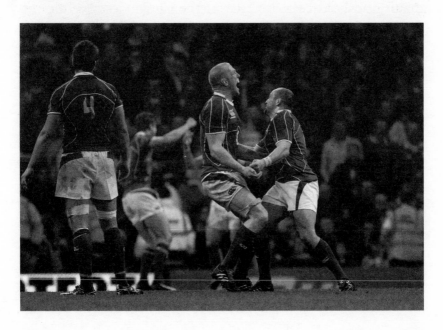

There were only fine margins between narrowly missing the Grand Slam in 2007 and doing it in 2009, but it must have helped that we got more out of our pack.

Personally, it was the best Six Nations I ever played. I went into every game with a list of goals written down.

3 impact carries
3 impact tackles
5 positive support lines

I had a thing about the support lines. Dougie Howlett was always running them, taking short cuts to be ahead of play and support the ball carrier when line breaks were made. Mervyn often showed me footage of instances where I could have made my job easier and made a bigger impact by predicting where the ball carrier would be or where the line break might end up. I was trying to play like a seven once the set-piece was over. I tried to get my foot in through the middle of rucks and kick the ball. I wanted to spin out of mauls and hold two or three of their guys down while the maul moved on. When I was doing all that stuff, I felt good.

Once in a while I'll see a replay of a try we scored in that Six Nations, and I love the doggedness we brought up front. From Ulster, Stephen Ferris had come into our back row. He did serious psychological damage to teams with his level of aggression, and his ultra-physical style lifted us.

I don't think Gordon D'Arcy's try against France would have been scored if we didn't feel we had the licence to keep picking and jamming, before Tomás O'Leary flashed it – as Deccie Edwards might say – and Darce did incredibly well to twist and turn his way over.

When I got back to Limerick after the win in Cardiff, there was a bit of a Monday-night club at Austin's. Back then, there was no name over the door, just the Young Munster crest. It would have been easy not to celebrate, because we had big games coming with Munster, but I allowed myself the pints and a cod and chips at Luigi's across the road later on.

By the first Saturday in May, when Munster went out to play Leinster in the Heineken Cup semi-final, we had won ten games in a row. One of those victories had come against Leinster in the league, but the best of them was the one that came next, a 43–9 win over Ospreys in the European quarter-final.

Under Deccie, there was never a time when you could have said: 'This is the brand of rugby we've been working towards.' But that day at Thomond Park, it felt like we had really kicked on. We were never going to win a third Heineken Cup without bringing something new to our game, and it all seemed to come together for us that Sunday. Apart from Paul Warwick at fullback, it was pretty much the same side as the year before, but we had found new ways of beating teams, and we produced probably the best rugby I was ever part of in my time at Munster.

People said we might have allowed ourselves to get complacent before the semi-final against Leinster at Croke Park. I didn't agree back then and I haven't changed my mind. Nothing went right for us that day, and everything they'd been working towards in the three years since we'd beaten them in the first semi-final paid off. They brought in good, hard players and got rid of the ones who didn't have what it takes.

When it comes to our rivalry, those two Heineken Cup games tower over everything else. Very few of the league matches we played stand out in my memory. We played them twice a season, and while those fixtures always had something extra, I was conscious that we could lose both of them and still be able to lord it over Leinster at the end of the season, by winning the Heineken Cup.

People have described the 2009 game as pivotal – a turning point in the rivalry. There's obviously a lot of truth in that, because Leinster went on to win three Heineken Cups, but I don't think what happened that day led to us falling apart and them going to another level.

The truth is that, by then, they had good plans in place to be better and we didn't. That summer they signed Nathan Hines, who was exactly the kind of combative player they needed in order to drive on. They already had the massive advantage of being based in the capital city, where most of the money in the country is. Success brought them new sponsors, new supporters, better training facilities. Their time was coming.

Had we won that game at Croke Park, we might have retained our title and made it three in four years, but our lack of planning would still have hurt us down the line.

12

The night before I was announced as captain for the 2009 Lions tour, I met up with the coaches at a hotel near Heathrow airport. I was delighted to be there, but even then I was only thinking about winning the series. Being asked to lead the Lions is a big honour, but you can't put it in a trophy cabinet. Captaincy isn't a prize, it's a tough job.

Ian McGeechan, the head coach, had called me the previous week and offered me the job. I took the news in my stride, because I knew I was in the running, but as soon as he came out with it I was looking forward to calling my parents. My father's life is all about family and rugby. If a guy got one cap for Ireland in his day, he was a legend. So for his son to go on a second Lions tour and be captain – it was great to be able to hear the excitement in his voice. My mother has only ever wanted me to be happy and safe, no matter what I was doing. Whenever rugby brought me fulfilment I knew she was just as proud as Dad, even if the game itself wasn't as important to her. I knew I would never have received such an amazing honour if it weren't for her drive and work ethic. It was never something she encouraged in me; her example throughout my childhood was all I needed.

The other coaches in the hotel room were Warren Gatland, Graham Rowntree, Shaun Edwards and Rob Howley. When I arrived they were sitting around a big desk with Ian and Gerald Davies, the manager. John Feehan, the Lions CEO, was there too.

At that stage they were putting the finishing touches to the touring party. There had been a selection meeting before I arrived in the room and thirty-six names had been written down, but there was still a bit of to-ing and fro-ing going on and it was fascinating to be part of it. It struck me that the selection process had been very difficult for them, and I couldn't get over the range and detail of the situations and possibilities they were trying to cover.

Ian sat back and listened as the others kicked it around again and again. Some people coach by formula; others are all about instinct, and I got the feeling that these guys were in the instinct camp. It was obvious they were a very tight group.

McGeechan has a special way of talking. He'll start to speak ... then inject a pause and you're left hanging on what's coming next. I couldn't believe how much like the 1997 Lions video it all felt. Just hearing his voice did it.

We flew to Johannesburg full of hope. We knew what we were playing for. Some of us had won Heineken Cups and a Grand Slam, but we wanted a forever moment, as Jim Telfer had described it – the kind that only a winning Lions tour or a World Cup victory can give you.

*

I'd had nearly three years of captaincy experience by then, but I was probably still taking too much on myself. If the team failed, I thought it was my responsibility. It was one of my faults as a leader, but it might have been a strength as well.

As captain on that tour, the stakes were so high I felt like my credibility was hanging in the balance every single day. We spent forty-three days together and never once did I think: *It's going to be all right – we're going to come out of this OK.* From start to finish, it was a tour on the edge.

I look back on it as a great life experience, but at times it was very difficult. In a way it was like one of those tough training sessions you're delighted to have done, something you feel great about afterwards because you know how much it took out of you. It's hard to captain a group of men you haven't built up a relationship with. The trust that can earn you the captaincy of your club or country just isn't there. On a Lions tour, it's assumed. I wasn't filled with confidence that what worked with club and country would translate here. I had to work through those feelings of uncertainty. Declan Kidney's words whenever a young player was picked to start with Munster were in my head: 'You've been picked for what you've been doing and what we've seen from you. Don't try and reinvent the wheel. Be yourself.' I told myself that I'd been offered the captaincy based on who I was – and it was important to remain true to that.

In the first game, against a Royal XV, we were twelve points down with not much more than ten minutes left and I started seeing newspaper headlines.

You don't get much time to think in games, but under the posts once or twice it wasn't looking good.

Fucking hell! This is poor.

We ran in three late tries to save ourselves, but in the press conference after the game I barely bothered to hide my feelings and I didn't care that they were showing. I was thinking:

Is this going to be like New Zealand all over again?

If this goes wrong, a lot of it is going to be down to me.

I remember sitting on my own, halfway down the tour bus, heading back to the Wigwam Hotel outside of Rustenburg. I looked a state. My head was strapped to keep down the swelling in a cauliflower ear. Under the bandage around my eye was a scratched cornea that hurt every time I blinked.

The next day I started getting texts from home about criticism of my captaincy in the English media. I didn't pay much attention, but the criticism didn't help and neither did the texts.

Things picked up after that first game. We bonded well and we got better. Lions tours are massive logistical operations. It was clear that the coaching staff had given a lot of thought to how we could spend time together and become a team quickly. The lessons of the 2005 tour had been learned.

We generally trained at schools, and a full gym was transported around the country, ready to be set up for us whenever we reached a new training venue. The weather in South Africa meant the forwards could do weights pitch-side while the backs worked on set-piece plays. Then we'd swap over, the backs doing weights while the forwards did scrum and lineout practice, watching each other all the time, laughing and joking and enjoying each other's company. We would then break for a fifteen- or twenty-minute snack. Paul Stridgeon, our strength and conditioning coach, would serve smoothies with great fanfare. Then we'd have a very short meeting, where the coaches would roll in a box housing a 50-inch analysis screen. We'd huddle around it before going out to train for forty-five minutes. It meant we were always done by lunchtime, allowing the players the afternoon off to spend more time together and relax. I'm sure that moving the analysis screen and the gym from place to place wasn't easy logistically, but whatever effort went into it was more than repaid: by the time we got to the Test series, we were an extremely tight group.

Test places were wide open and I felt proud to be captain of a squad full of class players who were doing everything they could to become a team. Those three Test weeks were the ultimate for me. It was the best of our best, up against the world champions. It was no-holds-barred rugby, quality players taking one another on, three weeks in a row. For me, Brian's massive tackle on Danie Rossouw in the second Test was the defining moment of the tour. It put both of them out of the game, concussed. In all my time playing rugby, nothing hit the same level of intensity and physicality as that game.

Even when we lost the first Test in Durban, narrowly, we still believed in ourselves. I thought if we could come back and win the series, after being 1–0 down, we'd be happy for the rest of our lives. I broke my front teeth in that game. I was going over the top of Mike Phillips' head in a ruck when he pulled back and smashed into me. I could feel the teeth loose in my gum and I ended up having three hours of surgery on the Thursday evening before the second Test.

In Pretoria, for most of that game they were kicking the leather off the ball. We had them under pressure in the scrum. We were ten points up at half-time and confident. In his first Lions Test, alongside me in the second row, Simon Shaw had a huge game.

When I think about it now, it feels like we threw it away. We were better than them in that game and we didn't do it. But they were world champions for a reason.

We lost our tighthead, Adam Jones, to an injury, five minutes into the second half and it went to uncontested scrums. We were fitter than them, but their front row had no scrummaging to do and they started carrying a lot of ball.

We trailed by three with a couple of minutes left, when we got a penalty. Straight away I was thinking: *Take the points.* Martyn Williams came over to me and said we could still win the series if the game ended in a draw. When Stephen Jones kicked us level from out near the touchline, I thought we'd got out of it alive.

Rog was on as a sub and what happened next has haunted him – the penalty conceded after he chased his garryowen, trying to win the game, then Morné Steyn's kick straight through the posts from inside his own half, with the clock already in red. When the whistle blew I took my gumshield out and stood there for a few seconds, but when I saw Rog I felt more sorry for him than I was for myself. I knew how much he was hurting.

The dressing room was utter devastation. Rog was taped up and covered in blood. If anyone said anything, I don't remember it. All I remember is the silence. I felt completely crushed but I didn't shed a tear until I got a text message from my friend Timmy Lane, who was at the game. When I won, a lot of texts came through. When I lost, there weren't so many. I was picking up my bags when Timmy's message arrived. He doesn't throw out many compliments, so maybe that was part of the reason I got emotional.

> Well done today, it was an incredible game, the greatest I've ever seen. I've had a ball. I wouldn't have come over here if you weren't involved, so thanks very much. Head up and I'll chat to you during the week.

I wasn't the only one who thought we'd been the better team for most of the two games, but I was already questioning myself by the time we got on the bus. I knew that if we didn't win in Johannesburg, my Lions Test record would be played six, lost six.

At half-ten on the following morning we took off in a couple of buses for a two-day safari trip to Entabeni. Except some of us didn't make it that far. A few of us wanted to ditch the safari and head back to the hotel. I had no interest in seeing elephants and lions; all I wanted to do was deal with the disappointment by tipping away at a few beers. I thought most of the others felt the same way.

I started walking down our bus, asking if guys wanted to turn back. A few others did the same. There seemed to be enough of a buy-in to convince me it was the right thing to do, but when it came down to it only around twelve of us were on the bus that turned around for Pretoria, while the other one kept going.

Up until that moment, there had been a real feeling of togetherness in the camp that wasn't quite there in New Zealand four years earlier. Friendships were made that I know will endure. As head coach, Ian had done really well in making it work with a much smaller squad. It's a hard one to balance, but it makes you very tight as a group.

I was sitting beside Stephen Jones, and our bus hadn't gone a hundred yards before I started doubting my decision.

Are we after splitting the tour a bit here?

Stephen was a really good pro and he was asking himself the same question. I remember texting Donners:

Fuck it, I shouldn't have done that.

He replied and said it was no big deal. But it was a mistake and I was unhappy with myself over it. Back in Pretoria, nobody stayed out late. We weren't in the mood. The guys who went back were the bones of the team who started the third Test – whether there was something in that or not, I don't know.

We knew we were staring down the barrel of a 3–0 defeat. The prospect of losing in Johannesburg and suffering a whitewash as captain was enough to make me feel physically sick.

Two days later I was on a physio bench at the Sandton Sun Hotel, Johannesburg, filling my lungs with deep breaths and feeling a burst of pain from the top rib on my right-hand side.

We were shipping injuries all over the team. We'd lost both our starting props in the second Test – Gethin Jenkins and Adam Jones. Brian was still shaken up after the Rossouw tackle and he was flying home the following day. It wasn't looking good for his centre partner, Jamie Roberts, either: together, they had probably been our two best players on tour.

I wasn't exactly fighting fit myself. My back hurt and I hadn't been sleeping well, but the rib I'd popped in Pretoria was giving me the most discomfort. I was examined by a physio, Prav Mathema, and then by a doctor, Gary O'Driscoll, Brian's cousin.

The truth was that my ribcage was sore – but not sore enough to keep me out of a Test match for the Lions. I knew that, but Gary had a duty of care to the players, and he'd been shaken by the level of attrition in the second Test. He offered me an out: 'This is serious, Paul. This could possibly rule you out.'

I can remember allowing myself to think, for maybe five or ten seconds, that missing the game wouldn't be the worst news I could get.

You wouldn't have to go through the build-up.

If we lose, it won't be down to you.

You won't have to beat yourself up as much.

It bothered me for two or three days that I'd allowed those thoughts into my head, but they were nothing new and there was no way I was ever going to allow myself not to play.

I told Gary: 'It'll be fine.' And it was.

I've read enough psychology books since then to know that thoughts like that don't amount to anything. It's only when you act on them that it begins to define you.

Before we flew out to South Africa, when I'd spoken to the squad in England, I had said there was no worse feeling for a Lion than not filling the jersey and doing it proud. I had experienced that on the 2005 tour. On that tour, we didn't become a team. We stood off, sussed each other out, and by the time the Tests came around we weren't ready to take on a group that had been a team for a long time. In South Africa, we had to assume the guy on our left and our right was the type of player and person that was good enough to be selected for the Lions. The challenge was in becoming a team.

I thought we had done ourselves justice in the first two Tests, but we desperately needed to win the third Test, for a lot of different reasons. The players had gone to the well, emotionally and physically. We were a team, and we deserved at least one Test win. Ian told us it was about reputation and respect. It was obvious how much he wanted us to go out and earn it.

Apart from feeling bad about being 2–0 down, the disappointment over my decision on the safari trip hadn't left me. I was still carrying a little bit of guilt over the feelings I'd had, however briefly, about the rib injury. But I also knew that we had fought tooth and nail for the jersey and people were giving us credit for that. I always wanted any team I was involved in to be seen in that way, so I was proud of the spirit we had shown. Nobody could say we hadn't given it everything, but we needed a win so much it was almost suffocating. Another defeat would have meant eight in a row for the Lions and most of that record would have come under the watch of players like me, who'd been there for more than one series. I knew there would be talk about what that level of failure meant for the future of the Lions.

In the team talk on the night before that game I felt myself getting emotional and my voice started cracking. There was no camera in the room because I wouldn't allow them into any of my meetings – I didn't want guys thinking I was saying stuff for the video. Our backs were to the wall and that probably came through in what I said. I told the players that our performance the next day would be the Lions' legacy for the next four years.

Speeches in sport are over-rated, even if they make for good reading in newspaper articles. The right words can set a tone and can add something to a team that's motivated and ready to win – but the players have to be there already themselves. If you're a bit nervous, I think players respect that. So I never liked being too rehearsed when I spoke to a team before a game – I just let it come out whatever way.

I knew we would have to dig a performance out of God knows where, and that guys would have to come in and do a massive job. That's what happened. For a battered team, it was a great win and an excellent performance. There was elation in the dressing room – we really had become a team and we felt proud. It was a win for mental strength and belief and doggedness.

I went into the South African dressing room and swapped jerseys with Victor Matfield. It wasn't so much about the jersey, though. We had gone on a lap of honour after the game, to thank the Lions supporters, and I wanted to say to Victor: 'Look, we know you won the Test series – we were just thanking people who'd spent a lot of money to come.'

I said it to John Smit, their captain, as well. He was good about it. He said: 'I appreciate you saying it – we'll leave that kind of talk to the papers.'

It came out later that they were riled up about something that happened around the first Test. There was a new thing in Super 14 rugby around then which we'd never heard of: the two teams sharing a drink in the home dressing room after games. When the invitation was made to us before the Durban Test, I didn't feel it was something we should accept. Brian agreed with me and we sent a message back: 'Let's wait until the last Test and have a big night out then.'

We were in their country, we were underdogs and we needed all the edge we could get. We thought we needed to be digging in mentally until the series was over, not socializing with them with two Tests left to play.

I'm not sure how that message was delivered, but it turned out they had taken it badly. We had our night out after the third Test, but at midnight they got on their bus and headed away. I was having a few drinks with Matfield and he didn't have a problem staying on, but they were already under orders: on the bus at twelve.

After the tour I went on safari with Emily. They took us out early each morning, and there was a four-hour break in the afternoon. I slept for the entire afternoon break, every day.

I'd come away with a reasonably good feeling after the third Test, but a few months later all I could think about was the opportunity that we'd missed. The frustration faded over time, but I still see it as a big regret. It wasn't that I wanted to dine out on it forever, but it's only every twelve years that the chance comes to win a Lions series in South Africa, and it's only going to get harder to do.

I remember thinking back then that if I'd picked up a serious injury in the first game of the new season and been forced to retire, I would have been happy with my career if the last thing I'd achieved in it was being part of a winning tour with the Lions. I would have told myself that I could walk away without a bother.

Being around for the next tour, in 2013, felt like a long shot then. I was about to turn thirty and I thought I might have two or three years left, if I was lucky.

13

Towards the end of my career, people often asked me if I'd go into coaching. There were days when I thought it was the only thing I wanted to do, and days when it was the last thing I felt like doing.

I used to see Tony McGahan and Laurie Fisher working twelve or thirteen hours a day, seven days a week. After we'd played on Saturdays they had to put in the time on Sunday to prepare for the review the following morning – there was no let-up, and very little time in the week to relax. The losses weighed heavily on them and the wins gave them very little reprieve.

I had studied computer engineering before turning pro-fessional. In 2009, thinking I should prepare the way for an alternative career path, I enrolled for a business degree with the Open University.

I bought into the distance-learning concept.

I bought all the books.

I was excited by what I was going to learn.

B201 – Business organizations and their environments

B204 – Making it happen! Leadership, influence and change

B291 – Exploring innovation and entrepreneurship

But I also had a concern at the back of my head, after reading the advice to prospective students.

It's important to bear in mind that any higher education course of study is rigorous.

Make sure you can commit the time and dedication that will be required to your chosen course of study.

A week before I was due to start I found I was spending a little less time focusing on my next game, which bothered me. Then I started worrying that I'd get competitive – that it wouldn't be enough for me just to pass, I'd want the best results I was capable of achieving. I felt like I was having an affair outside of rugby, that I was two-timing my ambition to be the best player I could make myself.

So I pulled out.

Five months after their win against us in the Heineken Cup semi-final, Leinster beat us 30–0 in the league. They were stronger than us all over the pitch, and especially up front.

Tony was devastated – we all were. It was supposed to be the game when we put the Croke Park defeat behind us. At the time I couldn't put a finger on what was wrong. None of us could. All I knew was that things were somehow different. It was around then that the thought occurred to me that maybe Munster had just got lucky with a really good group of players, and that things might not be the same when they were gone. I thought about the Saracens team we'd beaten in the 2008 semi-final. They had excellent players, they were a match for anyone on their day, but they'd been going for so long that the great performances were happening less and less often. Any time I found myself thinking negatively like that, I had to fight it off and hold on to the belief that our team still had what it took to win Heineken Cups. And we did.

When we lost games during our most successful years, it wasn't because we were technically off; it was usually down to us not being right physically and emotionally. There wasn't as much technical detail in the game then, but, at our best, we were always in the right place mentally. We never over-analysed – if there was a ruck, we just tried to blow anyone near to it out of the way.

Back when I played for Munster Schools, we were desperate to get set first in the scrum. We wanted to show the opposition we were fitter, hungrier. We didn't know anything about the science of scrummaging, which says you should let the other pack go down first, because the less time you're in the squat position the more power you retain in your legs.

Later on, when we had a do-or-die Heineken Cup pool match at Ospreys coming up, I remember Frankie Sheahan's response when I suggested getting set for every scrum before them.

'That's a great idea!'

We hammered them in the scrum and won. Technically, we were only making things harder for ourselves. But we believed – even if it was just for one week – that we had stumbled on something.

Once I became a senior player I was always big into trying to figure out what we had to do, but it used to be a subconscious thing. When I thought about it more, I realized I was spending every week trying to find something, anything. When we did find something, we'd cling to it and build our week around it.

When Leinster outplayed us at the breakdown in that semi-final, I felt it was down to their aggression and our lack of it. It was the simple answer, but not exactly the right one. Very often our solution to being beaten at the breakdown was to go harder, to be more aggressive. But the game was moving on. There was more to it than hitting bodies as hard as you could. Advanced coaching was bringing a technical element to the ruck, and we didn't manage the transition from being a passion team to being one that could combine emotion with the precision in the way Leinster under Joe Schmidt did.

When you're not sure where you're going you can end up getting a lot of the basics wrong. A few weeks later we got beaten in Edinburgh, our third defeat in four games. There was only a score in it but we were really poor – just flat. We were missing guys in the front row, but apart from that it was more or less a full-strength team. On paper it was one of the best backlines we'd ever had: Warwick; Dowling, Mafi, De Villiers, Earls; O'Gara, O'Leary. Six of them had played unbelievable rugby against Ospreys, six months before. The seventh – our new signing Jean de Villiers – was a world-class player.

The time was right for us to develop. Rog was eager to play with more width and exploit the quality of our backline. He was massively ambitious for the team and he wanted to run the ball a lot more. That was fair enough: Rog was an onfield captain too, and the out-half dictates so much of what you do. As well as that, the personnel were there to develop what we were doing.

Still, there were times when I felt we should have been using our tactical kicking game more. It used to frustrate me because Rog was the best tactical kicker in the world. He did it on autopilot. I loved how he could run flat out and then

spiral a ball into the corner. Even if there was a winger closing in, he wouldn't get near it – the ball would hit the turf
and skid into touch. He still had every ounce of that ability,
but it wasn't the first thing we were looking for any more.

Rog's tactical kicking was a massive ingredient in Munster's winning formula and at times I felt I admired his
kicking game more than he did himself.

We had countless conversations about the best way forward
for the team, and sometimes we didn't agree. I loved discussing things with him and arguing with him. More often than
not, when we needed somebody to step up and win a tight
game for us, it was Rog who did it. And when we fought our
way out of that particular slump, he was there again.

We'd already lost a pool game at Northampton, and when
Perpignan came to Thomond Park everyone said we needed
a bonus-point win.

We didn't get one try, let alone four. Perpignan scored
three, but we still beat them by a point, 24–23. We were losing inside the last ten minutes, until Rog kicked another
penalty. He had been dropped by Ireland for the game
against South Africa the previous month. From that day on,
he was in a battle with Johnny Sexton for the rest of his international career, but he had so much mental strength he was
always going to deliver once he got back to Munster.

People didn't rate our performance against Perpignan, but
I could see a lot of good things. I knew we'd be feared up and
in the right place mentally going over to play them in the
reverse fixture the following weekend. The Stade Aimé Giral
is a tough place to go to, but I liked having that feeling among
the group.

The day after the Thomond Park game, we had a tenth-
anniversary reunion of the Young Munster Junior Cup team.
We all got a bus up to Galwegians to support the Cookies in

the All Ireland League, and on the way up we watched clips from our cup run in 1999. All the lads were cheering when the two massive fights from the final came on. Later on, we had a brilliant night back in the Corner Flag and I can remember Justin asking me how I was feeling about playing Perpignan away from home.

'We will kill them next week,' I said.

A few months after I'd played my final game for Munster, I did a Q&A with the supporters' club in Cork. Somebody asked me to name my favourite away match. People could ask that question on five different days and I might give five different answers, but the one that came to mind that night was Perpignan away, December 2009.

Tony had brought Mick Galwey in as a mentor for the week. Gaillimh was with us when we went around town the night before the game, handing out Munster pins and badges to people on the streets and in the Christmas market. It was all about letting their supporters know we were there to do a job and that we'd come to win.

We went in at half-time with a one-point lead, 10–9. Gaillimh said a few words. We heard afterwards that the South Africans in the group – Wian du Preez and Jean de Villiers – didn't know who he was and couldn't understand why a stranger was giving a team talk in our dressing room.

We won 37–14.

As soon as the whistle blew, I was feeling certain we could win another Heineken Cup, that we had the beating of any team. It felt like we had come through a difficult period and we were stronger as a result of it.

Denis Leamy had a stormer, but in the last play of the game he injured his knee and it put him out for the season. I was devastated when I heard the following day how bad the injury was.

In January, we dug out a home win against Northampton and qualified for a home quarter-final. I had to watch ten minutes of that game in the bin. I was locked down on a totally legal poach but Romain Poite didn't see me. He took out the card just as the lads started patting me on the back, thinking we had the penalty. They were camped on our line for scrum after scrum, but we survived.

There was some atmosphere in the new stadium. The capacity had doubled to 26,000 and it was full for every Heineken Cup game. A few people said to me: 'Did ye notice the crowd?' It was like they were really proud of playing their part. We hadn't played particularly well, but the point was they didn't need us to give them a reason to shout: all we had to do was empty ourselves in the pursuit of victory.

That Sunday some of us drove up to Carton House in Kildare to join the Ireland Six Nations camp. It was the third weekend in January. The next time I played for Munster, there were three weeks left before Christmas Day.

PART THREE

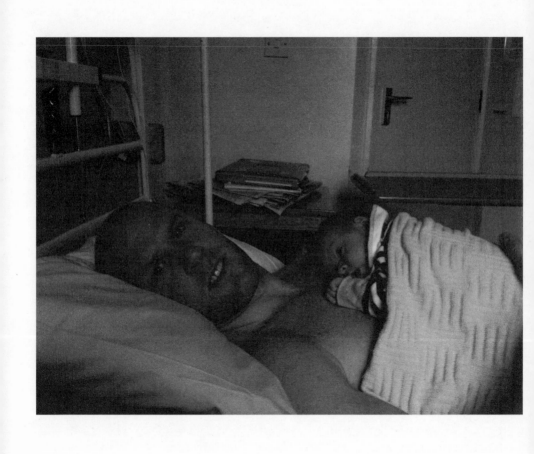

14

The drug was called Tazocin – an intravenous antibiotic. It was supposed to attack the tiny pools of pus that had appeared, from out of nowhere, in my groin. I'd been given it three times a day for a week at the Bon Secours Hospital in Cork, until I told them I needed to go home.

I had a new son. Paddy was just a few weeks old and I wanted to be with him and Emily, not staring out the window of a hospital room, sixty miles away, when I didn't even feel sick, or trying to pass the time by watching DVDs I wasn't in the mood to enjoy.

They let me go home, and a woman from the Baxter medical company came to my house, put the antibiotics in a portable fridge and showed me how to administer the dose myself, using the PICC line running along my left arm all the way to my heart.

After a week of this, there was minimal improvement and

I noticed that my body was beginning to react badly. It started with pains in my knees, and after another week of the IV treatment it was worse. When I opened the valve to let the fluid into my vein, there was a throbbing pain in my jaw, in my knees, in my elbows. The only way I could fight it was to keep everything moving. And twenty minutes later, when the dose was all in, I was sitting on a bench at my kitchen table feeling frustrated, asking myself why nobody seemed to have any answers.

I can't do this any more, it's making me worse.

Why isn't it getting better?

How did this happen?

Before they put me on Tazocin, I had been taking strong oral antibiotics, which gave me diarrhoea for three weeks. The weight kept falling off me. I lost ten kilos in the end. I looked ridiculously light, pale, downright ill. I noticed people were looking at my shoulders and I could see the question in their head.

Is there something wrong with him?

At first nobody really said anything, until it was too obvious for them to ignore.

Mostly they were subtle when they first came out with it:

'Did you lose a bit of weight?'

Then not so much:

'You're after dropping a good few pounds, Paul – are you?'

And then, after they stopped asking me what game I was hoping to make it back for:

'My God! You've lost so much weight!'

When I left school I weighed fourteen and a half stone, or 92 kilos. At twenty, I met the Connacht coach, Steph Nel, and he told me I'd need to be a minimum of 110 kilos to play professional rugby. That became a magic number for me, and it wasn't easy to get there because I'm not a naturally big man, unlike a lot of the second-rows I've played with and against.

I found out that I was an ectomorph, or a slow gainer. It meant I couldn't eat enough. I needed two grams of protein a day for every kilo of body weight. I remember, during Eddie O'Sullivan's time as Ireland coach, wearing a calorie counter for twenty-four hours while training in Spala, Poland – we had weights, fitness and skills all in the one day. I burned 7,900 calories. I needed to force-feed myself and take supplements just to stay at the same weight.

To see all the hard work it took to keep my weight at around 112 kilos go down the tubes was demoralizing. And all that time, in the back of my head I was resenting how it had come about.

This isn't even a real injury!

I didn't get it hitting someone in a tackle, or even being hit!

A rumour went around Limerick that I had cancer. Somebody walked up to Dad in town and said it to him, straight out. And Dad, he's a worrier. I'm sure there was a part of him that wondered if I was holding something back from him.

I got a text from a friend:

I know it's just a bad rumour about you having cancer but I just want to double check it's not true

Another friend called me.

'Look, Paul, this fella today was saying you've a heart condition. I'm only ringing you because he sounded so convincing. He had a load of information about it . . .'

It wasn't the first time I'd been the subject of rumours, and they usually start that way, with somebody pulling something out of the sky and making it sound so plausible that others can't help themselves from spreading it around.

Listen, this mightn't be true now, but . . .

Somebody else let me know my medical condition was being discussed on a web forum. Sure enough, someone had put it out there that cancer was the reason I'd lost all the weight.

People go on these websites under an alias. There are no names, no pictures, no contact details, nobody accountable for the false rumours about players' lives. I contacted the site owners and told them to take it down.

I look back now and think how lucky I was that Paddy came along when he did. We named him after Emily's grandfather, a lovely gentleman who passed away while she was pregnant.

I can still see him in the delivery room, flinging out his arm as it came free and then spitting out blood, while I was thinking, *This is the most incredible thing I've ever seen.*

In the middle of it all the thought came into my head that the midwives must have been trained in positivity, because they were brilliant with Emily.

Taking him home from the hospital was special; something as simple as putting him in the car is a nice memory. There were flowers and balloons everywhere and I worried that he might be allergic to pollen or something. There was the daunting feeling that you're taking responsibility for another human being, but when we strapped him in and pulled out of the car park it felt like, all of a sudden, you're a family. Then you shut the front door behind you and lock it and it's just the three of you, heading into the unknown.

Crikey – we haven't a clue here!

At first, Paddy didn't sleep at night. I remember thinking that if you didn't want a baby – or if you weren't ready for one – it must be a nightmare. Me and Emily, though, we were ready. And it's true what they say: being a parent changes how you look at life.

Every night Emily breastfed Paddy around half-nine and then I looked after him as she got some sleep upstairs. I gave him his bottle around half-eleven, a big feed to make sure he'd sleep. Then I lay on the couch with him until half-two or three, cradling him in my arm, with his head nestling in my hand as I fell in and out of sleep. I loved that feeling – the warmth of his tiny head on my palm, the two of us there together as he slept.

Sometimes, during those late nights, I thought about what the future held for him. I wanted him to grow up knowing that anything is possible if he believes in himself and his abilities. I wanted him to feel that even if he came across people with all the skills in the world, he could still figure out a way to get the better of them.

I thought about taking some lines from *When We Were Kings*, the documentary about how Muhammad Ali beat George Foreman in the jungle, and putting them up in his bedroom when he was a little older, to remind him that the right attitude will overcome anything. In Zaire, Ali was up against a guy who was better than him, stronger than him, fitter and seven years younger – a fighter who wasn't intimidated by him, who had every box ticked to beat him. But Ali still figured out a way to win.

Even when Paddy was very young, I was looking forward to the day when I could bring him into the dressing room with Munster or Ireland and let him play away. I wanted to carry him on to the pitch at the end of a big game, after we'd won. When that happened, more than once towards the end of my career, it gave me some of the best memories of my time as a player. I found that those great moments are even more special when you have your son with you after a tough game and you're walking down the tunnel together.

In those first weeks and months, though, when nobody could figure out how to fix my groin infection, just looking at Paddy put me in a better place and took my mind off the injury, at least for a while.

In the newspapers, people were writing about my injury, but it never felt like an injury to me. You get injuries playing in a game, or training. This was different.

I'd noticed a tiny bit of pain in my left groin during the Six Nations. Nothing to stop me training, just twinges when I sneezed or coughed – you wouldn't even call it pain. I got tested for a hernia: nothing showed up.

In the Scotland game I only felt it once, chasing down Johnnie Beattie as he went in for their try. It was a bit stiff afterwards, but not serious. Next day – nothing. But by Wednesday it was at me, and a scan showed a slight cleft tear. It was tiny, it could have been there years. I could have played with it, but it was niggly – something I needed to get right.

I went for a scan, and they said the pubic symphysis muscle between my pubic bones was under stress.

'What we're going to do,' said the doctor, 'is inject your groin with some cortisone.'

He reckoned it didn't massively need it – but an injection would prevent problems in the future.

So I thought, fine – if it's going to help long-term, let's do it.

In it went and I felt grand. Then I drove back to Limerick, went to bed and spent the night in agony.

I'd gone from something that I could play through, to being in serious pain. Straight away, that should have said 'infection', but for weeks it threw everyone who looked at it off course.

The next morning my physio at Munster, Neil Tucker, thought it was 'steroid flare' but he said we'd check for an infection, just in case. He pulled out a textbook and showed me: when cortisone goes into your muscle it can sometimes antagonize it for a day, maybe two.

Fair enough, I said – it looked right. But nobody could tell me much about steroid flare – there seemed to be very little medical knowledge about what exactly it is. Four days later I was still in agony and there were new symptoms on my right-hand side.

I asked the medics: 'How can this be happening? I came in here with a left groin strain – how can I have this?'

I told them I couldn't put on my pants without bending over in pain. I couldn't sneeze without having to lean against something and then wait ten seconds for the pain to ease.

They were starting to think it was an infection, but when I got bloods taken there were no indicators. They put it down to a condition called osteitis pubis: an inflammation of the pubis symphysis. But they put me on an oral antibiotic, Augmentin, just in case it was an infection.

By then we were into the week of a Heineken Cup quarter-final against Northampton and I thought I was in with a shout of playing. I went into intensive rehab and trained on the Thursday. In agony. It hit me whenever I changed direction or slowed down from speed. Three-quarters of the way through the session, I stepped off the pitch. The following morning, I could barely get myself out of bed, so I ruled myself out of the game and stopped all rehab.

After four weeks, another scan showed the symptoms were getting worse, and by then the medics were starting to become convinced: it was an infection. What I had to fall back on, when I was struggling with it, was that they were doing everything in their power to figure the thing out. I knew that Neil Tucker, in particular, was giving it his all, Skyping doctors in Adelaide on his day off and working long hours trying to get things right for me. Eanna Falvey was working his socks off too. But it threw us a lot of dummies. I'd have three good days and then a twinge out of nowhere, just walking up the stairs.

On and on it went. I was bobbing along from one diagnosis to the next, and the frustration kept building inside me. Every person I met, out of politeness, asked the same question.

'How're you doing, Paul – how's the injury coming along?'

I had two stock answers.

1. 'Nearly there now. Nearly there.'
2. 'On the mend!'

They usually had a follow-up:

'When are you back to us?'

Us. It was a friendly question, the kind you'll always get in a rugby city like Limerick. I knew they were just being nice to me, but there were days when I was boiling after being asked the exact same question over and over, and I felt like saying:

'Do you not realize I've been asked that about twenty or thirty times already today?'

There were other questions that really bugged me:

'Do you think your body is trying to tell you something?'

Actually, it is – I think I'll retire. Thanks for pointing that out to me.

If my family asked, they got the look of death, or an answer so short they knew the topic was out of bounds. I knew they were anxious every day to know more, and that it was probably considered a very delicate process, asking me about it. I felt like an asshole when I could sense them bursting to ask a question, but I wouldn't give them a chance. I wanted to wait until I'd made big gains, rather than give them daily updates. But even when it looked as if I was making progress, I didn't like talking about it much, in case I jinxed it.

When the Tazocin didn't work, they switched me to a new intravenous drug: Meropenem.

That meant another three weeks in hospital, in Limerick this time, which at least gave me the chance to go home during the day, in between the IV treatments.

That got rid of the infection, finally, but it was really only the start of the recovery. By then the bone looked like a piece of Swiss cheese, with holes going through it left, right and centre, and the only thing the new drug had done was to take the pus out of the holes.

They told me it was going to be another twelve weeks before I could put any stress on the bone.

When you're injured, someone else takes your place in the team and the lads get on with it, always concerned when they meet you, but with their own games to concentrate on, their own lives to lead.

It's a hard place to be, when you're on the outside looking in. When you're starting, the team's problems are your problems. When you're injured, you end up living – at least a little bit – the life of an individual athlete. You miss being part of the team – sharing problems and fixing them, being in it together, getting ready for a big performance on Saturday.

That was how I felt in those weeks and months: it was like a void. When you've got a long-term injury and you're watching from the stand or at home, you feel bad for the lads if a game doesn't go well. You'd like to think you could have made a difference. And when the team wins, most of you is delighted and a small part of you thinks: *Are they moving on without me?*

Munster's season ended, a second year without a trophy.

Ireland flew to New Zealand and then to Australia – two more caps left behind. I thought then I'd never get to a hundred caps, the way John Hayes had in the Six Nations just gone.

Pre-season training came around again in late July, only I couldn't train with the rest of the team, couldn't run, couldn't even jog.

When we won the Heineken Cup in 2006 I used to do a weights circuit with high reps and high speed – it was so hard that I felt like getting sick the whole way through it. In that first week of pre-season in 2010, when all the senior players were back in, I was so desperate to fight my way back to fitness that I told Neil Tucker I wanted to try that high-rep session. I wanted to do something I knew was really hard and see where I stood. He said OK, although he looked hesitant.

I arrived early the following morning, psyched up to train until I was ready to vomit. I wanted to feel like I was earning my wages. I wanted the lads to see me coming out of the gym covered in sweat, to feel like I was one of them again, training hard in pursuit of our goals. I'd built myself up so much it felt like my whole rehab hinged on finishing this session, but then Neil told me I wasn't doing it at all. Instead, he gave me a different programme.

A light bike, rowing and a weights session with 10kg dumbbells.

I felt like I'd been shot. I lost it.

'What about the session we decided we were doing?'

'You're not ready for it yet.'

'And you're just telling me that now?! Have you any idea how much I wanted to do that session? I have to go home every night and deal with this injury!'

Tension had been building between us because that's what

sometimes happens between physios and injured players. All the frustration came out in one go and we ended up having a row.

When I was injured I wanted to be back playing yesterday. Neil said he was doing everything he could to get it right, which was nothing but the truth. I knew he had spoken to the best people in the world and – more than anyone – he had a handle on what was best for my recovery. I think I always said sorry in situations like that, when I knew I was in the wrong. Ten minutes later we were having a good chat.

Maybe it's only when we're no longer injured that we regain the perspective to see the bigger picture and appreciate the dedication that the physios and the medics bring to their job every day. But I couldn't resist asking Neil that day:

'Am I the worst patient you've ever had?'

No, he said. He named a couple of other injured players: 'They were worse than you.'

Hearing that from him made me feel good – or better, at least.

Back in the gym, I turned a stationary bike over at a pace that wouldn't have taken the breath out of a sixty-year-old housewife, going so slowly I had to put my wet top back on.

When I was done, I walked over to encourage the lads doing a fifteen-minute fitness hit at the end of training. They were still picking each other off the ground and high-fiving as I headed to the changing rooms, the first one there before lunch.

I agreed to do this book in late 2009, and it started then with conversations. I'm not sure that I gave much thought to how long the process might go on. I was probably thinking a couple of years. I'd had only one serious injury at that stage and I remember thinking that if I made it to the 2011 World

Cup and then retired, I couldn't complain. Anything after that would be bonus time.

The groin infection happened very early in the process of working on the book. Because I had a lot of time on my hands, I put some thoughts down on paper. I wrote about how I was feeling when the frustration of that infection was probably at its worst. It was later in pre-season, on a warm-weather training trip to La Manga in Spain. I'd only just been given the all-clear to start jogging. The minute they gave me that news, a feeling of excitement swept over me. Straight away I started seeing myself doing hard fitness sessions with sweat dripping off my face. But it wasn't like that. I had two sets of five 30-metre jogs, and I struggled even with those.

In La Manga, my first training 'session' lasted four and a half minutes. It was a start, but when I looked across at the rough-and-tumble training the lads were doing – wrestling each other in different events for three-quarters of an hour – it made me feel further away from a comeback game.

I remember looking over what I'd written on my laptop and thinking, a week later, *That reads too dramatic*, but maybe it gave a sense of the frustration and vulnerability that affects us in sport when we're injured.

Sunday 15 August 2010

Today was one of the worst feelings of my career. We had yesterday off so a big night was planned for Friday but some of the lads are so absorbed by their training that they're not drinking – even the Coke they are having makes them feel guilty. Other guys had a few beers and headed back to camp for food, a protein shake, water and bed.

A few on the injured list gave it a lash and I joined in, safe in the knowledge that I won't be playing any time soon. I ended up the drunkest I've ever been – I had to be carried back to bed. Today the lads were killing themselves on the pitch, awash with positivity about the work they're putting in. I was watching from the sidelines and my hangover from Friday night still hadn't gone.

The guilt was overwhelming.

The lads are doing two rugby sessions and weights every day. All I'm doing is running. The 30-metre runs change to 50 metres and the number of sets goes from two to three and then four. The progress is too slow for me and I'm still on Difene [*an anti-inflammatory*]. It's a crutch and if I'm honest I know it. It's a great drug, but I need to be able to run without it. After all the IV antibiotics I want to be medication free.

In my head I feel my credibility with the lads fading away. Sure, I have respect from past seasons but there are new faces now, younger guys who don't really know me.

There's no buzz or energy in anything I'm doing. This injury is battering away at my confidence like nothing before and there's no end in sight. What I'd give for a comeback date, instead of having to keep explaining that I don't really know when I'll be back.

I haven't been putting my opinions out there amongst the lads for a while now, because I keep telling myself I haven't played for the team in six or seven months, and so why should they listen to me now?

I often have an opinion on different things – sometimes a firmly held belief, other times just an idea to throw in and spark a bit of debate. But when I'm sitting on the sidelines while the lads kick lumps out of each other in training, I don't feel I have the right to an opinion. I'm not the one going out on Saturday to fix things. But not contributing anything makes me even more pissed off with the injury and probably does nothing for the healing process.

My big fear is that when I do get back I won't be at the level of fitness that I'd like. For this reason I really considered giving up the captaincy. I'll have to play my way back to fitness, which is OK at the start of the season, but when it comes to the stage when every game counts it's very different.

Captains are picked for what they do on the field. The cliché that you're only as good as your last game is very true. When I'm not playing well as captain I feel my leadership becomes hollow. People give you the benefit of the doubt, but only for a certain period of time.

I'm worried about coming back and not being the same player – and maybe people in the crowd giving out about me. Having to listen to that would kill Dad.

I know those first few months back are going to be full of fellow players' doubts, coaches' doubts, fans' doubts, media doubts. But these are the things that make the big days special.

Three-quarters of the way through rehab for the groin, my knee came at me out of nowhere. I went for a scan and it showed an osteochondral lesion – a small bit of cartilage was flaked off, like a piece of eggshell. It was just a little flick, about 7 mm wide, but it was painful. They said it was a bad injury and they reckoned I'd had it for a while. They told me two things.

1. It doesn't get better by itself. You either learn to manage it, or
2. There's an operation, but most people don't come back from it.

I was now almost thirty-one and I felt I had no choice but to get on with it and hope for the best. The knee delayed my comeback further, but on the positive side it gave the groin more time to get stronger. I knew I needed games to get fit.

A Friday-night game for Young Munster in the All Ireland League was ideal and I appreciated the club giving me the opportunity. Three times when I came back from injuries as a professional I managed to play for Young Munster. I always enjoyed it and I think they did too.

I trained with them on the Tuesday evening and I couldn't get over the physicality – they were going at it hammer and tongs. I enjoyed it so much I started thinking about playing a season for the Cookies after I'd retired as a professional – just playing for the fun of it and knowing that winning or losing wasn't going to be the decider of my mood for the rest of the week.

Dad raised me as a Young Munster diehard. On the last Friday in November, three hours before the kick-off against Shannon, he sent me a text.

> Best of luck tonight, hope it goes well for you. Remember you
> have been out for eight months so take it handy.

He wanted me to amble around. It was an important game for the club, but his only concern was for my well-being. Obviously I wasn't going to take his advice, but I appreciated the sentiment behind it and the blatant bias. Having him in my corner no matter what was always so comforting.

I came on for the second half and in the dressing room afterwards my groin felt great, my knee was fine and on the inside I was thrilled to have gotten through it. Still, we'd lost the game and I was also devastated for the lads. Two of them were in tears. It was great to see, that passion.

Afterwards I went into the Shannon clubhouse for a curry with the lads, and a past president of Young Munster, Brendan Collopy, bought me a pint of Guinness.

After a night-time game I rarely went to bed until 3 a.m.,

because I was too wired to sleep. Then again, normality went out the window when you had a seven-month-old baby in the room next door. I stayed up until half-four, catching up with the neighbours and buzzing about what was to come against Cardiff at Thomond Park the following Saturday night. I was thinking about extra skills sessions during the week, extra weights, video analysis, eating well, sleeping well, getting ahead and building confidence.

When Paddy woke at six, I realized the game had taken more out of me than I'd thought. It was my first introduction to the realities of actually playing rugby when you're the parent of a young child.

I went to his room and it was the first time I ever got cross with him.

But that didn't last long.

My first game for Munster in ten months and thirteen days went like this.

Five minutes into the second half, I was on the bench alongside Wally, bursting to get on. I was expecting the call, any minute. Shaun Payne came our way.

'Wally! You're going on at fifty.'

I give him the look.

'What about me?'

Partly joking, partly serious. Mostly serious.

'Nothing for you yet, Paulie.'

The longer the game went on, I knew I wasn't going to have enough time on the pitch for a second wind. Finally, the call came and I could hear the crowd cheering as I opened my tracksuit. I was coming on for Donners. He ran towards me in the freezing fog and there was a roar which lasted less than a second in my head, because straight away I was on my way to a lineout near our line.

By the time I got there Mick O'Driscoll had gone for a four-man. I called it on myself. Damien Varley's throw was a little low, but I took it, drove on, went to ground and we box-kicked it clear.

Maybe it looked like business as usual after sixty seconds, but there was no intensity in my play, no zip. I laid into a few rucks that I didn't really need to go to, rather than stepping off my foot and getting back outside Rog.

I knew the road back wasn't going to be easy.

I'd arranged for one of our best supporters, Dominic McNamara, to come into the dressing room afterwards. He had lost both his arms when he was younger and he had a hook at the end of a prosthetic limb, so we called him The Real Claw. He was always messing, slagging, making people laugh. And now he had pancreatic cancer and less than two weeks to live.

His best buddies rented a corporate box, took him out of the hospice and brought him to the game in a limo. His eyes were sunken and he'd lost a lot of weight. Two of his friends were crying while he was going around getting his jersey signed, delighted to be there.

It wasn't the only piece of perspective we got that night. Later on, at the Strand Hotel, there was a party organized for our head fitness coach, Paul Darbyshire. A couple of months before, Paul had been told he had motor neurone disease. He was married, with four young children, and he knew then that he had less than a year left. He used to be one of the fittest guys in our whole set-up, and watching him deteriorating in front of our eyes was heartbreaking.

I was glad to have come through another test of the groin and the knee. I left early, because I hadn't felt well all day. Back at home, I threw up and went to bed.

Maybe it's easy to say it now, with the benefit of hindsight, but I remember feeling at the time that I was entering a new and final stage of my time as a player. I was aware that I was going to have to play the rest of my career injured, or at least never fully fit. I didn't know that other injuries would come along and nearly finish me – especially the one to my back, two years later. But I did know that the knee was going to bug me – at least on and off – until the day I retired.

I was always going to struggle with being reminded by an ever-present injury that I wasn't the same player who won the Heineken Cup in 2006 or the Grand Slam in 2009, but I saw it as a challenge as well – it was something to keep fighting against.

In a lot of ways, the rest of my career was all about that battle.

15

The only red card of my professional career came in my second game back for Munster, against Ospreys at Thomond Park in the Heineken Cup.

I'd come on as a second-half substitute. With eleven minutes to go we were leading by six points, having come from behind. We just needed to drive another nail into them.

At the side of a ruck, the Ospreys Number 8, Jonathan Thomas, grabbed my jersey with his left hand. The referee, Christophe Berdos, was five metres away, with a clear view. I had my back to Thomas. All I wanted to do was get him off me. Deliberately, I swung my right arm backwards, hard and high.

He was a little closer to me than I'd thought, and because he had his eyes on the referee he didn't see it coming and he walked into it. I turned around at the precise moment when my forearm connected flush with the side of his face and he went down like a ton of bricks under my legs.

I didn't think the referee had seen it but I knew straight away that I had a problem and within a second I was already rationalizing it.

I'm probably going to get cited here, but at least I'll finish the game.

As I stepped away, Berdos looked straight at me and brought the whistle to his lips.

This could be red.

He headed for the assistant referee, came back and called me over. He was avoiding eye contact. He wanted me to stand and wait until our captain on the day, Denis Leamy, got there.

Thomas was still on the floor and there was blood spurting out of his mouth.

I knew what was coming, which is probably why I said something stupid.

'He was pulling me back, I swung my arm – I barely touched him!'

He had no interest. He pulled out the card. Red.

Mick Galwey was on the touchline. Tony McGahan had felt he could add something on match days: big-game experience, a calming influence. I walked off the pitch and stood alongside Gaillimh, embarrassed and a little bit shellshocked.

Tony had brought me on to make a positive impact and I'd done the complete opposite and let myself and the team down. If I'd swung a foot lower, it wouldn't even have been a penalty against me. But I'd been careless and clumsy and I felt a massive burden of responsibility.

If the lads get beaten here, it'll be down to you.

Don't let them score.

I looked up at the clock: seventy-three minutes.

Gaillimh leaned into me.

'When did you go off?'

'Sixty-nine.'

'Jesus. You'll get back on for a minute anyway.'

'Mick, I got a red card.'

'Was it red? I thought it was yellow!'

For a split second I felt a little hope rising. Then I turned around to the bench.

'I got a red card, didn't I?'

'Yeah,' someone said. 'Red.'

'Bollocks,' Gaillimh said. 'I just assumed it was yellow.'

Ospreys threw everything at us. We lost two lineouts out of three. In the final minute they kicked a penalty into the corner, looking for a seven-pointer, but Quinny made a big turnover and brought my agony to an end.

Afterwards I sought out Jonathan Thomas and apologized.

'Sorry there, I never meant to get you in the face at all.'

'Not to worry, not to worry,' he said. 'I got a few stitches but I'm fine.'

I got cited but Shaun Payne told me I mightn't get a suspension. 'You didn't see him,' he said. 'He wasn't in a vulnerable position. He was obstructing you.'

Four days later, I walked into the boardroom of the European Rugby Cup offices in St Stephen's Green, Dublin, wearing my best suit, shirt and tie.

The guy deciding my fate was Jeff Blackett, the Judge Advocate General of the British Armed Forces. Even before I sat down I didn't like the mood in the room. By the time I saw the judge, I'd already shaken hands with the prosecutor, Max Duthie, and the ERC's disciplinary officer, Roger O'Connor. Neither of them had objected, so I walked towards the judge and offered a handshake

He wasn't having any of it. He told me to go back.

The last time I'd attended a disciplinary hearing, after I was cited for a scrap on the ground with Robert Sidoli of Wales five years earlier, the atmosphere had been more encouraging. Jeff Probyn, the former England prop, was part of a three-man disciplinary panel. I'd been worried going in because anything more than a two-week suspension would have put me out of Munster's Heineken Cup quarter-final against Biarritz.

When the thing was over and they'd given me two weeks of a ban, Probyn stood up.

'Does that mean you'll be able to play against Biarritz, then?' he asked me.

I didn't want to let on that I knew, even though I was already feeling happy about the outcome.

'I'm not sure when the game is on.'

'It's on Sunday.'

'Right. I suppose I will, so.'

At the 2010 hearing there were seven people in the room and Christophe Berdos was on the telephone from France. The only chance I had of avoiding a ban was to overturn the red card.

Donal Spring, my solicitor, said that the ref could be heard three times using the word 'elbow'. Striking with the elbow is an immediate red card but the DVD proved no elbow was used. The contact was accidental and just above the wrist.

Then Berdos came on the phone.

'I made a mistake,' he said. 'It wasn't an elbow.'

It was obvious that Max Duthie had been expecting our line of defence.

'Do you believe it was still a sending-off offence?' he asked Berdos.

'Yes.'

Twenty minutes later Judge Blackett handed down his verdict. He said he was satisfied that the red card was justified, for deliberate foul play.

He didn't accept Donal Spring's claim that a first red card

in nearly ten years as a second-row forward amounted to an exceptional record.

He banned me for five weeks and took off one on account of my 'reasonably good' record.

I lodged an appeal, which was heard through a conference call at the ERC offices a week later. The judicial officer, Professor Lorne Crerar, listened to our arguments. He said he'd call back with his decision. When the call came, his secretary was on the line. The four-week ban stands, she said.

After I'd walked out on to St Stephen's Green, Tony rang me to commiserate. I was frustrated all the way home on the train back to Limerick. It was a month since Keven Mealamu of New Zealand had had a four-week ban, for a flying head-butt on Lewis Moody at Twickenham, reduced to two weeks. I felt there was one law for some, and another for the rest.

The old Munster team was beginning to fade away. Quinny and Hayes were in their final year. A lot of us were into our thirties. We needed fresh blood from the academy but there wasn't enough of it coming through.

The great players, the ones who'll make something happen when the team needs someone to step up, don't come along often. Wally was thirty-four and still a class act, but he'd been putting his body on the line for twelve seasons with Munster, and for Garryowen before that. For years he'd been our power runner, the guy who got us over the gain line more than anyone else, and for all that time he was a freak in the gym. Powercleans, squats, jumps – he was better than everyone, all the time. I was always trying to catch up with him, so I kept an eye on his scores. There was a jump we did, a test of explosiveness. You propelled yourself straight up from a standing start with your hands on your hips. No matter what shape he was in, no matter how hard a game he'd had the previous weekend, Wally's score used to be 57 or 58. I wondered if it played on his mind when his score started falling, because it played on mine. Even then, he was always excellent – but he used to be untouchable.

His knee was bad, he had problems with his ankle, with his back: there was compensating going on all over his body. And even still, there was nobody better to get us a try from ten metres out. There were rucks that season when I'd get myself off the ground to see where we were going next and I'd catch sight of Wally with his hands on the ball, sprinting towards the try line, running over people.

On the first day of 2011, Flannery played his last game for Munster – we just didn't know it then. His calf had been giving him problems for a long time and it made me shudder every time I saw him limping. Other players would have retired after so many setbacks, but he wouldn't let it beat him.

Sometimes you think you couldn't have any more confidence in someone, but with him it kept building, even when he wasn't playing. The way he talked about himself – it was like he'd taken it out of a psychology book. Somebody else saw the negative, he saw the positive, and as a result he gave the people alongside him belief.

If Fla and I disagreed on something, I'd always try to see it from his point of view, because I knew he would have thought about what he was saying – he wasn't just throwing it out there.

To train for a week alongside Flannery – and take him on – made you fitter and better. Even when you beat him at something, he wouldn't let you have it. If you benched more than him, he'd find a way to turn your victory into a moral defeat. And he was a withering slagger, one of the best.

'How many shoulder reconstructions have you had?'

'I haven't had any.'

'Well, I've had two.'

'So?'

'So, you only benched two and a half kilos heavier than me. You'd want to look at yourself.'

Ian Dowling was also fighting a losing battle against a hip injury. He hadn't played in months and soon he'd retire. He had incredible self-belief too and he'd come into the team at just the right time, when we needed guys who were training like there was no tomorrow. His example led the team in so many ways. He won two Heineken Cups, but his career was cut far too short. At twenty-eight, he needed a hip replacement. There was something very wrong about that, and it made the rest of us think about the long-term impact on our bodies of all the big hits and the collisions.

When an injury was bothering me, I could see the concern in Dad for my long-term well-being. Every so often, he expressed the worries that must have been at the back of his mind for a while.

'You're going to be wrecked after you retire!'

'What if it stops you from playing golf later on?'

'What if you're not able to kick a ball with Paddy?'

'Maybe you should be getting out at this stage, Paul.'

If I'd walked into the kitchen at twenty-eight and told Dad I was being forced to retire, he would have been really disappointed. But once I was in my thirties, after so many injuries, I knew he wouldn't be upset in any way to hear that news.

I felt that I was actually in very good physical shape, all things considered. If I'd had to do an office job, instead of tackling seventeen-stone rugby players, I wouldn't even have noticed most of the things that caused me discomfort from time to time and restricted the kind of movement I needed in training and during games.

Around that period when Fla was struggling with his calf, my knees were sometimes achy from lineout jumping. Not sore, not restrictive, just achy. It felt like the ache was there to remind me of my age, to chip away at me.

When I trained well, it was easy to ignore the aches. When I didn't, they bugged me, but I looked on it as another test. I felt I couldn't allow it to get the better of me. In that little battle with my own body, anti-inflammatories were my friend. After taking Difene, I felt like I could play for another five years.

Towards the end of my career, for a Saturday game I took Difene on Friday and Saturday. It was like a miracle drug, except it could disagree with my stomach. So I took Zoton, an indigestion tablet that dissolves on the tongue and lines the stomach. By kick-off the body felt – at least for a while – pretty much symptom-free. No aches, no pains, nothing.

I was always conscious that anti-inflammatories needed to be taken in moderation. I hated it whenever I had to take Difene to play. Rugby needs to exert vigilance over legal painkilling medication, because when people's livelihoods are at stake it's human nature that some will go too far and do themselves long-term harm chasing short-term goals.

Rugby today is an attritional game in which power is king. Apart from physical freaks like Jamie Heaslip or Donncha O'Callaghan, it's inevitable that any player at international level is going to pick up more than a few injuries over the course of a career. But even though rugby became more and more of a physical contest during my time in the game, with bigger and increasingly athletic players, the injuries I got over the years were rarely caused by massive tackles. They were mostly just bad luck.

Players today have more hits to take, but they get far better medical treatment too. Long after he'd stopped playing rugby, Dad learned that he had broken the AC joint in his shoulder at some point. He'd played away with the injury for Young Munster and nobody had noticed.

Because of Ireland's player management programme, those of us who made our living here had fewer games in an average season than other international players. Even though the restrictions on game time sometimes frustrated me, I knew it was for the best in the long run. Later in my career, more teams employed hard line speed in defence, and this made the collisions heavier. The whole point was to get in front of your man and catch him full on as soon as he collects the pass. That requires three things: power, technique and timing.

Back in the day, you showed a guy the outside and then took him round the ankles. Now, that gets put down as a negative tackle in the stats, because you're soaking for a few yards instead of coming up hard. So, instead of chasing guys across the pitch and tackling them side on, we were hitting them right in front – and taking the same hits when we carried the ball.

Sometimes the impacts looked like nothing, but they'd result in stingers that made me a defensive liability until the pain subsided. Going in to hit a maul, my head might glance off someone and I'd feel fire down my arm for maybe fifteen seconds. I lost all the definition in my right trap muscle from those stingers. After the harder games, I might feel a nerve in my shoulders shutting down and restricting my range of motion.

I played a lot of games injured, but I'd like to think I always knew what I was doing. I always knew the risks. If a doctor had said to me, about an injury: 'If you play another year with this, you're not going to be able to walk properly when you retire,' I would have walked away.

Six days before Munster's Heineken Cup pool game in Toulon – one we needed to win to stay alive – Tony told me I was starting. I hadn't played in four weeks, because of the suspension. And because of the groin problem, I hadn't started a game in ten months.

Thinking about the game, I started feeling very, very nervous. I was worried that I'd play it in my head all week and end up wrecked on the pitch. I was thinking that if we won, people would say it was a great decision by Tony to play me. And if we lost, I'd probably get the brunt of the criticism.

After I heard the news I spoke to Axel.

'He's playing me.'

'Yeah. He has to.'

'How'd you mean?'

'This is our cup final. If we lose, next week doesn't matter. So he has to start you.'

Rog said he just assumed I'd be playing as soon as my suspension was served. It was a great thing to hear. I couldn't believe people thought starting me was a no-brainer. It made me appreciate that some people thought I was needed, even after being out for so long and looking like I was finished.

I don't know if other leaders got a good feeling when someone said something like that to them. Did they need it, that bit of reassurance? Maybe I lost some belief in myself after being out so long, but I do know that I was desperate to justify Tony's faith in me.

We were well beaten. What hurt most was that we played straight into their hands. They didn't even have to be that good to hockey us. In the end we were flattered by the score-line: Toulon 32, Munster 16.

All week the atmosphere in the camp had felt strange, muted. There was nobody bouncing ideas around, nobody speaking with conviction.

I did a lot of talking, hammering home the key points as I saw them.

'We're not beating ourselves this time!'

'No cheap penalties!'

But for a guy just back after suspension for ill-discipline, I wasn't coming from a good place.

The game was on a Sunday, and by the Friday I was worried. I felt like I was coming back into a completely different team from what I was used to. Guys were so quiet I found it unsettling. It was like the passage of time and a succession of bad losses had eaten into our belief.

Five defeats in a row to Leinster, losing the quarter-final to Biarritz the previous year, sluggish performances in the league – in sport you've got to draw your belief from somewhere, and that day we didn't have the confidence to go toe to toe with a big team like Toulon, away from home.

We coughed up penalties and Jonny Wilkinson knocked over the kicks. Confidence went out of us, our scrum creaked, and we stopped kicking tactically.

Our pack used to dominate teams through fast ball. We decided when to take it on ourselves and when to leave it out to the backs, depending on what we saw in front of us. But against Toulon, every time I got up from a ruck the ball was being passed across the line until we were tackled into touch.

With six minutes to go they put my number up. I sat on the bench with a jacket around my shoulders. I had my head down and I was wrecked tired, but there were a million things going through my head.

Where are we going?

This is happening during my time and on my watch.

At the airport we got a great reception from the supporters. I felt like dropping my head when I was walking past them. They were incredibly good to us. I was ashamed.

The following week, Flannery told me he couldn't get over how happy I was in the dressing room after we beat London Irish. 'Because we were *bad*!' he said.

With ten minutes left we were 14–7 down – at home in the Heineken Cup. Ten minutes away from a fourth defeat in six pool matches.

We dug in and fought our way back. We scored three tries by playing relentless, high-intensity rugby. Like we used to do. We just made good decisions and a lot of them were pure instinct. We got back to some of the things we used to do, got away from playing off nine all the time. The game plan goes out the window when you're fighting for your life and calling on whatever it was that got you a pro contract in the first place.

And that was what made me happy.

Three months later, Harlequins beat us in the semi-final of the Amlin Cup. They didn't have to play fabulous rugby to win. We made it easy for them.

It was our second European defeat at Thomond Park in sixteen years. Because my knee was at me, I watched the first forty minutes from the bench. It was as bad a half as I'd seen from us. We just weren't physically ready to do a job on them. And that was everyone's fault, including mine.

Tony and Laurie were both excellent coaches. They were technically brilliant. The more the pressure came on them, the harder they worked. In the team meetings before that game, they presented their ideas perfectly and conveyed a clear message.

'Know your role. Do your own job. Do it with physicality and aggression.'

It was all very logical and everything they gave us was probably right. But when I thought about it afterwards – when I was trying to figure out why we hadn't put it into practice on the pitch – I kept coming back to the fact that there was very little interaction in the meetings.

The Munster culture I was used to, fostered by Deccie, was very much about player ownership. Back when the players were running things more, a guy would hold his hand up in a meeting and say: 'Look, I messed up there and I know why. It won't happen again.'

Healthy debate was always a good sign. Now, nobody was saying anything as the coaches were presenting to the group. Feedback was encouraged, but we were a quieter group than the one that had been there before, a little less sure of ourselves.

I said it to Tony after that Harlequins game: to me it was like the coaches just assumed that the whole room was taking what they said on board. It was really good information, but guys weren't participating. Instead of discussing it, or asking questions, we were nodding our heads. And then, when things went wrong, it wasn't much of a surprise that guys were slow to admit they didn't know their role as well as they should.

Harlequins knew our record at home. They probably started with massive fear. Once they'd won the first collision, that fear was gone.

We treated it like any other game. On the same day, Leinster beat Toulouse and made another Heineken Cup final.

They were in a different place to us by then. The years when they were behind us had served them well.

At Thomond Park, it was fairly easy for us to put a team under pressure straight away. Go long from the kick-off. Pressure them into putting it into touch. Win the lineout and send up a garryowen. Then maul them. Let them make mistakes. Play for penalties and go three, six, nine in front, then pull away from them. The time to play would come. It was simple, but it had served us well in the past.

But we didn't do any of that. We had the ball seventeen times in the first half and turned it over fifteen times. Knock-ons, dropped balls, it was like an epidemic.

On our first move we put up the garryowen. Old school in many ways, but it's always been an important part of Munster's game at home: a solid kick-chase and hitting them hard. It's a statement of intent, so it needs to be executed well and with intensity. It wasn't. Our chase line was all wrong – James Coughlan went really hard but the next guy to him was six metres away and so James got sidestepped. If everyone else had been in a hard-chasing line, their guy would have stepped into another Munster player and got smashed. Instead, he fielded it comfortably, beat a few men, set up a good ruck and they were back on the attack.

At half-time in that game, it was unbelievably quiet. We weren't the problem-solvers we had been before. There were no solutions. Even if someone is talking and they don't have an answer, at least they're showing a bit of belief in themselves. There was none of that.

Axel cut to the chase with his defence review the following week. He put three things up.

Not Professional.

Not Munster.

Not Acceptable.

After the game people were talking about Harlequins' physicality. Axel showed the first ten or twelve breakdowns and pointed at their players.

'Are these guys being aggressive?' he said. 'Is this guy? That guy?'

They weren't. They were high in the breakdown and we weren't at the races.

I said it in the meeting: 'The only team not playing like Munster is Munster.'

After that game, we had a going-away night for the players who were leaving.

Ian Dowling had announced his retirement. Paul Warwick had got a better contract offer from Stade Français and Sammy Tuitupou was moving to Sale. Quinny's final game was the following week.

On what should have been a special day for them, we'd put up a very un-Munster-like performance, and our mood reflected that. Different guys spoke. Flannery made the speech about Dowling and broke down. Then Dowls choked up. By the time I got up to speak about Quinny, there was a lot of emotion in the room and I broke as well. I couldn't get the words out at the start. I had to ask Rog to speak while I composed myself.

There were a million stories I could have told about Quinny. Funny ones and crazy ones. I had a very special relationship with him. He looked after me when I first came into the team, and his astute advice gave me a head start. I still remember being in the old 33-metre swimming pool at UL when he told me that my chance would come – and when it did, I had to be as fit as I possibly could. He had seen guys through the years trying to break into the Munster team, but after four weeks on the bench they wouldn't be fit enough or sharp enough to take their opportunity. I took it on board, and whenever I sat on the bench for Munster, I argued with

Deccie to be allowed to play for Young Munster the following day. I'm convinced that played a massive part in me breaking into the Munster team in that first season.

Quinny and I fought like brothers at times, but we developed a great friendship. I told the lads that when I first came into the squad, he epitomized everything I thought was great about Munster – he was a savage trainer, a fantastic footballer, incredibly committed and unbelievable craic.

The weeks after the Harlequins game gave me hope. As players, we took on more ownership, more responsibility for our performances. We held players-only meetings. We had excellent coaching and were now making that information our own. For those two weeks, it became more our thing, and to me that made a massive difference.

We played Ospreys in the Magners League semi-final and that week we had the hardest scrummaging session in a long time. The team wasn't picked and guys were scrummaging for their places. Marcus Horan made it, and in the game he was really strong against Adam Jones. He was hungry for it, he was bitter. He'd had two tough years and it all came out on the pitch.

Sometimes a negative image can motivate you more than a positive one. Leinster came to Thomond Park for the league final four weeks later as two-time Heineken Cup champions. Since Joe Schmidt's arrival they were unrecognizable from the Leinster teams we had played in the past. They had climbed a mountain mentally in the European final against Northampton the week before, coming from 22–6 down at half-time to win it. They could hardly have been more confident and, for us, the worst possible end to our season would have been standing aside on our own pitch and watching them being presented with another trophy.

Shortly after half-time, they were pushing hard on our line. It was an arm-wrestle. We won it. We kept them out through desperation and desire and being in the right place mentally. After that, we dominated the rest of the game and beat them three tries to nil.

Hayes was still on the field in the last minute of the final, when our scrum won a penalty try. Against a seriously good Leinster back-row of Sean O'Brien, Shane Jennings and Jamie Heaslip, Wally was man of the match.

At the end there was relief, but I was very proud too. I lifted the trophy with Paul Darbyshire's little boy, Jack, and we all gathered round for a photograph that will be a nice memory as the years go by. Paul was in a wheelchair at the front. He hadn't got long left and we were all so glad that we could share that moment with him. He died just over three weeks later.

Every guy in that photograph had his own story to tell about the season we'd just had. For me, there were very

few games I enjoyed because I never felt right for them, never felt fit.

Towards the back, Paul Warwick was holding his little girl, Éire. He had the biggest smile you'll ever see, on his last day as a Munster player. Over on the far left, John Hayes's two daughters, Róisín and Sally, were hanging out of him. Right at the front, Lifeimi Mafi had an arm wrapped around his daughter, Cassidy.

When I saw the picture the following day, I thought: *Some day I'll have Paddy in a picture like that and hopefully there'll be a trophy there with us.*

Over on the right, Barry Murphy had a big smile as Jack and I lifted the cup. Like the other guys not involved on the day, he was wearing a suit. Ten days before the final, Barry had been forced to retire. He was twenty-eight, the same age as Dowls. They'd played a big part in our story: we were losing standard-bearers left, right and centre. More than anyone, I was pleased for Tony. Laurie, too – he was leaving to go back to Australia and the ACT Brumbies, and Axel was taking over as forwards coach.

I could see how stressed Tony was before the final. I congratulated him afterwards, and said I knew how much pressure he'd been under.

He said it didn't bother him. Maybe when the buck stops with you, that has to be your attitude. You have to keep fighting it off in your head.

That season everyone was writing Munster off, but we still finished thirteen points clear at the top of the Magners League table. When things weren't great, we were still winning.

That gave me a good feeling, but when I thought about all the good players who wouldn't be around the following year, I worried about how much we were losing.

16

Three weeks before we flew out to the 2011 World Cup in New Zealand, I had an epiphany.

I'd been struggling with my fitness all year. In those first weeks back after being out for so long, I didn't have it in the tank to play the way I wanted. Conserving energy was the only way I could get through the games. In the Six Nations, I was still pacing myself. Only by our last game, against England, did I feel any way close to an acceptable standard. Then I did my ankle against Leinster and finished the season back in survival mode.

Whenever the going got tough in our World Cup training camp at Carton House, I listened to the little voice in my head:

You cannot maintain this pace!

One day we had to do three 30-second runs at the end of training. The front-rows, second-rows and back-rows were all given minimum distances they had to cover. Off we went. On the first run, I reached my marker comfortably, but well behind the back-rows – and I'd always been there or thereabouts with them.

On the second run, I went five metres further and the back-rows came back to me by another five.

I made up more ground on the third run. I was right beside them.

Then I walked off the pitch with an uneasy feeling. I didn't know what it was, but something wasn't right. A few days later it suddenly hit me.

They had emptied the tank on the first run.

I had paced myself. I'd done what was required and no more.

I saw Donners alongside me. He was superfit, someone I always competed with, viciously at times. I should have been looking to take him on. But my head was telling me something different: I didn't trust my fitness.

Just sit on his shoulder here. Sit in behind, you're fine.

I never trained like that.

I hated guys who trained like that.

The penny had dropped: I was clear of my injuries and I had to retrain my mind so that I got out of the habit of pacing myself in training sessions.

The following day, I went as hard as I could from the off. I faded badly at the end, but it made me feel better that I wasn't holding anything back.

I remember thinking the World Cup would be my last big tour. I hated the thought of leaving Emily and Paddy for six or seven weeks. I thought about the Lions tour up ahead in 2013, and in my head I was ruling myself out already.

Rugby tours are toughest on your partner, especially when

you've got young children. As a player you're a long way from home and it's not easy if the games aren't going well, but you're among friends every night, never short of company.

On the day I left, my family said their goodbyes in the

kitchen at Justin's house and then Dad came out to the car to say his own. It was always a great feeling to know that someone else was as nervous for me as I was myself. He and Mam were following me down and I could sense he was thinking it could be the last big trip before I retired.

Watching my career was an intense experience for him and he always let me know what it meant, even though those words didn't come naturally to him.

That day he said: 'Who would have thought that you'd have eighty caps – isn't it just unbelievable?' Then he told me he loved me, and said how proud he was of me. It was a beautifully awkward moment from an old-school man. I pulled away in the car, highly motivated for what lay ahead.

Four years on from the disastrous World Cup in France, everything about our preparations felt better. We were based in Queenstown, in the south-west of New Zealand's South Island, a beautiful place buzzing with young people.

There was a serious setback early in the tournament when Jerry Flannery's calf went at training. I looked around and realized he hadn't been there for half an hour. When the doc told me the news I felt the energy drain out of me.

After I got back to the room we were sharing, I found him lying in bed with his hood over his head, watching old sports documentaries on his laptop. I got a bottle of red wine and we sat back and shared a few glasses, talking about old times. We barely mentioned the injury. There was nothing positive I could say – he had torn his calf for about the fifteenth time. People came to our room during the night and it felt like a wake for his career. He was on YouTube, pulling up old rugby clips. For the next six months he kept trying to beat it, but he never played again.

Before we played Australia, Fla presented the players with our jerseys. He was in tears the whole time. When I heard he was going to be handing them out, I knew he'd cry. That's just the way he is. But it was poignant and it was important. It lifted me.

I felt lucky to be on the other side. We were sharing a room, but now our worlds were miles apart. I'd felt emotionally flat in our first game, against the United States, and I decided to try listening to some music to get me ready for Australia. I spent the evening in Rala's room, asking the lads what songs they listen to before games and compiling a playlist. Shane Jennings suggested a track called 'Promontory', from the soundtrack to *The Last of the Mohicans*. Other guys chipped in with some great songs. On the morning of the game, I went for a long walk on my own, listening to the lads' playlist. I kept on walking until I actually got lost. A Fijian family in a banger of a jeep recognized me and pulled over.

'Sorry there, any idea of the way to the Waipuna Hotel?'

'Jump in!'

I listened to the same music in the bus on the way to the stadium. I walked around the pitch, listening to it. There were no big speeches, just reminders that the forwards had to step up. I said we could create a legacy for ourselves, with the whole country watching.

Australia went straight in. On their very first play they won a good lineout at the back and tried to send Pat McCabe into the heart of our defence. We had no tail gunner at the back of the lineout – we'd put an extra man in the backline. So they looked up and saw a five-man defence waiting instead of four, but still they sent McCabe in. We held him up in a choke tackle – turnover straight away. One of them tried to push Sean O'Brien. Seanie pushed him back in the face. It was the perfect physical start.

Our back-rows were everywhere. Having Stephen Ferris

back from injury was massive. Ferris didn't just make tackles, he smashed people. When he carried, he carried hard. I was in behind him when he picked up Will Genia and drove him back ten metres – Genia just folded into his arms. It was the kind of moment that wins rugby matches.

The scrum gave us huge confidence: they were coughing up penalties which meant fifty metres down the pitch for us or another three points on the board. It finished 15–6 and we were well worth the win.

Dad wanted to know everything when I spoke to him on the phone the following day, but he had news for me too. Rog was retiring, he said – finishing with Ireland after the World Cup.

I told him that was ridiculous. But he said no, it was in the paper, Rog had said it to the media after the game.

So I spoke to Rog.

'Did you announce your retirement last night?'

'I think I might have, yeah.'

'You're not retiring though – are you?'

'I dunno, I dunno.'

'That would be madness – you can't do that! You've got loads more left in you.'

'Thanks,' he said. 'I appreciate that.'

He'd come on for Johnny Sexton against Australia and played really well, but not starting was tough for him. He was never one to settle for second best. It wasn't in his nature.

Beating Australia meant we got some respect – for the first time – from the New Zealander in the street. I hadn't read any media since the beginning of the tournament, but I was curious to see what the Aussies had made of our win.

They had absolutely no respect for our performance.

Robbie Deans, their coach, said they needed to learn how

to play against teams that just wanted to keep taking three points off them. Will Genia said they played better against the bigger rugby nations, the ones who play a more open game.

Reading those comments made me hope we'd come up against them again later in the tournament.

After we'd won all our pool games, we drew Wales in the quarter-final. That week – and before a lot of other big games in my career, when I was trying to keep the stress at bay – I thought a lot about Lahinch. About swimming there. Playing golf. Drinking pints. Relaxing with Emily. Cooking food and spending time with my family. Resolving to spend more time in West Clare was something I did every time I had to deal with the build-up to a big game.

Dad said he never saw me as low after a game as I was the night Wales knocked us out. He was probably right. I didn't feel like talking. I didn't have a whole lot to say.

There was the option of trying to blot it out – for one night, at least – by going on the beer. But that didn't hold any interest for me. I had one or two drinks and sat back, listening to some of the lads, just thinking to myself: *What's the point? What's the point of even trying to figure out what happened?*

When we lost a Six Nations game there was another one coming up, or a summer tour to get things right. Even when we lost Heineken Cup semi-finals with Munster, I'd be on the phone with Rog practically the following morning, full of ideas and solutions.

Now, I was playing in my third World Cup and I assumed then it was my last. I was thirty-two and I didn't think I'd still be playing four years down the road. So it was black and white to me: we had let the greatest opportunity of our

Ireland careers slip and for some of us there wouldn't be a next time.

What really hurt was that it was there for us. We'd have been in the semi-final and the injuries were piling up for New Zealand. We'd have needed luck, but it wasn't beyond us – a chance to retire with brilliant feelings of achievement that would have stood to us for the rest of our lives.

Sitting in the team room nursing a beer, I didn't have any interest in figuring out why Wales had beaten us – what they'd done right, what we'd done wrong. Wales switched to a kicking game when they went ahead. But any team is liable to do that, and all the talk about Plan B or Plan C was just clichés. Never once in my career did I practise a Plan B. We were on their line six or seven times and we should have executed two or three of those. But I wasn't getting into that on the night they beat us – all I could think about was what we'd left behind.

Emily had been sending me little videos of every new thing Paddy was doing and they had kept me going, but once we'd lost that game I just wanted to go home.

The next twenty-five hours passed like this.

I was in bed before 2 a.m. Lying there, I wasn't looking back at the game – I was thinking about the following morning and how I'd feel then.

I started calculating my options. There were two.

1. I can try not to think about it – and if I'm lucky I'll fall asleep. I'll wake up with a clear head six or seven hours from now. After two seconds it will hit me like a train. I'll have to process it and start dealing with it.

2. I can postpone it. Get out of bed and go for a walk. Meet up with a few of the lads.

I chose option 2.

I got dressed, pulled my hood up and went walking. I texted Rog and asked where he was.

2.40 a.m.: Text from Rog: 'We're at Cully's bar. Come on down.'

2.50 a.m.: The Four Kings, on the corner of Taranaki and Dixon Street. Christian Cullen's place was empty apart from a few rugby supporters, Rog, Johnny Sexton, Sean Cronin, who was providing the entertainment, and a few more of the lads. I hadn't even been thinking about having a drink, but someone ordered me a beer.

5.30 a.m.: On my way back to the hotel I met a man from Drogheda dressed as a leprechaun. Then I ran into Fergus McFadden, so we had a couple more in the bar – me, Fergus and the leprechaun. Before we knew it, it was nine o'clock.

9.30 a.m.: The D4 bar, 143 Featherston Street. We ordered the $20 Big Brekkie – bacon, sausages, eggs, tomato, mushrooms and hash browns on toast, which read better than it tasted. Sometimes the leprechaun was full of chat, but other times he fell quiet and me and Fergus gave out to him for not contributing more to the conversation. I was drinking some kind of sparkling wine because I couldn't stomach anything else.

10.30 a.m.: The leprechaun ordered whiskeys all round.

1 p.m.: A few beers with Mam and Dad back at the hotel.

2.30 p.m.: I bumped into John Eales, one of the great second-rows, in the hotel lobby. We'd never met and we spoke for a few minutes about this and that, before I headed back to the D4 for a few more drinks.

5 p.m. (approximately): Some other place.

8.30 p.m.: The Establishment bar, on the corner of Courtenay Place and Blair Street: me and Fergus again.

11 p.m.: Subway restaurant, 23 Courtenay Place: one Chicken Temptation.

11.20 p.m.: I was on my way back to the hotel when I bumped into some of the staff from O2, the team sponsor. So we had a drink.

12.15 a.m. Monday: I was on my way back to the hotel when I bumped into Keith Earls, Damien Varley and Donnacha Ryan. I had a few more drinks with them, and then I felt hungry again.

2.15 a.m.: McDonald's, 200 Courtenay Place: one Big Mac meal.

Me: 'I'm definitely going back now.'

Earlsy: 'I'll go with you.'

2.40 a.m.: We came upon Electric Avenue, 132 Courtenay Place.

Me: 'Earlsy, look at this place! It's eighties music night!'

Earlsy: 'We're going home.'

Me: 'Ah come on! You know how much I love Eighties music!'

Earlsy: 'We're going home, Paulie.'

Me: 'Ah go on! We'll just go in for one and listen to the music.'

Earlsy: 'No. We've enough for one night.'

3.15 a.m.: I set the alarm on my phone for nine.

9 a.m.: After the alarm rang, it took me a few seconds to figure out where I was. Then came the realization that I had spent more than twenty-four hours escaping our defeat, not dealing with it.

We were due on the bus at ten. I mustn't have looked too good when I boarded it. I got a new nickname that day: The Corpse.

At Shannon Airport, Paddy recognized me straight away. I'd been worried that he wouldn't, but he pointed at me and smiled.

The three of us went to Portugal, to a lovely place down near Sagres with a balcony overlooking the sea.

On a beautiful cove beach during that week I found myself thinking that if I had to retire in the morning I'd be able to handle it quite well. With my family around me, I was dealing with World Cup disappointment much better than in the past.

17

When Munster became successful, expectations for us rocketed and it was hard to keep a grasp on reality. Success, year on year, was expected of us. People forgot how difficult it is to beat the best in Europe. They forgot that we'd come a long way in a short time. In 2004 Cardiff put sixty points on us, and we finished seventh out of twelve that year in the Celtic League, but people only remember our run in the Heineken Cup.

Once we'd gone three seasons without making the final, attitudes changed. When you're winning, you're able to tell people what you're doing right. When you're losing, everyone is able to tell you what you're doing wrong. Everyone was an expert and, while it really bugged me, in another way it just made me more determined to be successful.

We played Aironi, the Italian team, in my first game back after the World Cup. It was nearly ten years since my first

Munster start, away to Neath. Me and Rog were the only two players on the team-sheet for both of those games.

2001	2011
15 Dominic Crotty	15 Johne Murphy
14 John O'Neill	14 Doug Howlett
13 John Kelly	13 Will Chambers
12 Jason Holland	12 Danny Barnes
11 Anthony Horgan	11 Keith Earls
10 Ronan O'Gara	10 Ronan O'Gara
9 Peter Stringer	9 Conor Murray
1 Peter Clohessy	1 Wian du Preez
2 Frankie Sheahan	2 Damien Varley
3 Martin Cahill	3 BJ Botha
4 Donncha O'Callaghan	4 Donnacha Ryan
5 Paul O'Connell	5 Paul O'Connell
6 Jim Williams	6 Denis Leamy
7 David Wallace	7 Peter O'Mahony
8 Anthony Foley	8 James Coughlan

It was only two years since we'd played the best rugby of my time at Munster, and the truth is we still had a very good squad. Conor Murray had come from nowhere to become the best scrum-half in the country. Others who had been waiting a long time for their chance were taking it. Looking at the team sheet against Aironi, it's obvious we were in transition, but I didn't think we were too far away.

John Hayes came off the bench that day. He was about to retire after fourteen seasons of unbelievable service. Wally had a long-term injury and his knee never came right. He'd been going even longer than Hayes, but his body had taken a lot of punishment. Even before he retired, six months later, I thought he'd given enough – more than enough. A big part of me was desperate to have him back in the team, but I didn't want to see him suffering later in life from all the bangs he'd taken for us. Denis Leamy was only twenty-nine that Friday night at Musgrave Park, but after another six games we lost him to injury too.

I was beating myself up that season because I thought we had to judge ourselves against the standards we had set in previous years. I had it in my head that we were still the Munster of 2006, of 2008. I was thinking, *We're Munster and we should win* – even though we'd lost, one by one, so many great believers, trainers, players.

We didn't feel the loss of those guys straight away, and it wasn't something we spoke about among ourselves. That was a good thing, because there was nothing to be gained from dwelling on it, and in those tough weeks when we missed what they used to bring we knew we had to be out in front saying: 'There's two or three things we need to fix here and we're fine.'

We still had the quality in depth to field an excellent pack. BJ Botha had come in at tighthead and he was doing well. We had Axel as our new forwards coach and he was excellent. What we needed was new leaders – new voices, strong personalities, problem-solvers who could play for us and coach us as well.

Peter O'Mahony was coming through and we had seen leadership in him from day one. I could tell by the way he trained – he was hungry. You could see it in his carries – he was twisting, turning, kicking with his socks around his ankles, doing everything to get over the gain line.

The first day I met him he was just a kid in the academy and he was going around shaking people's hands. We'd just won a game with Ireland and he came up to me.

'Well done the other day – I was up there at it.'

I was taken aback by his confidence. It was impressive, and seeing a character like him in the academy was encouraging. I don't think he was even twenty-one when I had him down as a future Munster captain.

We played Leinster the following week and lost 24–19. There wasn't much between us but they were better at the breakdown, and that was the winning of the game. On the pitch I couldn't understand what they were doing – all I knew was we couldn't get near their ball at the ruck and we could barely secure our own. The combination of excellent players and top-class coaching was bringing them to another level.

It was obvious that many new habits had been drilled into them. A few years later, when Joe Schmidt got the Ireland job and I saw the detail of his work, I thought about how various Leinster players had improved massively under him and it frustrated me that they'd been given such an advantage over us when Joe was running things for them.

I always felt optimistic early in the season. I always felt it was on to win everything. But, for a while, I allowed that Leinster defeat to drag me down.

Are we going to have another season like last year?

Are we going to have to kick every penalty we get in order to win?

Somebody had stood on my hand during the game and when I woke up the following morning back in Limerick the cut was infected. I went to the hospital later in the day. The accident and emergency ward was rammed and I was on a trolley until three in the morning. I'd brought my laptop and I was trying to look at the game, but on one side I kept hearing the sound of a woman's sick hitting a cardboard box and on the other a guy was shouting, 'Get your hands off me!' all through the night.

As rugby players we were used to special treatment when we got injured, and I felt like an asshole for thinking that things must be bad if they couldn't find a bed for me somewhere. I got moved to a corridor until noon the next day, when they said there was a bed at the hospital in Croom.

Tony picked me up and drove me out there. We'd been due to talk about things and I didn't want to put it off. In my room, we went through the video of the game. For a long time he'd been frustrated that players weren't doing things the way he wanted them done.

It was one thing going on to the field wanting to be accurate and disciplined and fast off the line because that was what Tony had told you he wanted. It was something different – and more powerful – looking to be all of that because you'd thought about what the head coach had said, you'd done your own research, you'd decided 100 per cent that it was right, and you'd spent the week trying to develop good habits. The performance you were looking for was the same, but I felt your preparation was infinitely more powerful if you'd done it for the right reasons – if you believed what you were doing because you'd challenged it and debated it with colleagues. We needed to own the process of how we were going to win.

Until the end of my career, I believed that if you're not figuring stuff out for yourself – or trying to come up with some of the ideas – you won't commit with the same intensity and you won't know the game plan as well as you should. When things went wrong for us, as they did in that Leinster game, we were slow to come up with solutions. I think we were trying to be good at so many different things, we didn't

265

know where to look for the answers. We tried to cover many skills, instead of the critical few.

Years later, in Ireland camp, Joe Schmidt used to talk to us about the 'big rocks' of our game – the things we needed to be excellent at. When he reviewed a performance he looked at everything, but really it was the big rocks he went after. He used one-liners or buzzwords to get his message across. He wanted those words to jump into our heads when the situation called for them.

If there was a ball on the ground in training, everyone nearby shouted 'Scraps!' and tried to dive on it.

When we were on our backs with the ball after carrying, he wanted us to contort, rotate, swivel – it was about stopping a poacher from getting on us. Great coaching is often about imagery and cues. Joe told us he wanted us to be like a mackerel that had just been pulled in and was jumping around on the bottom of the boat. It was the first part of what he called 'Body Ball'. The second part was about making sure your ball placement was good. It was so effective that I used to find myself commentating in my head a split second before I'd hit the ground.

Body Ball!

If somebody didn't do enough to shake off the poacher, some of the more forceful guys like Eoin Reddan or Johnny Sexton wouldn't be long letting them know about it.

'That's bullshit! Fucking Body Ball!'

People coached those things in different ways. Some stopped the video and said: 'Look at Paul here. If he could just move his body around a bit more to stop this poacher and then maybe place the ball a little further out . . .' Joe gave the team a bunch of triggers, cues we could say in our heads, and he kept ramming them home until they became second nature.

266

All the good teams have their cues now, but coaching hadn't got there when I had that conversation with Tony at the hospital in Croom. All I knew then was that we needed to find better ways of packaging the excellent information he was giving us. All I could suggest was that we simplify things and stick to the main pillars of our game. We weren't going to become better players in a week, so we needed to work on the good stuff we had and make it better.

We went after that for the rest of the season. The following weekend, Rog kicked one of the most famous drop goals of his career to beat Northampton in the first pool game of the Heineken Cup. He knocked it over after we went at them for forty-one phases, with the clock nearly four minutes into red. It was pure doggedness and desire. My hamstrings and calves were cramping. My groin was at me. The crowd was going ballistic and I could hear Rog shouting at us as we went back and forth across the field.

'*Paul! Get up! Carry! Carry! Carry!*'

'*Leamy! Get the fuck up! Get up! Get up! Clean it out!*'

When it's all on one last play, you're just thinking about your job, the next place you need to be. I threw Rog a brutal pass when a drop goal was on, but we worked another chance for him. In that moment, as the ball went back, I wouldn't have swapped him for any out-half in history. Under the gun, he was incredible. He absolutely nailed it.

I was the only guy in the pack who'd played in the 2008 final. The night before the game, I'd spoken about our back-row and the journey they'd each been on to become first choice. Niall Ronan had been in the squad for four years, learning, waiting for a chance. James Coughlan had been overlooked and played AIL rugby until he was twenty-four. Peter O'Mahony, an academy graduate, had been through a lot of injuries. I didn't mention them by name, but I said: 'I admire your tenacity. You all fought tooth and nail to get into this team and we have to do the same tomorrow.'

As I sat at my place in the dressing room after the game, I was thinking that we'd shown ourselves the way forward. At the end of the previous season, when I'd had to fill out a voting form for our Player of the Year award, I could barely think of one name to put down. Six months on, a lot of hands were already up, early in the season.

We weren't going to have Wally scoring tries for us from ten metres out. Two of our best attacking threats – Keith Earls and Felix Jones – were out injured. But Rog's tactical kicking game and instinct always gave us a chance. So I felt we had the beating of most teams, if we weren't beating ourselves.

The European club game was changing and I thought the only way Munster could compete with the wealthier sides was by being different and more efficient. The big French and English clubs could sign great players and be sloppy at a load of things, without it costing them, because of the quality of their squads. We couldn't do the same things as them and expect to be at the same level. We needed to be different. We couldn't afford to be sloppy in any way. For us to win another Heineken Cup, we'd have to be unbelievably good at all the things that were controllable. And if there was anything out there that might give us something – even a small edge – I wanted to know about it.

I was reading books about the psychology behind team sport, about personality profiling. I was interested in the idea that teams can improve their performance – especially when the pressure comes on – by having a better understanding of their character traits. I was someone who could give out yards to a guy on the training ground and then feel so guilty about it later that I'd call him at home and apologize. Sometimes I wasn't sure why I did things, or whether they were helping or hindering the team. If it meant that greater self-awareness could improve me as a player and a leader, I wanted to understand myself better too.

I couldn't eat after that Northampton game. I had never been so physically wrecked in my life. I don't know if it was from the exhaustion, or the three days of antibiotics for my infected hand, but I threw up a couple of times during the night. Then I lay on the couch at home and wondered what the future held.

I'm not where I need to be yet.
How are the players coming in going to do?
Potentially we could be brilliant.
Potentially we could be average.
It's hard to know what way it will go.

If we won it this year, it would be incredible.

The following week, people came up to me on the street.

'Well done at the weekend!'

'Yeah,' I said, 'it seems to have restored the faith a little bit.'

Even though part of me was still thinking about all the criticism thrown at us in the weeks before that game, I was delighted to see the supporters so happy. I loved hearing stories about the craic in town afterwards. But I got frustrated whenever someone said we'd been lucky in the last play.

'How were we lucky?'

'I thought Nigel Owens might have given them a penalty a few times.'

'They were offside seventeen times in those forty-one phases.'

'Were they? Jeez, I didn't see that.'

Things were different. A negativity towards Munster was taking hold, but it made me enjoy it more. I was in a better place mentally because I had peace of mind going to bed every night. I knew I was doing everything I possibly could to make myself and the team better, on and off the pitch. I was very conscious that in order to keep having an influence, I had to be playing well. I couldn't hold someone to a standard that I wasn't maintaining myself.

In his great years, Roy Keane showed a lot of us the way. When he wasn't doing it on the pitch any more, Manchester United showed him the door. All of a sudden, his words didn't carry the same weight. They saw him as too opinionated, too much trouble. Once or twice I wondered, around that time, if Munster might have the same conversation about me one day.

'Actually, Paul now is more hassle than he's worth.'

Any time I spoke out, it was always about the team being

better, or about the long-term future of Munster. I wanted to make sure that when I had finished playing, we'd still be winning, or in a place where we could win. I felt the older players were protecting something important, something that had been started by other people, special people who came through a difficult period in the nineties and created an amazing culture in that 1999–2000 season. And I worried that what had been special was becoming diluted.

In every squad I was ever part of, there were guys who had the answers, guys who thought they had the answers, and guys who knew they didn't have the answers. We were never going to have thirty-five players who were fully focused on winning every game, but we needed more than we had.

I felt I had a great relationship with some of the younger players coming into the squad. But with a few exceptions it didn't seem like we were on the same level when it came to protecting the whole Munster culture. There were a lot more guys with contracts than before, more fixtures to fulfil, and even when players were only in the team a few times a year they were there in the background, wearing the gear. It wasn't anybody's fault, it was just the way things had gone. I always felt that a smaller squad, with fewer peripheral players, would be better. There were too many guys who were in one week and then out for three, drifting when not involved.

The academy graduates who had the required work ethic made the breakthrough. Many, however, didn't seem to possess the attitude to training necessary to succeed at the highest level. Not many of them scared me with the physicality of how they trained, or their fitness levels. When I looked to compete with someone in training, it wasn't the twenty-one-year-old coming through; it was still O'Callaghan, or Flannery before he retired.

I was lucky to have come up with Donncha and Jerry.

They put the team and a work ethic in training at the top of their priorities. That's the example I followed and became immersed in, so that it became part of my belief system.

The academy graduates all wanted success, to be in the first team, but they thought their natural talent and doing what they were told would be enough to get them there. I wanted them to figure out for themselves that being part of a Munster team good enough to beat the likes of Toulon and Clermont and Leinster meant you trained harder than them – and that was just for starters.

Peter O'Mahony was young, but he was old-school. He understood the responsibility his generation had to keep things going for Munster. As he became a regular starter I could see how heavily that began to weigh on him and the other young players coming through. The season after that Northampton game, we had Edinburgh at home. We'd already lost our first pool match, against Racing Metro, badly, so it was all on the line. Edinburgh were terrible that day and we won 33–0. I was going around chatting to the lads in the dressing room when I saw Peter in his corner, with his head down and his hands covering his face. I could tell he was emotional, and he didn't look up until he was ready. After that, he was laughing and joking with the rest of us, but I guessed where the emotion had come from. With the responsibility of being a senior player comes pressure – and the relief when you win can be overwhelming.

Going into the last pool game, away to Northampton, we'd won five out of five in the pool. We weren't playing great, but I thought if we could beat Northampton away from home and make it six, our confidence would rocket – no matter how well or badly we played. Outside of our group, nobody saw us winning. For most of that week, I was picturing what we would be saying to each other in the dressing room after the game, if we'd done it.

'That's six games in a row where people are writing us off – and we're still winning!'

'Even after this, people won't be talking about us – but we know we can beat anyone now.'

We put fifty-one points on Northampton. It was the day Simon Zebo showed what he was capable of as an attacking force, a back-three player who had something different. We were beaten in the scrum, but we ran them ragged.

Then we played Ulster at home in the quarter-final and lost. We gave them a 19–0 lead, but we should have had enough to come back. It wouldn't have been beyond us in the past.

When it was over, I had to do press. At times like that I always tried to say what needed to be said, and no more. It's hard to be 100 per cent sure of your thoughts on a game when you only have your own film of it in your head, seen from the second row. It's easier a few days later, having watched it a few times and discussed it with players and coaches.

That day I probably let my disappointment show a little bit.

'We weren't accurate enough when we had the ball.'

'The quality of player is there. Maybe that Heineken Cup nous isn't there.'

'A vital part of the game is not beating yourself – that's what we didn't do in the past.'

In the dressing room, we couldn't say anything.

Tony couldn't talk either. He just said: 'I've nothing, lads.' We could all see he was absolutely crushed by it.

When we let big chances like that get away from us, it was very easy to start thinking everything was wrong. But after a few days of suffering, I tried to stay positive when I was turning it over in my mind.

We've got some lovely players coming through – guys with good character and fibre.

I just have to be patient.

We can still be on a winners' podium with the Heineken Cup before long.

I do believe that will happen.

And days like this will all be part of the build-up for that.

We'd known for a while that Tony was leaving, going back to Australia for a job as defence coach with the national team. I was injured for his final game – a really bad defeat at Ospreys. He deserved a better ending after what he had done for Munster over seven years. I have a bag of special jerseys in my attic and before Tony left I pulled out the one I wore in the 2006 final as a parting gift for him.

That Ospreys game was Mick O'Driscoll's last time to wear the Munster jersey – he was retiring at thirty-three. I was only a year younger than him, and I wondered again how much longer I had left.

18

The first time I met Donal Walsh, he was twelve years old and fighting bone cancer in the leg. Not long after, he texted me from hospital, in between chemotherapy sessions.

Is there any chance you could get a Munster jersey signed for me?

I replied straight away.

Of course – I'd love to get one done for you

He corrected me.

It's not for me. I'm running a raffle to raise money for Stuart Mangan

That's the kind of kid he was – incredibly inspiring, mature beyond his years, stuck in a hospital ward and thinking about a young rugby player who'd been left paralysed by a freak accident – and who would pass away the following year. I stayed in touch with Donal and over time we developed a friendship that brought me more than it ever gave him.

He used to get a lift from the inspirational quotes his friends sent him when he was sick. When Munster lost, he would text them on to me. He couldn't play rugby any more, but he became head coach of his own age group at Tralee RFC and occasionally I'd get a message asking for advice.

One of my best players' confidence has gone to bits. How do I help him get it back?

When I tore my medial ligament at the end of Tony's final season, my friendship with Donal helped me to keep the frustration in perspective. His cancer had returned around the same time. They took away half his lung and he had more chemo. In the middle of it all, he sent me a text about my injury and it made me laugh. People tried to say the right thing whenever I was injured, but usually it was better to say nothing. Donal was different – he just had a great way about him.

I'd say you must be fair pissed off

We used to disagree about Lance Armstrong. He loved Lance's book. He believed in the fairytale about the cancer survivor who came back to win clean. Maybe I should have said nothing and let him believe, but I kept telling him the fairytale wasn't true. It bothered me that he was putting his faith in someone who didn't deserve to be a role model, but Donal needed to believe in somebody. He had to draw his strength from somewhere.

'He's never failed a drugs test.'

'He was just better than the rest of them.'

'He wouldn't cheat after beating cancer.'

Donal was a genuine hero. By the time of Armstrong's doping confession, he had already come through two bouts of cancer, but it was back for a third time. He had tumours in six places. I told him he should be writing his own book, the story of the boy who beat cancer three times. I said that after he'd written his bestseller, we'd go on the speaking circuit together. But I knew he was finding it harder.

A month before he went, he told me it was coming:

'Two weeks before I get sick and two weeks dying.'

Hearing that made me realize how lucky you are if your kids are healthy – it's all that really matters.

Donal became known all around the country in his last few months. He spoke out about young people taking their own lives, when he'd have given anything to stay alive himself. He made a massive difference.

I was desperately sad to get the phone call from his dad, Fionnbar, that Sunday night, just after he'd slipped away.

After fighting it so hard for so long, it would have been easy for him to throw in the towel near the end, when he knew there was no hope. I told him it would be a comfort to his parents to remember how brave he had been. I remember chatting to him on the phone one day, while I was driving home from training in Cork, asking him what he was up to. He said he was writing a lot, listing out all his cherished memories to make sure his family knew he'd had a fantastic life, even though he was only sixteen.

Emily and I went to see him at his home in Blennerville, just beyond Tralee, two weeks before he died. At one stage I asked him to join me in the living room – just the two of us. It was a big effort for him to get there, and it was only when

I saw him walking so slowly that I realized just how weak he was. When he sat down, he was so out of breath he couldn't talk for three or four minutes.

After he'd recovered, I said to him: 'You are doing a lot of good in the world. Everywhere I go, I get asked about you. Everyone thinks you are some kind of superhero.'

In a low, soft voice, he said: 'I never thought of it, now, like that. I never thought of it . . .'

I'd injured my right knee in the final league game of the 2011–12 season, against Ulster in early May, and it needed an operation. Nobody was sure about the recovery time, but Ireland's tour to New Zealand was only a few weeks away and I didn't want to rule myself out of it. The physios at Munster were against me touring, but when I went up to Irish camp it was left to me to make the call. There were three Tests. If I had a chance of being fit for the last one, Declan was willing to bring me. I was offered specialist physio in London, before the team flew to New Zealand. It was wing-and-a-prayer stuff, but there was a chance.

I went home and spent an entire day deliberating on whether I should go or not. For most of that time I was probably trying to convince myself it was better to give the knee more time to heal.

I can't play against New Zealand when I'm not right.

I could go down there, get my knee busted and my career will finish on this really bad season.

I won't be remembered for the player I was in 2006 or 2009.

Or worse – I could do damage, but not enough to retire over. I could spend the rest of my career feeling horrible because I'm not able to train properly.

So I made the phone call and pulled out.

As soon as I hung up, the guilt hit me.

You're putting yourself ahead of the team.

Other guys are bound to be carrying knocks – and they're going.

Then I started wondering about what the lads might think when they heard I'd ruled myself out.

Jesus, Paul has a chance of playing for Ireland against New Zealand and he's after turning it down – just because he doesn't want to risk his knee.

By then I was thinking about the 2015 World Cup as my exit point, if my body held up. I knew confidence for that tournament would be built on the back of the battles the team had gone through together. Nothing was going to instil belief like winning in New Zealand – which was a point I made to Emily over dinner at the Savoy Hotel in Limerick that night.

I spent the first half of the meal giving her all the reasons why I should tour.

'Well, go then,' she said. 'It really sounds like you should.'

Then I hit her with the counter-argument, and she bought into that.

'You're right – you shouldn't go! It's definitely the right decision.'

I woke at eight the following morning. I knew the Ireland players based in Limerick were leaving for Carton House at half-ten. From there it was on to London and then New Zealand.

I lay in bed until 9.55, turning it over in my head again and again. I was in turmoil over it.

Then I called Deccie and said I'd changed my mind. I wanted to give the physio treatment in London a try.

I was booked into a gentlemen's club in Mayfair, the Lansdowne. On the first morning I came down for breakfast and was asked to leave because I wasn't appropriately dressed.

On day two they kicked me out of a lounge for being on my phone.

On day three, after another physio session, I was told I had no business going to New Zealand – there was no way my knee would get through a game.

A few weeks later I was in Mike Prendergast's mobile home in Kilkee – Limerick by the sea in summertime – watching Ireland run New Zealand close in the second Test. A big part of me still felt guilty that I hadn't got on the plane.

I was carrying an engagement ring around with me all that week. I was planning to propose to Emily during a picnic at White Strand near by. I made sure the local off-licence had champagne. I staked out the Pantry café, and picked out the food. But every day it rained. It never stopped.

When we got back to Limerick it wasn't exactly picnic weather either, but I suggested we drive out to Curraghchase Forest Park. Emily took Paddy to see the ducks, and when they got back I had it all ready.

'What's the champagne for?'

'I was thinking we might have something to celebrate.'

'Like what?'

'Will you marry me?'

'Really?'

'Really.'

Our wedding was in Auch, a beautiful old town in the south of France, the following summer. Marcus was my best man. I remember one of my teachers at Ardscoil Rís, Bobby Byrne, telling us that the brothers we fought with as kids would end up becoming our best friends. I was thinking: *You don't know my brother.* But it turned out he was right.

Justin was groomsman. Because of the age difference between us, I never fought with him when I was young, like I did with Marcus. He has always been a close friend and my most trusted adviser. Even now, he still looks after me like a baby brother.

Ten minutes before the ceremony was due to start, I looked around the cathedral and there were dozens of total strangers in the pews. There were Japanese tourists and guys dressed in Bermuda shorts and wife-beater vests. There was a Frenchman wearing a Munster polo shirt who kept pointing to the crest and giving me the thumbs-up, in between taking photographs.

I asked someone when the crowds would clear out.

'The cathedral never closes,' he said.

Emily joined me at the altar, and after telling her she looked beautiful I said: 'Don't turn around but there's a massive guy with no top on in the middle of our wedding.'

She laughed. She thought it added to the occasion.

The craic continued at Château de Lartigolle. My biggest days playing rugby couldn't bring the happiness I felt during that week in the south of France.

Even before I got injured, I'd decided I wanted to give up the Munster captaincy. After struggling with the job early on, I ended up really enjoying it, but a new team was coming through and I was part of the old crew. I was very conscious that the players who had come in needed to create their own history and take more control over how we did things.

Most of the old team were already gone, and Peter Stringer was the next legend to leave, at the end of the year, without getting a chance to say a proper goodbye. He had to get away. He wanted it too much to sit on the bench. He kept the hurt to himself, but it was killing Strings not to be involved as much as he once was. Over the next four seasons there was no shortage of takers in the English Premiership for what he still had to give.

I knew Donners was hurting too. Donnacha Ryan had broken into the team ahead of him and had been our best player in the season just gone. Donners responded to being dropped by working even harder, if that was possible, waiting for his chance to come again. In those months he was everything that you would want in a Munster player: 100 per cent a team man, training hard, bringing the other non-selected players with him, never complaining, travelling to matches he wasn't involved in, texting players before games, always in good form, self-belief never wavering. Once or twice that season I asked him if he was all right and he just said, 'I'm fine. I'm fine.' I knew him too well to believe that, but it wasn't in him to bitch and moan. And he loved Munster so much he couldn't bear the idea of leaving.

I felt for guys who weren't getting picked – especially when I could see them killing themselves in training. Occasionally I thought about how I'd react if I was dropped myself, and I hoped my response would be to think: *Right, there's a reason this has happened. I'm going to fix it and hopefully that will make the team better too.*

I had one or two doubts about stepping down as captain. I wondered how I'd stop myself from talking to referees, but the more I thought about it the more it made sense. At first, I felt Peter O'Mahony would be the man to replace me. I liked the idea of the younger players thinking: *The guy I was in the academy with is now captain. It's time for me to step up and lead.* I wanted them to see me training with even more intensity and realize that the captaincy had nothing to do with how much I'd put in before.

Rob Penney had come from Canterbury in New Zealand to be our new head coach. Niall O'Donovan had replaced Shaun Payne as team manager. They felt there was already a lot of change in the group and that maybe Peter needed a little more time to step up, because injuries had got in the way of his progress. Doug Howlett had been with us for five seasons and he was still in incredible condition physically. He was one of the best signings Munster ever made, an example to the younger guys every time we trained. The day came for our squad picture to be taken, ahead of the new season, and Rob told Dougie to sit in the middle. He did it for a season and was excellent. He was approaching the end of his career then and the captaincy was always going to come Peter's way.

I'd met Rob before he was offered the job. I think Garrett Fitzgerald wanted to make sure a few of the senior players were comfortable with whoever was chosen. Axel was in the running for it, but I got the sense they felt it wasn't his time yet.

Rob was very impressive. He said: 'I've never seen a pack work harder – but you're committing too many forwards to the rucks. You're tiring yourselves out. You're going off your feet. And your backs don't have the confidence to go wide because there aren't a few forwards floating around to mind them.'

It was probably as good an indication as any of what he had in mind for us. It was essentially the New Zealand game plan – exploiting space and creating opportunities through accurate kicking and forwards holding width. I remembered Brad Thorn spending loads of time on the wing when we'd played New Zealand at Croke Park in 2008. Back then I couldn't figure out what he was doing there, but the way Rob explained it made sense.

At Canterbury he had coached the latest All Black second-row star, Sam Whitelock. On the weekend after we first spoke I watched Whitelock playing for the Crusaders in a Super Rugby game and I counted the number of rucks he went to in the first half – eight. Over the eighty minutes in the quarter-final against Ulster, I had gone to forty-five rucks. I could see the direction Rob wanted to take us in, and my first instinct was that I liked where he was going and I was looking forward to being part of something new and developing my tactical appreciation.

On his first day, he gave a presentation to the players and put a picture of Henry Ford up on a big screen, with one of his quotes underneath: *Whether you think you can, or think you can't – you're right.*

He told us there was any amount of research that showed positivity got results, whether you were coaching rugby players or teaching kids, and very little evidence that being negative with people was the best way to motivate them.

'That's my philosophy,' he said.

He had a clear and concise idea of how he wanted us to play, and how he was going to coach it. It was the most structured game plan I'd been given since Eddie O'Sullivan's time with Ireland. At the heart of it was the simple idea that if there wasn't space to run into, then there had to be space to kick into. Rob was putting three points into each of his presentations and we were going away having remembered all three. He was like a beam of positivity and within a few weeks there was a very good feeling around the place about his ideas.

I couldn't wait for the new season to start. In a perverse way, the less successful we were, the more I was enjoying the challenge. I loved it more than ever, loved being in the younger guys' company. A lot of my desire to keep playing came from wanting to achieve things before I finished up, and from wanting to be a better player. After he retired, I noticed that the bio on Wally's Twitter page said 'Contented rugby retiree'. When I saw that, I thought: *I wouldn't be content if I had to retire now*. I didn't want to go out when Munster and Ireland were struggling and I'd been going from one injury to the next.

So I told myself I'd have a really good pre-season – I'd arrive for work earlier and earlier every day, doing my own training and getting myself right. There was a Lions tour the following summer and I was going all out to be part of it.

I thought, if things went my way, I could have the best season of my career. And I thought that if I came back from my injury fresh and rested and in phenomenal shape, everything was possible.

19

Three months into the season I hoped would be the best of my career, I was lying face down at Cappagh Hospital, waiting for an epidural injection in my back. I'd barely trained in six months. I'd played two games for Munster, when I hadn't been anything like fully fit. And I'd pulled out of the autumn internationals when a scan showed that the bulging disc in my back was getting bigger.

The radiologist getting the needle ready was a friend, Steve Eustace. He'd got my back right before, five years earlier. Before he put in the needle, he said: 'You know, you don't owe anybody anything.'

It struck me there and then that somebody so medically close to me was talking about retirement, or at least hinting at it. I suppose he was letting me know that I didn't have to have another injection in my back, or put myself through a second operation. There was another option.

I appreciated his concern for me, but I wasn't ready to let go. If I'd made the decision to retire over that injury, it would have felt to me like my career had been petering out for three years.

As a player in such a physical sport, what killed me were the injuries that stopped me from training and forced me to take steps back, just as I was getting where I needed to be. So instead of being like a pro cyclist who, at thirty, has just gotten fitter and fitter over time, I ended up on this road where my fitness peaked and troughed. Injuries are part of the game, just as much as passing the ball or lifting weights. But a few of those injuries took so much rugby away from me, just when I should have been at the top of my game, that I was left feeling like I needed to make up for lost time.

I thought the announcement of my retirement would have been a footnote, that people would have been expecting it, more or less, and they'd have said: 'Well look, that's been coming for a few years now – between this injury, that injury and the other injury.'

So I told Steve: 'It's not about owing people anything. I still have things I want to achieve – for my own peace of mind.'

I spent that Friday night in the hospital. The season I had such high hopes for was falling apart and there was a huge frustration in me, but I kept it on the inside.

Before getting the epidural, I'd considered surgery, but it was only the physical demands of rugby that were putting a strain on my back. I could pick up Paddy and swing him around without feeling anything, and my back had come right in 2008 without surgery. After speaking to Keith Synnott, an orthopaedic surgeon, I decided to manage it conservatively and hope for the same outcome as before.

To pass the time after getting the injection I watched twelve episodes of *Californication*, one after the other, because I needed to stay on my back and I'd found that watching or reading anything about sport or high-performance training was making me feel more frustrated. They were constant reminders of what I was missing, when the best thing for me was to switch off and give my body a chance to get better.

I thought about the Lions tour, and it felt like I was already running out of road. I loved it whenever a doctor told me I could play with an injury, that nothing was going to make it worse – it was just gonna be sore. But a back injury was a back injury, and there was no rushing it – whether there was a Lions tour coming up or not.

It was mid-November and I knew it wasn't a good idea to set myself a comeback date when there were no certainties about my recovery, but I needed something to focus on so I did it anyway – 29 December, the home game against Ulster.

I tried everything and anything – magnets, massage therapy, hot-water bottles, yoga. It seemed like everyone I met had a story about their back, but Christmas came and there was no improvement whatsoever.

People who find their jobs or their lives tough often think that other people are sailing through, and it's rarely the case. I didn't want to admit to anyone how I was feeling, mainly because I was trying hard to stay positive. When I got home after another day without progress, I would try to leave my frustration at the front door and be a decent husband and father. Once or twice, watching TV with Emily, with my mind somewhere else, I let out a curse – but when she asked what was up I didn't go there.

'Nothing! Sorry.'

I'd had bad days before with injuries, but I was never actually unhappy. It was a part of the game, and the challenge in front of me was to get right. But in the two weeks before Christmas, when I knew I had no hope of playing before the end of the year, I was lower than I'd ever been.

I finally admitted it to myself on St Stephen's Day. I was watching a cycling documentary series about Team Sky. A rider called Mathew Hayman was being asked questions on a Skype call with the team psychiatrist, Steve Peters.

'What's your happiness level, out of ten?'

'Ahhmmm . . . probably about eight.'

'What would make it ten out of ten?'

'There's a couple of other things going on, with an injury that's dragging on a bit.'

'You've got an injury. Are you doing everything you can to deal with the injury?'

'Yes.'

'If you think about this logically, the injury is not causing you to drop to eight out of ten for happiness. Are you ready? It's very subtle, this. The reason you are dropping to eight out of ten is you are not accepting the situation. That's different.'

My happiness level then was maybe three out of ten. Normally, it's ten out of ten. For the first few months of the season I'd been telling myself to give it time and do my rehab to the highest possible standard. I knew that Warren Gatland, the Lions coach, liked big, heavy second-rows and at least I could still do some decent upper-body weights. I didn't want to look small on the pitch when he was there to see me. I told the Munster fitness guys I wanted to bench-press 155 kilos by Christmas, to build some aesthetic size. And I told myself there was nothing more I could do, apart from show up with the right attitude.

This is your life at the moment.

But the complete lack of progress eventually broke me.

Six weeks after the epidural I had the same symptoms and no comeback date. I was very, very disillusioned – going in for an hour's physio every day with my jeans on, because I didn't have the heart to get into a tracksuit. After watching that Skype conversation, I accepted where I was.

Right, this is disastrous. I'm actually miserable. And I'm miserable because of this injury.

Then I called Caroline Currid. I'd kept in contact with her since our first meeting in 2008, usually when things weren't going so well. Very little bothered me when I was playing great rugby, but when things weren't so good I found it a big help to talk to her and unravel the thoughts in my head.

I'd starting thinking about retirement, figuring out what I'd say if I was asked about it in an interview. With my injury profile, it would have been a fair question.

'Well actually, three years ago I thought I'd be retired by now, because the games were stressing me out too much.'

'And now?'

'I'll retire if I know my body won't let me train hard enough to be at my standard any more.'

Four months before, I had told Caroline I wanted to do everything possible to make sure it was a big season for me. Now, she told me that having such high hopes and expectations was part of the problem, because I was coming down from a greater height.

'Do you feel as if there's a weight over you?'

'Yeah, I do. That's exactly how I feel. I feel like I'm walking around with this cloud over me all the time.'

We spoke for a while and she told me to write down whatever was in my head, but that was too airy-fairy for me. I didn't need to do it anyway, because even when we were talking I was starting to feel better for having accepted the way it was. I was seeing things with more clarity and I thought I had a decision to make – either retire or look again at an operation. I had a lot of faith in Keith Synnott, but getting a second opinion was the logical thing to do.

The following day I flew to London and saw a surgeon at the Lister Hospital, Damian Fahy. 'Looking at your scans,' he said, 'I think you could be back playing in six to eight weeks after an operation.'

As soon as he came out with that, my form was better. I was plotting my way back. When sport is your job and someone says you can be back on the field of play in six to eight weeks, what you hear is six.

I wanted to have the operation the following day, but I had to wait until after the weekend.

Emily drove me to the Mater Hospital in Dublin at 6.45 on Monday morning – New Year's Eve – and I was off on a trolley twenty minutes later. Just before they put me to sleep, I got a little bit emotional. People had been saying and writing that my body was giving out, and that I should retire before it took any more punishment. I wasn't blind to the dangers of playing on too long. For a few years, as the game got more and more physical, I'd seen teammates and opposition players come out of the Six Nations broken up and badly in need of rest they didn't always get.

If my body was telling me it was over, I was going to listen. Maybe, if I hadn't missed so many games with various injuries, I wouldn't have felt like I still had more left in me. Physically, I knew where I was better than anyone, and I didn't agree it was time to call it a day, but on the operating table I got a little panicky before I went under. I started thinking about Emily and Paddy and asking myself if I was being selfish.

Should I be doing this?

Maybe everyone else is right and I'm wrong.

Should I be getting a second back operation, just so I can play for two more years?

But when I woke up, Keith Synnott was standing over me with a smile on his face, saying: 'It couldn't have gone any better.' I was on the comeback trail.

After a couple of weeks of lying flat on my back, I took my first steps outside the house – a short, slow walk to the local shop to buy a packet of Jelly Tots for Paddy. Over the following nights I went further, listening to music with my hood up, studying the Munster fixtures on my phone as I walked along, telling myself I still had everything to play for – a Heineken Cup, a Lions tour, a chance to feel good about my contribution to Munster after seven months of giving almost nothing.

We'd lost two pool games in the Heineken Cup, but the lads had dug in to qualify and we had a quarter-final against Harlequins on the first Sunday in April.

For a lot of reasons, it was the game I was building myself up for. So whenever the rehab got frustrating, I thought about it. When I had a target to go after, life with an injury was bearable.

In the end, it took ten weeks before I had enough conditioning to get back on the pitch, but I never really doubted I'd make the Harlequins game. What I did question, though, was whether we had it in us to win.

The week before the quarter-final, in my second game back, we were murdered by Glasgow. It was a shocking performance. We conceded fifty-one points and gifted them tries. I was in self-preservation mode again – mostly anonymous. I knew that if I went balls-out from the first minute I'd fall off the bus completely, but I needed to make a better stab of it than I did.

There was a lot of talk about Rob's game plan. People were saying it didn't suit us. They saw a second-row out on the wing and they didn't like it. If we'd been blitzing teams, it wouldn't have been a problem. But we had too many players showing no kind of form.

In a short period of time we'd gone from thinking, *How will we construct a situation where we get a penalty?* to *How can we exploit the space in front of us?* It didn't come naturally, that change of mindset. We needed to make the adjustment, but it was a difficult one. I met a guy one day who put it well.

'D'you know what the problem here is, Paul?'

'Go on.'

'When you've only ever used a hammer, you're going to find it hard to work with screws.'

I'm sure Rob was frustrated by all the unforced errors. Maybe he expected more from us, but we never saw him lose his patience. If somebody messed up, his attitude was 'You'll get it right the next time.'

I could understand why he didn't lose the head. The game plan required a team playing with confidence and self-belief. He wasn't going to achieve that by coming down hard on us, but it was still a big ask. The skill level he was looking for came more easily to New Zealanders, who had known nothing but rugby since they could first hold a ball, but Rob was a clever man. If he believed we had it in us to play that way, I didn't have a problem with where he wanted us to go.

I did feel, though, that we needed to marry some of what we were traditionally good at with this new way of playing. At first, Rob didn't get why we chose to maul when we were nowhere close to the opposition line. That was understand-able. But the maul had been a focal point for us in making a physical statement, through driving them back ten metres or drawing penalties. In the bad weather conditions of December and January, that mattered.

Doug was out injured and I was captain for the Harlequins game. When I spoke to the media during the week, I was very down about our chances. I didn't want to feign any optimism. It was almost like I felt we needed an antidote to Rob's relentless positivity, that we didn't have the track record as a team to justify being in any way confident. I *wanted* us to be worried. I didn't want to tell anyone it was going to be fine, because I didn't know if it was. I wanted the new guys to be feeling the same kind of fear the old team had experienced going over to Perpignan four years earlier, when we blew them away.

I could slag with the best of them in the gym, and a few of the lads noticed I wasn't my normal self.

'Is there no craic today?'

I just shook my head and gave them a half-smile. I didn't tell people I was seriously worried, that I was fearful of a thirty- or forty-point drubbing, and that I could see it happening if we conceded early and lost confidence in ourselves. I didn't say I was afraid the papers would be writing headlines about the demise of Munster.

The night before the game, I tried to articulate to the lads what I was feeling and where we needed to be, mentally – like nothing else mattered. I told them that the English teams coming over to play us in big Heineken Cup games used to say in the media: 'It's Thomond Park and it's Munster – it's going to be tough but we know what we're getting into.'

We used to love reading those comments. Donners would always say: 'Lads, they think they know us – and they don't.' But I felt our problem at that moment was that we didn't know ourselves.

It was nothing to do with the game plan, because I thought we could play any game we wanted within the framework Rob had given us – we could tighten things up, or spread it wide. I was talking about our attitude and our intensity, and the focus we brought on to the pitch.

Tommy O'Donnell spoke in the dressing room before we went out. He became emotional. 'Don't let days like today pass you by,' he said. 'I've worked so hard to be here – it's been too long coming.' He had been on a long journey to get to where he was. It was lovely to hear.

At the end of the first half, on the halfway line, the referee signalled an advantage to Harlequins. They were six points ahead and Danny Care, their scrum-half, was looking at the ref, checking that it was a penalty. The second Jérôme Garcès blew the whistle, Care quick-tapped it. We knew it was coming. We'd done the analysis – they'd been scoring tries from that position all year. Conor Murray had already gone back ten metres and when he shot up and made the tackle, James Downey went in and poached it. Penalty to us.

I always thought those were the kind of moments that shifted the balance of power in games. It could have been a thirteen-point lead for them at half-time, but we'd spotted it, worked on stopping it and executed it brilliantly. And as a result we were marching forty or fifty metres down the field.

We saw it out and won 18–12. A few days before, I'd felt we were in danger of falling off a cliff, and now we had pulled ourselves back from the brink. I was so proud. At the end of the game, I put my right hand in the air, with my index finger pointing straight up. I hated seeing that picture afterwards – it looked arrogant. I still don't know where the gesture came from. Maybe I was drunk on euphoria and relief. Whatever it was, seeing that picture bugged me and took away a lot of the satisfaction over the game.

Donners was on the bench that day. Me and Rog were the last survivors from the 2006 Heineken Cup team in the starting fifteen. We'd had so many great days, and we'd shared those big moments with the supporters and with our own families. Just seeing the absolute joy on their faces when we won big games was an amazing feeling – people thanking you and hugging you and wanting to carry your bag. And so the thing that made me most happy was seeing all that happen for the new team. They'd never experienced it, not really. And they must have felt that kind of reaction from supporters was reserved for the players from the other era.

I found myself getting emotional in a TV interview. I was embarrassed by that, but it's not always easy when you've just walked off the pitch. I couldn't help myself that day, because I knew what it meant to guys like Peter O'Mahony and Dave Kilcoyne, Conor Murray and Mike Sherry, and plenty of others.

In that moment I almost felt like we had won the competition. There was just euphoria everywhere when I walked back into the changing room.

An hour after the final whistle, I was already telling myself that it was just one game, and that Quins had been poor. There were no hard edges from them in the rucks or when we were mauling them. I wasn't bracing myself for someone to come in and hit me – a shoulder in the face or a dunt into the head.

I knew it would be a lot tougher for us in the semi-final, away to Clermont. On the day I wasn't as right as I would have liked to be, mentally or physically, because my groin was at me all week and it was in agony when I ran out for the warm-up. I'm sure the uncertainty over whether I'd play or not – and whether I'd be fit if I did – affected the team. It was disappointing because we ran them very close and we could have won, but we never gave it our best shot.

After sixteen seasons with Munster, it was Rog's last game, the end of an era. Things hadn't finished well for him with Ireland, but he had an unbreakable spirit and he fought his way back into form – typical of the man. Not many in rugby get the fairytale ending, but he was leaving with his head held high after an incredible career.

I have my own private memories of Rog, and that Clermont game is one of them. We were trying everything in our power to figure out a way to break them, while fighting for our lives defensively. It was only when Rog took over the game that we found a way back. His kicking and instinct were phenomenal that day.

At his best, he conducted games. He had a nose for winning rugby. He edged us ahead, slowly but surely. Maybe the thing that struck me most after he'd gone was how much he loved Munster. I found it amazing – and I don't think anyone else carried the torch in quite the same way.

A week before that semi-final, I thought I might be going out with him, more or less. I still loved the game, but I'm sure a lot of people nearing the end of their sporting careers tell themselves it would be better to go a year too early than a year too late. I was thinking:

Win this, win the final, get on the Lions tour, win that – retire.

If you want to feel good about yourself and what you've achieved, it would be a great way to go.

A couple of weeks before Clermont, in a game against Leinster at Thomond Park, Dave Kearney hit the ground hard after a challenge from Felix Jones.

I was five metres away and I only had eyes for the ball. I knew Dave was going to place it and my mindset in those situations, when the ball was loose and bodies were steaming in, was usually to kick it rather than pick it up.

He tried to place it but I was in too quick. When I watched it on YouTube later that night, and saw my right shin striking Dave's head just as my boot made contact with the ball, I realized it had been reckless. In slow motion, it looked terrible. But it was also completely accidental.

I had taken a hit from Brian O'Driscoll a split second later, but I was up off the ground and over to Dave straight away. I wasn't aware then that I'd caught him as hard as I had, but I knew he was in trouble. For a short time he was out cold, but I could see he was conscious when they took him off on a stretcher. I was relieved that he seemed to be OK, but he was on my mind any time there was a break in play for the rest of the game.

I went looking for him afterwards. I wasn't sure if the Leinster medical people knew how it had happened, so when I ran into Dr Arthur Tanner I said it to him.

'It wasn't the fall that knocked him out, Arthur. I actually booted him in the head.'

'We know that,' he said. 'But don't worry – we won't be doing anything.'

I was thrown by that. I thought: *Why would they even be thinking like that?* The idea that they might cite me for something I saw as blatantly accidental hadn't entered my mind. I played the game hard, but I thought it would be accepted that the incident was accidental: that I wouldn't intentionally kick anyone in the head.

I hung around, hoping to meet Dave so that I could apologize. When he came out he was fine about it, but I was conscious that he was still shaken up and groggy. We spoke again over the phone on the Monday. Brian had sent me Dave's number, along with a message of support. It was a text I appreciated, because by then it was already a big story and he must have known which way the wind was blowing in Leinster.

Another thoughtful text came from Deccie:

> Unfortunately it's going to be trial by media for a few days. Don't let it bother you.

Whether I was cited or not, the story was always going to get another few days of airplay. But then Joe Schmidt and Leo Cullen, the Leinster head coach and captain, gave it enough legs to carry it into the following week. They criticized the decision not to cite me and talked about a bad example being set to children.

It was a difficult week. In the end I forced myself to stop thinking about it. I told Dad to ignore it too. He was only upsetting himself.

However bad it was for me, it was worse for Dave, at a time when he was playing well after breaking through with Leinster. He spent a month out of the game.

I waited until I knew I wasn't going to be cited before I made the call to him. I didn't want him thinking I was trying to curry favour ahead of a disciplinary hearing. I told him again that what I'd done was completely unintentional, and I was grateful that he took me at my word.

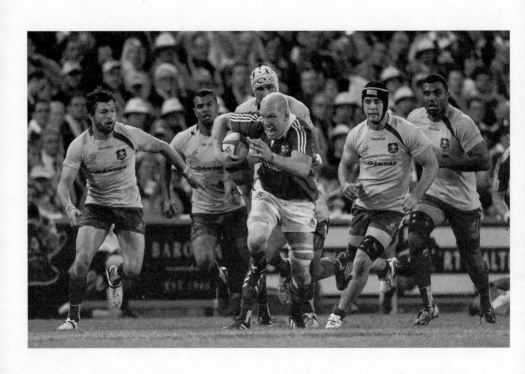

20

Not making the cut for the Lions tour to Australia would have disappointed me, but I would have moved on from it quickly. I'd come back from the operation and done everything I could to be on the plane. Anything after that was beyond my control. I wasn't confident, though – at all. Warren Gatland liked his second-rows to be 120 kilos, or close to it, and I was a stone off that. But when the announcement was made, I was in. From then on it was about making the Test team and winning the series.

The first few weeks were a rollercoaster. My left knee kept coming at me, chipping away at my confidence, and it was still in my head that I might retire at the end of the tour, if we'd won it and I'd played my part. But when the painkillers and the ice did their job and I couldn't feel it as much, I was excited about what I was learning, and I couldn't wait for training the following day, working with Graham Rowntree and Andy Farrell, or the extra tackling practice with Dan Lydiate, an expert chopper.

It was a pretty quiet group of men. The longer I played, the more I found that to be the case: the younger players weren't as vocal as my generation had been. The coaching got better over the course of my career and there wasn't as much scope for the big motivators, or the guys who could bring their own ideas and opinions to the group. There was very little of the old school left in professional rugby. The emphasis switched to players knowing their own jobs and the game plan backwards. It was a dynamic that couldn't have been much further from that of the Munster team I grew up in.

I had my work cut out to get in the Test team and I'd never felt under so much pressure for my place. I loved the battle of just trying to get picked. It focused my mind on playing and training well. I knew they had a lot of faith in Alun-Wyn Jones, so I thought I was in a tussle with Richie Gray and Geoff Parling for the other spot. I threw myself into it. I was setting goals for my training sessions, ticking them off in my notebook later, and then coming up with new ones.

I liked the way Gats did things, simplifying the game and encouraging people to play. He talked about the short cuts that could make a difference – reducing the distance from one ruck to another, winning a kick-chase by being ready to fire as soon as the ball left the out-half's boot, and taking the shortest possible route. He said they were the small things that made a player like Richie McCaw great when you added them all up. And I knew I'd be judged on how I delivered on them.

The game plan was about tiring the opposition out and then making them pay. I liked Andy Farrell's defensive system and the way he wanted us to stay focused on the ball, with maximum line speed. Neither Munster nor Ireland employed a lot of line speed in our defence. It was a habit that didn't come easily and I had to stay on top of myself to deliver what he wanted to see.

I was writing things on my hand, so I could constantly remind myself in training, or during the early games.

SC (short cuts)

LAB (look at ball)

GOTFL (get off the fucking line)

The coaching set-up and environment that Gatland had created was a pleasure to be part of. He thought there was nothing worse you could do to a player than subject him to long meetings or training sessions that went on and on. He was into fitness hits, short and sharp, with high intensity. He came over to me one day and I swear he was trying to do a job on me mentally, for the next time Wales played Ireland. Mind games were part of what he brought to the table and his track record showed he was good at playing them.

'Have you noticed how incredibly fit the Welsh boys are?'

'I dunno about that, Gats. I'd love to do a fitness test against them.'

Sam Warburton, the captain, was carrying a knock before the first game, against the Barbarians in Hong Kong. They didn't risk him and I led the team out, but I struggled in the heat and the humidity. We were wary of that game – and not just because of the brutal conditions. The Baa-Baas had just been walloped by England, so we thought there might be a reaction to that. They had some serious players – Sergio Parisse, Joe Rokocoko, Schalk Brits – and nobody wanted to be part of a team beaten in the tour opener. Being a losing captain would have been ten times worse. We won easily, but other guys handled the heat better than me. I was so wrecked near the end I thought I wouldn't be able to lift in the line-out, so I called it away from myself.

Gats had spoken to me a lot in the couple of weeks before that game. He was encouraging me to talk, to keep driving guys on, but once we landed in Australia he didn't have a whole lot to say to me, and once or twice I wondered whether it was because of the Baa-Baas game.

Does he think I'm not fit enough?

We played the Waratahs a week before the first Test. Gats picked a strong team and I was in it, alongside Alun-Wyn. In the team room before the game, at around eleven in the morning, Gats came up to me.

'Just to let you know – Alun-Wyn will be playing in the Test. So it's between you and Geoff for the other second-row position.'

'Right. OK.'

That was the full extent of the conversation. It wasn't something a coach would normally say to a player, but Gats went with his instincts.

I played well against the Waratahs – the work I'd put in paid off and I felt sharp all the way through. That was good enough and I was picked for the first Test. It was my seventh consecutive Test start for the Lions and I was pretty sure we had the firepower to get the job done this time.

The scoreboard said Australia 21, Lions 23 when the whistle went at the end of the first Test. They had a kick to win it, but Kurtley Beale slipped and it dropped well short. I didn't feel much inside – maybe relief, but nothing beyond that. I didn't feel like celebrating. For the whole game I had tried to keep a lid on the frustration I was feeling over the decisions going against us, especially at the breakdown. But we'd made mistakes too. We should have been out of sight.

Watching Beale line up the kick, I was thinking about the penalty shot Stephen Jones had to deny us our Grand Slam in Cardiff. I was resenting the fact that Australia were in a position where they could win the game at the death. So when it was over I was already starting to process that frustration, rather than allow myself to enjoy the moment.

Around five minutes before that, I had broken my arm, only I didn't know it then. Wycliff Palu was carrying the ball and when I went to tackle him my forearm smashed into his head. I felt something straight away and I went down, but I was also thinking it wouldn't do any harm to run down the clock.

James Robson, the Lions doctor, asked me to squeeze his arm. I couldn't at first, but after a minute he said: 'That's it, you're squeezing it. It's just the nerve that's dead.' You get twenty bangs a game and they fade away after a minute, so there was no big deal about seeing it out. At times like that there's so much adrenalin going you barely notice pain.

It turned out that I had a hairline fracture, but for a while I held on to some hope. I thought they could strap it up and let me play, that maybe it was old scar tissue. It wasn't like I was twenty-two, with my whole future ahead of me. I was prepared to take my chances with the arm, but when they were looking at it they found another fracture down at my wrist, from a separate incident. It was sore after the game, but I didn't think it was going to be a big problem. I still don't know how or when it happened. But that, more than the forearm, ended my series.

There was a Land Rover Discovery with Lions branding waiting outside after the specialist told me the story. I climbed in with Eanna Falvey, the Ireland doctor. Ray, the driver, must have guessed there was no point in asking how I'd got on. There wasn't a word spoken on the journey back to the hotel. I just needed to let the disappointment sink in, but I was OK after that. I accepted my fate. I couldn't talk the talk about Donal Walsh's death giving me perspective and then not find any in a situation where it was needed.

Nobody holds candlelight vigils for you when you're out of a tour. They say hard luck and they move on without you. It's the only way a team can operate when the next game is the only one that counts. When the management offered to keep me on tour, I knew there would be times when I'd feel like a food bill they didn't need to pick up, but I stayed because I wanted to be there if and when we won it. A big part of me felt that I wouldn't be a real Lion unless I'd been part of a winning series. It didn't matter what the players in the 1997 team did or didn't do after they won in South Africa; just having that achievement on their CVs was enough to guarantee they'd always be remembered. I knew it wasn't going to feel the same, wearing a suit, but I still wanted to hang in there for whatever good feeling it could give me.

Australia won the second Test, but in the third, in Sydney, we proved we were the better team. It was tough on Brian, in his fourth tour, to have to watch it from the stand, too. I'm sure his feelings were more complicated than mine, after being dropped for the first time in his career, but lifting the trophy with him at the end is a great memory. We'd both had our tough days with the Lions. After the 2005 experience, I wondered if they'd can the whole thing, on our watch. Even if we weren't on the same buzz as the players wearing jerseys, there was a lot of satisfaction in knowing we'd been part of a team that had finally put things right.

Any thoughts of retirement went out the window after that injury. Playing no part in two of the Tests wasn't the script I'd had in my head. But really, once I'd realized I was on the pace in the run-up to the first Test, I'd already decided to play on. I thought: *I'm back to being good again – the next World Cup would be a good time to leave.*

So I started my rehab. I got a small operation done on my knee while I was at it. I told myself I had to be due a run without injuries, that I'd had more than my share of bad breaks.

2002
Back, four months

2003
Broken thumb, three months

2005
Broken thumb, three months

2007/2008
Broken thumb, seven weeks
Back, four months

2010
Groin infection, knee: eight months

2011
Ankle, four weeks

2012/2013
Knee, four weeks
Knee/back, five months
Back, five months
Arm/wrist, six weeks

On my second day back running, just as I was finishing the session, my right hamstring came at me. I just upped the pace and that caused it to tighten. That cost me another month, which pissed me off massively, but it was early in the season and I sucked it up as best I could.

I tried to think about it logically, rather than feel sorry for myself. There had to be things I could do in my training that would give me a better chance of staying injury free. There had to be somebody – an older player, at the top level – who'd thought about the best way to prolong his career and found some answers. Rob Penney put me in contact with Brad Thorn. He was thirty-eight and still one of the world's best second-rows. I spent more than an hour on the phone with him, asking how he got his body ready for games.

Brad was a big help. He told me he knew what worked for him, and he got on with it himself. Before games, he did his own warm-up. He didn't worry about people thinking he wasn't a team player – out there by himself, doing stretches. He knew he needed to prepare a certain way if the team was going to get the best out of him. If anyone didn't like it, including the physios, that was their problem.

It was great information and after that phone call I changed a lot of what I was doing. I didn't even try to do the same stuff as the other players. I'd messed up by being too competitive in the past, taking on weights I had no business lifting, just to get the better of guys who were eight or ten years younger, and who'd never had a back operation or a knee that creaked when they got out of bed. So I made changes. I didn't squat. I didn't do a lot of weights. I did my own warm-up, in empty stadiums. I found different ways to stay in good shape, and they started working for me.

My contract was up at the end of the new season and I knew my bargaining position with the union was weaker, because of my injury profile. I'd missed the 2013 Six Nations. I'd pulled out of the autumn internationals the previous year. I'd started the new season injured. If the union thought I wasn't giving them enough bang for their buck, they probably had a point.

For years, I did very little hard negotiating. My agent and I always had a figure in our heads when there was a deal to be done. Once we got there, I signed.

I had dug in a bit at the previous negotiations, after the 2011 World Cup. They offered me a hundred grand less in the second year of the contract. I had no intention of taking the cut, so I checked to see if I could get a concrete offer from France. I didn't want to be bluffing. I wanted to be able to say: 'Pay me this – or I'm going.'

Word came back that Racing Metro were interested. Emily would have gone in a heartbeat and I nearly wanted the union to force my hand, like they did with Johnny Sexton a year later. I never ruled out the possibility of going abroad. As much as I loved playing for Munster, there was a little piece of me that loved the idea of living and playing in France. My house was ten minutes from the one I grew up in and I'd never lived outside Limerick. I knew it would be an unbelievably sad day for me, leaving Munster, but there was a big attraction in the idea of experiencing a different kind of life.

In the end, I agreed a contract with the IRFU, on the same terms as the previous deal.

The new Munster team needed to kick on, but in the Heineken Cup opener at Edinburgh we were seriously poor. I was only just back in the side, but I played badly and our lineout malfunctioned.

We had beaten Leinster the previous week and we'd had the intensity right for that game. Maybe we assumed it was just going to come out on to the pitch at Murrayfield.

Peter had stepped up to the captaincy, but he was injured and I was given the job again. In training during the week, I left it to the coaches to get us right. I had one and a half games under my belt and I just wanted to dig in and try to play well myself. In my notebook at the beginning of the season I had written 'Show – and then speak'. I wanted to lead through my actions, not through what I said.

In the week of the game, Rob did a presentation on 'victory disease'. It was about the Japanese military in World War II. They bombed Pearl Harbor in 1941 and then won so many battles that they became completely cocky and got smashed by the Americans the following year, in the Battle of Midway. Success had made them complacent, and vulnerable.

It was a brilliant presentation, but I was thinking, *We lost to Treviso two weeks ago. I don't think there's any danger of victory disease overtaking us.*

My thoughts and feelings around that Edinburgh game were a constant battle between wanting to take a step back from leadership and look after my own game – so that I could gain the credibility to lead again – and knowing that we were a team short on experience and leaders.

Most of the lads were young; they were still learning. They didn't really understand yet what it took to win a Heineken Cup, how few mistakes you could make, how efficient you needed to be at every opportunity – things the players from the old team had learned the hard way.

In weeks like that I was left thinking that Rob's ultra-positive approach needed a counter-balance. I felt that a lot of the same errors were cropping up, week on week. We had to figure out the fine balance between being positive – building guys up – while eradicating errors.

I felt we needed to be held to a higher standard, but we couldn't figure out how to make permanent changes to some of our bad habits. When I look back at that time, I think of players being tackled into touch. To me, that's the sort of thing that, if it happens once, should never happen again. For some reason it continued on, week after week, month after month.

After Edinburgh, we won five in a row in the Heineken Cup. We beat Perpignan and Gloucester away from home, and it was enough to get us a home draw in the quarter-finals. We were definitely moving forward. I was delighted and proud of the way the pack was performing, but I wondered too if the victories were papering over some of the cracks that hadn't gone away.

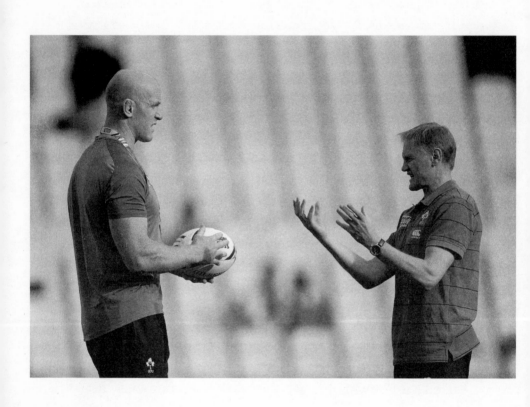

21

Joe Schmidt was pretty much the unanimous choice as Ireland's new head coach when Declan's contract wasn't renewed after a disappointing Six Nations. I wondered who would be captain and I thought long and hard about whether I wanted it. Not having the job would allow me to focus more on myself, for however much time I had left. As well as that, there was incredible detail in Joe's game plan. The captain needs to be driving the head coach's philosophy, but during the first days in camp I felt a long way off the pace.

I liked a lot of what Joe was doing: he was completely different to every other coach I'd had before then. After six months of working with him, my way of thinking about playing and preparation had been turned on its head. He generated a buzz about the processes that went into making our game work. Perfecting these processes on Tuesday in training was as important as the match on Saturday.

He trusted players to do things off the cuff, if they saw an opportunity. His plays, though, required total accuracy, a level of precision that I had never experienced. When a player made a line break, and then threw an unbelievable pass without even looking around, it was nothing to do with peripheral vision. It was because he'd pulled off the move four times in training and he knew the exact line the support player was running. The detail was amazing to me. There were plays where I knew, three rucks in advance, not only which of the rucks I was supposed to hit, but also the player I would be rucking.

Joe was big on everyone being a team player. If you weren't in the match-day squad, he needed you to take the job of preparing the starters as seriously as if you were starting yourself. The players Joe had coached at Leinster had spent three years listening to him drilling his key points home, and sometimes it was like they were speaking a different language. They were completely familiar with what he wanted from them. The rest of us had to play catch-up – and fast.

He reckoned he wasn't a psychologist, but psychology is a massive part of his coaching. He was the first coach I worked with who spoke of visualization and made it sound like something worthwhile to me. He packaged it in a way that made it simple to do and easy to apply to the game. You saw yourself running the support lines on the night before training, so when you ran them for real the next day you weren't doing it for the first time.

The emphasis went from the team owning the game plan to individuals owning their own roles first. Once someone had that – and the players around him had trust in his knowledge of his own role – then he could start helping other people out. Johnny Sexton knew his role inside out – and everyone else's, from the tighthead prop to the fullback.

Those guys who could be both player and coach were very powerful in any system, but particularly Joe's.

Brian told me Joe would make a late decision on the captaincy. It was his final season as a player, and he'd lost the captaincy in the previous Six Nations, when Deccie had gone with Jamie Heaslip. Sure enough, it was the Wednesday night before the first of our three autumn Tests when Joe came to me in the team room at Carton House.

There was no big deal made of it. It was just: 'Oh, I wanted to ask you to captain the side. We're looking at you doing it through to the World Cup, if you wanted.'

I asked if I could think about it.

'Yeah, no problem,' he said. 'I've got a management meeting now, so I'll give you an hour.'

Once it was offered to me, I was probably never going to turn it down. The more I thought about it, the less pressure I felt. With the way Joe coaches, there isn't a lot to captaining the side. You don't have to worry about the players showing a high level of intensity and work rate – he will just put a line through their names if he doesn't see it. It doesn't matter who they are, because the team is everything to him. If a player spends even a couple of seconds longer than he needs to getting back into position after being tackled, he will notice it – and he won't tolerate it.

So I knew after one training session that the job of getting the team right for games wouldn't fall back on the senior players or me as much as it did under other coaches. I never found captaincy easy, but I settled into it once I had a better handle on what Joe wanted.

Before our third game that autumn, against New Zealand, I was walking through the lobby of the Shelbourne Hotel when Denis O'Brien, the head concierge, called me aside.

'I've a little something for you here,' he said. He handed me an envelope and said it was from Rala, our bagman – the greatest character I ever met in rugby.

I used to see Rala fifteen or twenty times a day in camp. He could have given me the envelope whenever he wanted, but he found a way to do it with a touch of class. Inside was a card, with a handwritten message in old Irish script.

On the morrow, cause havoc and let slip the dogs of war. Good luck and God bless, R.

I loved the way he used words. I loved it that he felt he had a contribution to make. He was right, too. To beat New Zealand, we needed to tear into them like dogs. If we'd won the game, I might have framed that card and put it up at home, but it wasn't to be.

Down in Doonbeg, a week later, I met Jamesy Rael. He told me he'd been at the game with another old-school Limerick rugby man, Ken Lyons. With seven or eight minutes to go, when we led 22–17, Jamesy tucked his match ticket into his programme and said: 'I'm going to be one of about eight hundred people who have the match programmes and the tickets and who was there the two times an Irish team beat the All Blacks.'

'Where did you get the eight hundred?' Ken asked.

As play went on, they spent the next five minutes wondering how many of those who'd been at the famous game at Thomond Park in 1978 had died since, how many of the ones still alive would have kept their programme and ticket, and how many of those might be in the Aviva thirty-five years later. They even cut the number on account of our bad defeat to Australia the previous week, because they figured nobody could have expected a performance from us after that.

I was in the moment for all of it, even if I wasn't as fit as I needed to be. When we were 19–0 ahead I never thought of winning, or losing. But by the time Jamesy and Ken were having that conversation, as we tried to see out the game, I felt like I had nothing left to offer. I was worried that if something fast and dangerous came my way I wasn't going to deal with it. My body was hurting, my legs were gone, I could taste the blood on my palate and feel the pain in my lungs. And then, on top of that, there was a fear:

I'm going to be the guy who costs us . . .

I was breathing so heavily I could hear myself over the noise from the crowd. I remember being worried that the lads could hear me as well. After that thought came into my head I stopped breathing for a few seconds. I should have been telling them to keep going, to keep getting off the line and around the corner. Fifteen seconds later I heard myself blowing again. It was that kind of game – relentless. When I had a chat with Richie McCaw afterwards, he told me he was in the same state for the last ten minutes.

Most Irish people saw that game like Jamesy did – if we had held on, it would have been historic. They would have said: 'I was there.' That made me uncomfortable, because

there was no silverware at stake. The autumn internationals were a good measure of where you were, with the Six Nations around the corner. When there was a World Cup the following year, they had more significance. But we'd come a long way during my time with Ireland, and we hadn't done it by getting too carried away by winning one-off Tests, when the southern hemisphere nations were sometimes out on their feet after a long season.

For me, beating a great team would have been memorable – a massive first step on our journey with Joe. Conceding a try in the last play was devastating.

Once we'd left the dressing room, I had to make my way through hundreds of people in a big reception area to get to my family. They were grabbing my arm and asking for pictures, but I just wanted to see Dad so that I could feel his pain. I knew he'd be thinking the same way as Jamesy Rael. For his son to have captained the first Ireland team to beat New Zealand in 108 years of trying would have meant more to him than to me.

When we lost big games like that, people tiptoed around us, trying to say the right thing and ending up saying the wrong thing. Dad always said exactly what he was feeling, and it was so biased in my favour that I found it comforting.

Towards the end of my time at Munster, a player from our academy asked me to meet him. He was a nice kid and I wanted to help him, so I spent time thinking about what might be useful. I wanted to get the message across that if he wanted it enough, it didn't matter if he wasn't the most naturally talented player in the academy. I felt that rugby intelligence could be developed, with the right attitude. Players with a growth mindset embrace challenges. They cope better with setbacks. People with the opposite – a fixed mindset – might have all the ability in the world, but talent will only take them so far in our game. A guy who doesn't see the value of hard work will give up more easily when things go against him.

I remember Doug Howlett saying to me once: 'Good people make good All Blacks.' That stuck in my mind, because I was always trying to make sure the teams I was part of had good values. It annoyed me if I saw guys parking their cars in an ignorant way, or if they weren't respectful enough to turn up wearing the right training gear, when the coach had made it clear it was important to him that they did. Sometimes, standing up for the values I thought were important made me feel I was forever on some people's case, but they were what I stood for and I could never step back from that.

One of the first things I took from Joe Schmidt was that he saw it as his job to make sure players turned up with the right attitude. One of the first points he made to us in camp was 'win the moment in front of your face'. I wrote it down in my notebook. He'd meant it in a rugby context – don't worry about what happened five minutes ago, just focus on your next job; win that moment and move on to the next one with the right attitude. It struck a chord with me and I realized I could apply it to every part of my preparation for rugby. It was a simple idea and I found it helpful in getting myself right.

There were Monday or Tuesday nights when I felt I hadn't trained well earlier in the day and I decided I'd try to win every possible moment from there until the next game. I could start by going to bed early, after a protein snack, with a plan for the following day written out – goals I wanted to achieve in training. In the morning, I'd try to win all the moments in front of my face for the rest of the day – a good breakfast, a review of my plan from the night before, getting to training early with the right gear on, taking notes at the team meeting, being on the training pitch twenty minutes early and doing my own warm-up, and some extras.

At the end of training there were still moments to be won. As players we were part of a big team and we had to have respect for everyone in it, so I could help Rala clear stuff from the pitch, and then do some recovery in the pool, watch training back on the laptop, review my own performance and see if I'd done what I said I would. Later on, at home, I could turn off my phone so that I could relax, have a really good meal, then switch off, watch television, allow my body to recover – then write a new plan for the next day.

Once I'd done all that – when I wasn't rushing out the door in the morning feeling unprepared, or realizing at 10 p.m. that I hadn't done a piece of analysis that suddenly felt unbelievably important – things wouldn't play on my mind. I could get to Thursday and Friday, knowing I'd tried to win all those moments during the week and there was nothing more I could have done to be ready to play well.

This was how I prepared towards the end of my career. I wish I'd had it from an early age.

I started coughing phlegm and blood the night before we played Scotland in the first game of the 2014 Six Nations. At half-four in the morning, when I couldn't sleep, I knew I wouldn't be playing. The team went well without me and won, which made it easier to take. I just about managed fifty-five minutes in the second game, against Wales, after being on antibiotics all week. We won that too, again comfortably.

We had England next, at Twickenham. I still didn't feel fit and I struggled. The first twenty minutes was like an Ireland

324

v. New Zealand game from the old days, when we used to start at a hundred miles an hour – only it was England making all the running. We came back strongly and took control of the game, but handed it back to them with some bad penalties. It was a three-point game and we were on the wrong side of it, but we knew there was big improvement in us.

Beating Italy by thirty-nine points put us in a good position going into the final game, against France in Paris. Walking out, we knew that any kind of victory would win us the championship. We were hanging on at the end, 22–20 ahead. When the whistle went and the lads were jumping around, I just stood there. The crazy finish had been similar to how we'd lost against New Zealand and it disappointed me that we hadn't shown the instinct to kill off the game.

That feeling passed quickly, though. I had never won against France in Paris. To finally do it, to win a championship there and lift the trophy, was an amazing experience.

I came to feel the satisfaction of that achievement, but

I had very little interest in going on the town to celebrate that night. I really wanted to play for Munster against Treviso the following weekend, so I was thinking about that. I didn't feel like I'd played very well in the tournament, especially in the early games, when I wasn't nearly fit enough.

A couple of weeks later I read an article that I identified with. It was about how we react differently to experiences as we get more balance in our lives. Our highs aren't as high as before, but what we do feel can last longer, so in a way it's just as satisfying. Maybe more so.

When I read that, I thought about how much I was still enjoying the journey – the battle to be better. In a lot of ways, still having that feeling about the game, despite all the injuries, was as good as winning things.

It was my last time to play alongside Brian. I talked about his best qualities in my speech afterwards – mental and physical strength, honesty, brilliance. I said I agreed with people who thought he had a talent that was impossible to replace, but the flip side of that was that for years he inspired so many to follow his lead.

We came up against each other one last time, in the Leinster v. Munster fixture, two weeks after Paris. He always had a good strike rate against us and he scored the only try, which was the winning of the game.

They were better than us – again. We couldn't get the ball off them. When I got back to Munster after the Six Nations I was a bit wary of putting my opinions around much. I thought some people might think: *He's been up in Irish camp, working with Joe.* So I tried to bite my tongue, but I didn't make a very good job of it.

A week after that, we played Toulouse in the European quarter-final. I knew we'd need massive passion and intensity, a little bit of the amateur ethos that should always have a place in the game. We weren't going to win by being technically better, or busting them with clever moves.

It turned out to be a magnificent day for us. Toulouse were massively psyched for the game, and the first ten minutes were the most physical I'd experienced in a long time. They weren't fit enough, though. They blew up, and we took over. We didn't get a lot of ball out of the scrum, but we killed them mauling – it was top-class. They couldn't live with it. We walloped them 47–23.

We had Toulon in the semi-final, at Stade Vélodrome in Marseille. I don't know what it was with those semi-final draws. During my time, we played French clubs in five semi-finals, and all of them were away from home. We should have beaten Toulon, though. The scrum hurt us, and sometimes we tried to play rugby in our own twenty-two. We were handing momentum to them all the time. It just felt like there was a vagueness about what we were doing.

We were an average, up-and-down team all year. So in the end we got what we deserved.

A few months before the end of the season, we were told Rob was leaving. He had been offered another year, but a better offer came from Japan and he took it. I was surprised when I heard. Maybe if we'd been further down the track in playing the rugby he tried to introduce, he'd have stayed. We reached two Heineken Cup semi-finals under him, but things never really came together like they had the potential to.

I was pleased for Axel when he got the head coach job, and excited when he brought Jerry Flannery into his coaching group.

On most days, as the new season came near, I was feeling good. When I woke up and got out of bed, my knees worked fine and all sorts of plans were on the cards.

I could play past the World Cup.

I could go to France for a season — just go over and see what it's like. Emily would love it.

Could I manage two more years?

Maybe I could coach in the second year and really learn the language.

I saw the World Cup as the natural point to finish with Ireland. After that, I was either going to join a club in France, or decide to retire. Either way, I knew it would be my last season with Munster.

Unless I was injured, I always felt optimistic in August. We didn't need to win a trophy for me to believe I was leaving Munster in a good place, but I was also thinking: *If we can avoid having a lot of injuries, we could have a great year.*

When I was having a cup of tea with Flannery during pre-season, talking about the team, it almost felt like it was 2008 again and we were looking for answers.

PART FOUR

22

Wednesday, 3 September 2014

I usually wake up a little before the alarm goes off, and these days I'm always curious to know what my first steps in the morning are going to be like. How will my back feel when I stand up? How will my knees feel, going down the stairs? Today my body felt really good. I'm a week or two away from playing, but I feel like I'm ready to go well, once I get myself match-fit.

This will be my fourteenth season as a professional and I feel hungrier than ever. I want to train harder, eat better, go to bed earlier than I've ever done. I want to be fitter than all the guys I'm playing against – and with. Wishful thinking maybe, but a target. Fitness, power, strength – I need to be better, and I think I can get there. It's about leading the tackle count, leading the line speed.

I have all these plans, all these ideas in my head. If I can get myself where I want to be, I think I can be as good as I ever was at the World Cup.

I feel like I'm behind other players at the moment. It's like I've written a script in my head where I need to do extra to get even with them and then more to get ahead. I still have injuries from last summer niggling at me, and it looks like they won't all clear up, but with the right training I can avoid aggravating them.

I'm not doing stupid weights. I'm not doing the same fitness programme as the other forwards. I'm sitting down with the S&C guys each week, letting them know how my body is. We talk about where I can add bits in and where I need to take bits out. That came out of the chat I had with Brad Thorn, and it's working for me.

For me, this season with Munster isn't necessarily about winning anything. I'd like to leave on a high, but the high doesn't have to be silverware. It can be consistency – being as good as we can be, and seeing where that leaves us. We might get some breaks and pick up a trophy, but most of all I'd like to go out having the knowledge I was consistently striving to be my best and trying to help others along the way.

Our coaches couldn't be any more up for it. As a group, they don't have a lot of coaching experience at this level, but they're massively hungry, and that counts for a lot.

It's two years now since I stood down from the captaincy of Munster. I've asked this year to not be considered whenever Peter is injured or not involved. It's time to bring a few other guys along and to give them responsibility. It also takes a little bit of pressure off me and allows me to prepare and play well myself, which is the most important piece I can add.

People know I'm coming near the end of my career and

I'm often asked if I'm dreading the end, whenever it comes. I'm not. Not at all. Whether I play on for another while in France or not, I'm looking at the next World Cup as the end of something huge in my life. My last game for Ireland, the last time I play for Munster – I'm not sure how I'm going to feel, but I'm not dreading it. I'm almost looking forward to it. It's like waiting for the end of my own movie, to see if the good guy wins. (I'm the good guy.)

Monday, 8 September 2014

I think the coaches need to hold us to a higher standard in training. We talk a lot about consistency, but probably not enough about the habits that lead to consistency. Without that pathway, it's just a word. People performing their jobs, moment by moment, to the best of their ability, both on and off the pitch, is what leads to consistent performances, not a piece of paper with the word 'consistency' written on it.

We lost to Edinburgh by a point on Friday. It was our first game of the season and everyone was really deflated after it. I wasn't playing and I'm a terrible spectator. You see things in a different light and the mistakes are harder to watch, especially at home. It makes a massive difference when there's a big crowd that's really up for the game. When the stadium is less than half full, there isn't the same fear factor for the opposition, but it's our job to produce rugby the fans can identify with. I don't think they want to see us score length-of-the-pitch tries necessarily, but they need to see something in how we play that they can relate to. It was so obvious the other night that they identify with CJ Stander. He's going to be a huge player for us if he can stay injury-free. He's powerful, he's fast, he scores tries. He's been waiting a while for his chance and every time he gets his hands on the ball you can see how much he wants to take it.

Axel was always scoring tries from the back-row as well. He didn't have CJ's power, but he had a great instinct for when it was on. In my best years for Munster I scored tries – five in six games in the season when we first won the Heineken Cup – but then it all dried up. I haven't scored for Ireland since 2006 and I don't know why that is. Playing for my school and Young Munster, I had a good nose for the line. They were mostly unspectacular tries from a few metres out, but I loved scoring them. I think a little bit of the greediness was coached out of me later on. I'm better at looking at a game and seeing things happening, but am I a more rounded player? I used to offload more and carry the ball more in wider channels, but I suppose rugby was a lot less structured then. Still, I often think I was better when I was just playing my own game as hard as I could.

Monday, 22 September 2014

We beat Zebre on Friday and I played OK. It wasn't a particularly good team performance but we scored five tries, which should give us a bit more confidence. Getting a win puts everyone in good form.

Life after the World Cup drifts in and out of my mind. I will definitely be retiring from international rugby and from Munster. That is concrete in my head and probably has been for a while. Coaching or playing in France interests me on some days, and not so much on others.

Last week I was walking around the gym, thinking about the future. I think a lot about what's coming next – whether to play on in France or not, whether I'll stay involved in rugby. I still don't have any answers. I love competitiveness and high performance. I can get as much enjoyment out of seeing a young S&C coach or player working his socks off as I do from winning games. So I think I could apply that to different things.

Monday, 29 September 2014

We've lost two of our first three home games. Whatever confidence there was in the squad has gone now. We should have beaten Ospreys by seven or eight points on Saturday, but we coughed up too many bad penalties and lost 19–14.

There was a time when we'd have solved the problem and won, but these days we get penalized for the same things, week on week. I cannot understand how we can repeat identical errors, game after game.

Sometimes I feel like I'm having the same conversation with myself year after year, but I still long for the coach-led, player-driven, problem-solving culture we used to have. When you've experienced at first hand the power that that combination can lead to on the field of play, it's impossible to forget it. The phrase 'play as you train, train as you play' has been around since forever, but only in the last few years have I learned how powerful a mantra it can be when it's applied properly. I don't think we're doing that as well as we could, and so our habits are letting us down on match days.

I think we need more players who turn up every day thinking, *This is* our *team. Whatever's wrong, we can fix it.* They're the ones you can hang your hat on. When we adopt that mentality, we'll be playing to our potential again.

The penalties we're giving away in training are the same ones we're conceding in the games. The discipline we need on the training ground isn't being enforced. We need to get to a situation where a video analyst looking at our training sessions would struggle to find penalties. If we get to that place, a referee will struggle to find them on Saturday. Right now, anyone looking for our infringements in training would have a busy day's work ahead.

We're doing a lot of things wrong that are easily fixable if we have respect for the ball and a genuine fear of making unforced errors – I don't mean knock-ons, because they can happen, but penalties for being ahead of the kicker, or for being isolated on the ground when all you have to do is roll over a few times to free yourself up to place the ball.

We're not expected to sidestep four people, fend off three more and chip the fullback. It's as basic as placing the ball back properly at a ruck. Some days I feel like I'm doing a lot of giving out. It's not something I want in my last year here. There are so many things we can be better at, things that don't require any talent and have nothing to do with ability: fitness, work ethic, being prepared, being on time, attitude, body language, passion, doing extras.

Watching a game, I saw one of our players get clipped in the head by a boot. It was no big deal, just a glance, but he stayed down for at least ten seconds before getting back into the defensive line. I feel it's my place to make the point: *We cannot do that and expect to win.*

So I asked him, 'Why stay down there? You weren't unconscious. You didn't have any broken bones. You know you can get back up straight away.'

I knew we couldn't have that the following weekend, because we were playing too good a team. We've got to be hoping that the opposition has a culture that tolerates that, not us. If they do, there's an opportunity there: for those ten seconds, we have more players than them. And those ten seconds can produce the half-chance that releases an Earls or a Jones.

To me – and so many other people at other clubs who think the same way – things like that matter when your ambition is to be the best.

It's frustrating.

Wednesday, 8 October 2014

We beat Leinster at the Aviva on Saturday and we deserved our win. Some of the work we've been doing at the ruck came out in force and led to us scoring some great tries.

It's been a long time since we won up there, but it would have been really disappointing if we hadn't done it. They were missing some big players, like Cian Healy and Seanie O'Brien. They didn't have Shane Jennings, who always plays well against us, and it's their first season without Brian O'Driscoll. So we needed to win, but ten minutes into the game I wouldn't have been surprised if we'd lost. We were just going along our usual path, making unforced errors and allowing them into the game.

We were delighted with the win, but I've been down this road too often to think we'll definitely kick on now and keep producing the goods. There have just been too many false dawns, where we've put in really good performances and then gone straight backwards.

Tuesday, 21 October 2014

My knee was at me all last week. We had Sale away in our first Champions Cup pool game and I shouldn't have played. I've done it a few times over the last couple of years, because the squad isn't as deep as it used to be, but I had a really poor game. We were sixteen points down at half-time – and then we came back to win it. Ian Keatley's drop goal at the death was just like old times: we found a way to win.

I haven't allowed myself to think about winning the tournament, because it doesn't feel like the same kind of campaign as before. My mental approach has changed. I'm just trying to get myself in the best shape I can to play well, so the knee coming at me again was really disappointing, especially when I know that rest is a big part of getting it right. I want to do more, not less. So, today, I had to work hard to fight off the negativity, because there's a fear at the back of my mind all the time now: *Am I gonna go to the World Cup and be average, because I can't train as I need to?*

Monday, 3 November 2014

Lola, our second child, was born on Friday – a Halloween baby. I felt like an old hand in the delivery room: didn't need any gas or anything.

Paddy is fascinated by his new sister. In weeks like these, it's tough being away from home in Irish camp, but it's tougher on Emily. I'm getting two days off from tomorrow and I can't wait for us all to be together.

Thursday, 6 November 2014

One of Declan Kidney's biggest strengths was being able to recognize where players were at mentally, before games. If he didn't think the team was in the right place, he'd do something. In his Munster days, he was into *The Lion King*. He thought the movie had a lot of powerful messages. He knew

that a Munster team playing one of the big French sides away
from home was going to have a fear factor, so for him it was
about finding ways to confront that. The scene from *The Lion
King* that stuck in my memory was the one where the hyenas
are talking about how much they fear Mufasa, the biggest and
most powerful lion in the kingdom. He played it for us once,
before we played Toulouse.

'I just hear that name and I shudder,' one of them says.

The hyena beside him goes: 'Mufasa!'

The first one cowers. 'Do it again,' he says.

'Mufasa! Mufasa! Mufasa!'

For us, Mufasa is South Africa. On Saturday, we know we'll be up against massive players, and that they'll come with a huge scrum and a strong lineout. We know it will be hard to maul against them. So I've always had that fear, playing against them, which is both good and bad. You can't give them too much credit, in your head. But sometimes it's not easy to avoid that, especially when you're unsure of how well prepared your team is.

I had a really good chat with Eoin Reddan today. He made it the hard way, leaving Munster for Connacht, going back to Munster and on to Wasps before joining Leinster, all with the goal of increasing his chances of playing for Ireland. Playing with people who have gone on that journey fills me with confidence.

Redser is very deep about his rugby. I've always enjoyed talking to him about the game – he's an astute brain, a great guy to confide in. He also understands Joe's philosophy. Today he said: 'It's great, isn't it? As long as I know my job inside out, Joe will make sure everyone else is prepared. I don't need to stay on top of you and you don't need to stay on top of me.'

At an elite level, all the coaches are trying to do very similar things. What makes the difference is understanding players well enough so that you get them to do things right on the day of the game. In the past, me and Redser have spoken about how you sometimes think you're really well prepared – and then you go out, and you're flat. On other days, it's the other way around.

'How do you think we're set?' I asked him. He said he didn't know, but I read from his facial expression that he was worried. I was too.

I try not to fear any opponent, but any international second-row will tell you that Victor Matfield has the ability to destroy your lineout. He's the best lineout operator I've played against. He very rarely makes mistakes and his restart work is excellent as well.

In the autumn of 2009, after we beat South Africa, a lot was made of the fact that Gert Smal, our forwards coach at the time, had taught me some numbers in Afrikaans. I had also downloaded an Afrikaans counting class from YouTube. The Springboks had the same lineout calls for years on end. In the video room I listened to Matfield's call on the ref mic and then tried to guess where the ball was going. By the end of the week I was able to look at a sequence of around a hundred of their lineouts and know where each one was going, based on the call.

It worked. There were a few lineouts where, after Matfield had made the call, we were lined up defensively before they even got to where they were supposed to be. Their lineout had been the bedrock of their success for years. They cleared their lines excellently, they scored tries off their drive. They drew a lot of penalties, and their box-kicking game off lineout drives was incredibly effective. Attacking that meant we were hitting them at their strongest point. In the second half, they started calling lineouts in a huddle, but we still got after a few of their balls.

They stole a few of ours, too. On the opposition's throw, Matfield moves around the lineout a lot, with pace. He upsets the caller and the thrower. No matter how good a day I had against Matfield – and that was the best one – I was never 100 per cent on our ball. He told the media that Gert Smal was man of the match in that game. It was a fair point.

Against a competitor as good as him, you only get to do something like that once. After retiring from rugby he is back playing again, at 105 kilos – six or seven kilos down on before. He's light and fast, and he has big men lifting him. The lineout will play a massive role at the weekend, again.

Thursday, 13 November 2014

On the Friday night before the South Africa game, I pulled up on my phone something Jerry Flannery sent me a while ago – a page from Mike Tyson's autobiography. Cus D'Amato, his mentor, used to get into his head before fights. He understood the fear that can take hold of people in sport when they're about to go into a physical battle.

> Your mind is not your friend, Mike. I hope you know that. You have to fight with your mind, control it, put it in its place. You need to control your emotions. Fatigue in the ring is 90 per cent psychological. It's just the excuse of a man who wants to quit. The night before a fight, you won't sleep. Don't worry, the other guy didn't either. You'll go to the weigh-in, he'll look much bigger than you and calmer, like ice, but he's burning up with fear inside. Your imagination is going to credit him with abilities he doesn't have.
>
> Remember, motion relieves tension. The moment the bell rings, and you come in contact with each other, suddenly your opponent seems like everybody else, because now your imagination has dissipated. The fight itself is the only reality that matters. You have to learn to impose your will and take control over that reality.

I read it two or three times. It made sense to me. If Tyson could feel like that, whatever fear I was experiencing myself was normal. The fear of failure is natural and it needn't be

debilitating, if I use it in the right way. It makes me prepare better and work harder. It eliminates complacency and gets me to a place where I'm ready to compete, particularly when I know it's going to be a physical battle. By the time the game came round, I was building my belief.

They're in Ireland, in November – and it's cold.

They're at the end of their season – and it's summer back home.

We're getting better all the time.

In the dressing room, I was feeling better about us being mentally ready to win. Joe has a way of getting you to walk on to the pitch completely focused on your job – and not the result, or its consequences. That focus reminded me of how I was on the 2013 Lions tour, in the games before the Test matches. I knew there were things that Andy Farrell, the defence coach, had to see from me if I was going to make the Test team.

We were using a new tactic to defend South Africa's maul.

It came from our forwards coach, Simon Easterby, but I was worried about it. The idea was to stand off their lineout maul. Once they transfer the ball, you send a guy around the back. So you're avoiding the confrontation, in a way, which didn't sit well with me. I thought it was saying to them: *You're stronger than us, you're better at mauling. So we're going to look for a trick to stop you, instead of facing you head-on.*

But we went out and played some great rugby. Their scrum put us under pressure and our lineout struggled, but we did a lot of things really well and put them away fairly comfortably. We're never going to be the biggest team, but we're big on trying to be more disciplined, more clever, more together. The maul tactic worked a treat. If a team does something like that to us once, we deal with it, but they never fixed it. They did score a maul try against us, which was a real disappointment, but overall it really worked.

They scored a consolation try in the last minute, and we still won by fourteen points, 29–15. In the past, after a big win like that, we'd often go backwards the following week. So I went into Joe's presentation on Monday wondering: *How is he going to dampen expectations?*

It was a brilliant meeting, edge-of-your-seat stuff. When I first started going to Joe's reviews and saw him making all these points, I used to think I'd have to watch the game for six hours just to see the same things he saw, but eventually I copped that he's looking at it differently. He can communicate what he sees incredibly fluently, so that guys who have been playing rugby for most of their lives are looking at things that they've seen a thousand times before – but in a whole new way.

Just as it started, I could sense he was about to go to town on us. The whole meeting was about the try we conceded at the end. So much of what we delivered in those last minutes was not up to the standards that are demanded of us and we demand of each other. Joe was holding us to a very high, exacting level, no matter the scoreline. He was setting the tone for the following week's training and performance.

At the end, just as we felt we'd had the shit kicked out of us, he said: 'Lads – fair play! An outstanding result! I was very happy. But this try – every single error here is easily fixed. So if we fix them, imagine where we can go to.'

At the end of the meeting I was sitting there thinking, *When it comes to coaching, this is the standard.*

Monday, 24 November 2014

People talk about the gap between the northern and southern hemispheres, but to me the real gap is between New Zealand and everyone else.

When I was watching Ireland in the 1990s, beating South Africa and Australia in November never happened. We beat Australia on Saturday. It was an excellent win, even though we were hanging on at the end. In one way it was a game that hinted at our potential, and in another it showed how far we still have to go. They were hammering away at our line but we defended really well.

I was very happy with how fit and strong I felt all the way to the end. It was the best feeling I've had on a pitch since the Lions tour last year. After a slow fifteen months, I feel like I'm at the level of fitness required for international rugby for the first time since Joe took over the job. I felt better with five minutes to go than I did five minutes in. The work is paying off and I'm moving to a place I've been chasing for a long time.

Thursday, 4 December 2014

I've found the build-up to this weekend really, really tough. We have Clermont back to back, so there was always going to be a fear factor, but I haven't felt like this for a long time. I know it's been a consistent theme for a lot of my career – feeling the stress for the big games against the big teams – but it's something I thought I had got on top of. Up to a point, anyway.

In professional sport, we all have different ways of getting ourselves mentally ready for the weekend, and when they stop working we find something new. Then we'll go back to what worked before, and hope it's the answer again.

When I think back to what I was like at the beginning of my rugby career, that guy is almost a completely different person. He's raw, driven, competitive, naïve. He thinks Limerick is the greatest place on earth. He thinks Munster are the greatest team in the world and Ireland is the best country. He believes the Young Munster approach to the game – hard and physical – is the way rugby should be played. And he hasn't had much life experience to challenge any of those beliefs.

When I was young, I thought there was only one way to do things. And it was a great way to be, because I didn't doubt people, or myself, and my head wasn't full of questions. So back then I showed up to training, did as I was told, trained as hard as I could and went home. But I loved what I was doing and I was ambitious and curious. I wasn't going to bob along without looking to improve how I played or prepared mentally, or without asking questions about how the team could be better. So I kept changing my logic. One season I'd embrace the stress, the next I'd try to fight it. They

346

were just different ways of getting by, of coping with the pressure and the self-doubt and the fear of failure which sometimes crept in.

For years I thought I needed to go through the stress to play well. I remember Munster playing Glasgow at Musgrave Park in the Magners League. It was the last game of the season and there was nothing on the line except pride. After the pre-match meal you get an hour and a half to lie down and pack your bag, and it was the only game of my life when I actually fell asleep. I slept like a baby. I remember waking up and thinking: *Jesus, I mustn't be up for this! I'm not prepared!*

I went out and played unbelievably well. The game seemed easy. I read it well and everything flowed my way.

At the time it made me question my approach, and I tried to repeat it but, for whatever reason, it never happened again, maybe because there seemed to be more at stake when I put my head on the pillow.

The bigger the game, the more detail I'd try to cover off. There were times when I couldn't have been more prepared – and that was when I hated it most, because I'd be thinking: *I have everything done, I'm ready to be my best.* And that was the fear – that I wouldn't be.

When you think about it, negative feelings like those don't make any sense. I was working as hard as I could in training, I'd have crawled across broken glass for the opportunity to play for my province and my country. And then when I got the chance that I'd been working so hard for, it was daunting. It seemed so big that if I didn't deliver, I'd feel like a failure.

The closer it got to the Saturday of a big game, the worse I became. Once, when I tried to slag my brother Justin about being a perfectionist, he wasn't slow coming back at me: 'I'm supposed to take that from the guy who can't function as a human being two days before a game?'

Forty-eight hours before kick-off, the only kind of questions I wanted to give brain space to were:

Is my head right for the weekend?

Have I got the work done?

Has the team?

Am I fit enough?

Do the lads know why that lineout move went wrong in training today?

Have I got my gear washed for training tomorrow?

Am I organized?

If my phone rang, even if it was a friend calling, I'd get annoyed.

Jesus Christ! Does he not know how important this game is?

Sometimes I granted myself a licence to snap at a family member, when I wouldn't have dreamed of it with someone less familiar. And that made me feel guilty because I knew they were the last people who deserved it.

I finally copped that, whether I'm uptight or relaxed before games, my performance isn't affected one way or the other – and being relaxed makes life a little bit easier.

What the pressure I'm feeling right now is, I can't put my finger on. I was good in the build-up to the Australia game. I played well too, so it might have something to do with that – knowing I'm capable of playing really well again and worrying that I won't deliver. But it's probably more down to being aware of how important the next two games are for the future of Munster.

I know I shouldn't be thinking that way, and putting pressure on myself, but if we can win on Saturday it would be massive for our confidence going down to France.

Tuesday, 16 December 2014

I struggled again the night before we played Clermont away. We should have drawn with them at Thomond Park, but I lost an attacking lineout near the end, and all we got out of it was a bonus point. We'd never lost to a French team at home, but they scored a try off a maul in the first minute and it was a big dent in our belief. Ten years ago, we would have been psyched up not to allow them to make a physical statement like that, but this team isn't used to success yet.

Last Friday night, in my hotel room in Clermont-Ferrand, I was really, really nervous. It was probably as bad as I've felt before a game in my whole career. You can be aware of all the psychology behind high performance and the techniques that help you to prepare well. You can try your hardest to stay relaxed and positive and in the moment. You can read all the inspirational books about developing a winning mindset and how different people confront and overcome their fears. You can take in those lovely words, but sometimes that's all they are: words. Sometimes there are no guarantees that any of them are going to put you in a better place. And that's how it was in my hotel room last Friday night.

I knew it was going to be a war. And belief levels were low – we hadn't trained like a group that was expecting to win.

We were playing a physically massive team, full of inter-nationals, with more coming off the bench. With ten minutes to go we were 26–9 down and going out of the competition. But we brought it back to 26–19 and that was enough to keep us alive. It was like the bonus point we got at Clermont the second year we won the Cup, when I was injured.

I don't think there are many teams out there who would have done what we did, because it took unbelievable heart. It was more than just that, though – there was a lot of intelligence as well. Duncan Casey's intercept try at the end came from coaching, fitness and smarts as well as heart – so that gave me a lot of hope that we can still take the big sides.

When I walked into the dressing room, I was devastated to have lost two in a row. The more I've watched the game back since, the more confusing my feelings get. We had two massive games, we were beaten in both of them and I've been sitting there in front of the video getting a kind of tingle of excitement, thinking that maybe in the malaise of these losses, there is hope. We did so many things well. There's so much potential. I never thought I'd be able to lose European games back to back and feel like this. What does that say about me?

Over the last few weeks Felix Jones has blown me away. We've needed people to stand up – and he has been phenomenal. He is the ultimate role model for everyone in the squad. Because of the mental strength he has shown to come back from his injuries. Because of the way he trains, and the way he treats people. And because of the way he plays: skill, passion and emotion, perfectly balanced.

He was always a great tackler, but in the first Clermont game he hit Nick Abendanon so hard in the chest that he knocked him unconscious. I heard afterwards that it was the heaviest impact ever measured by the GPS devices we wear. On top of all that, he's incredibly committed to our success. And I love it that a guy from Dalkey, who went to St Andrew's College and UCD, has bought in to Munster in such a huge way.

We have a player management programme under the IRFU that mostly works well, but sometimes it doesn't make any sense. I'm not allowed to play against Leinster on St Stephen's Day. The stadium will be full, there'll be a great atmosphere and I hate missing a game like that. Instead, I played against Glasgow on Saturday. We flew home from France, then I had to travel to Cork for training during the week, before flying to Glasgow, all within a six-day turn-around. That kind of travel is not conducive to high performance for a thirty-five-year-old with my injury profile. My head was wrong in the build-up. I was making excuses for myself before we ever stepped on the pitch. I think I almost talked myself into not playing well.

I shouldn't be playing this game.

Three travel days in less than a week – I'm not twenty-five!

I've had two back surgeries.

This could fuck up my knee.

I did some good things, but my work rate dropped off during the game and I was left thinking that the result could have been different. I had the feeling that other guys who had also played against Clermont might have been thinking the same way, so what I needed to do was to make sure nobody was infected with the same negativity.

We're always learning, but I should have led that. Instead, I descended into the kind of mental weakness I've tried to fight against all my career.

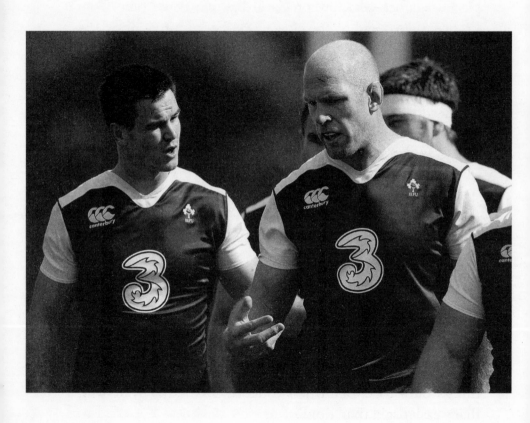

23

When I started out with Munster, I was able to make progress without being too conscious of what supporters or the media thought of us. That was a good thing, but for a young player now it's very different. Social media, websites, blogs, far more coverage in newspapers: everyone seems to be banging a drum, and as players we can't allow ourselves to be affected when it's negative. We need to ignore it and fix things ourselves. But when you're only finding your way, that's easier said than done.

We have followed up the two defeats to Clermont with losses against Glasgow and Connacht, with a win against Leinster in between. It probably isn't a bad thing to be shutting out what people outside the group are saying about us. Right now it's all about us fixing the problem, but the little bit of optimism I found in the Clermont defeats has been extinguished.

I didn't play against Leinster, so it's the fourth game in a row I've lost. Connacht are a good side, but defensively we were poor, very soft. When I take time to think about our situation – which isn't very often – I'm despondent and pessimistic. I don't enjoy contemplating where we are because in the past I've always had answers.

It's tough at the moment, but I'm still enjoying the battle to turn this spell around.

Friday, 23 January 2015

Donncha O'Callaghan always makes me laugh. If I'm out for a stroll with him and we pass a very old couple, he'll turn to me and say: 'Not long now.'

I met a couple in Cork today, outside the Passport Office on the South Mall. They must have been seventy. The man smiled at me and said: 'Thanks for all the memories.' It was as if I'd just retired from the game, or he was expecting me to announce the news any day now. I'm sure he was probably thinking it: *Not long now.*

It must have sounded the same way to his wife, judging by her reaction.

'Shut up, you eejit!' she said. Then she turned back to me, and it was like she wanted to reassure me I wasn't finished.

'Best of luck for the future!'

I could see where he was coming from, though. It's almost a week since we were knocked out of the Champions Cup, by Saracens. Billy Vunipola, their back-row, seemed incredible to me on the pitch – like a machine. He was making massive hits, big carries, running into tight channels and creating space with his power. Most players like that – explosive ball-carriers – tend to drift in and out of games, but he kept going. He was fit, hungry, relentless. I know he's twenty-two and I'm thirty-five, but I want to be as good in my position as he is in his. And I felt miles away from that.

Yesterday I went to see Catherine Norton, our nutritionist. I wanted to ask her about Novak Djokovic's diet. In 2010 he went gluten-free and dairy-free – it transformed his career. He started winning Grand Slams and he hasn't stopped since. So I was half hoping that Catherine might say: 'Let's get you tested for a load of allergies. There might be something in that.' I thought I might find out that I'm allergic to something. Then I'd go off it and feel unreal.

But she told me Djokovic's parents owned a pizzeria and an ice-cream parlour, so he grew up with a really bad diet.

'You've got a great diet,' she said. 'There's not a whole lot you need to change.'

I kind of knew it. But I was still a bit disappointed.

I think I can be every bit as good a player as I was in my best years if I can just negotiate my injuries and get into proper shape. At least before Saturday I thought that. Now it's a struggle to even believe that thought, let alone achieve it.

It's only two months since I said to myself, at the end of the Australia game: *I'm there. I'm where I need to be.* How can I have gone backwards since then?

I think back to the time when I used to have six or seven carries in a game. I'd kick and bullock my way over the gain line somehow. These days, my ball-carrying disappoints me and the more I try to be the player I was, the further away it seems to me.

I think about the possibility of letting myself down, or that I should have retired a year earlier. I'd hate not to perform at the World Cup. It would be a shame, after all these years. And nobody wants to go out on a low like that, seeing people's memories of you as a player tainted by the way things ended. The longer you hang around as a second-rate version of what you once were, the longer people remember you as that. I've seen guys at the end of their careers playing poorly because their bodies were giving up on them. And I'd think: *I played against him three years ago and he was just incredible.*

There's only so long that you can hang on and compete when you're doing very few leg weights or power weights, things that make a big difference to your fitness. I don't want to be hanging on with Munster or Ireland because I expect to be at a certain level. I'm supposed to drive standards and I can't do that if I'm not maintaining them myself.

I'm not able to train hard for three days after a game. I have to spend much of the week recovering in order to be right for the following week. And so I'm always thinking: *Am I ever going to shake this off and be able to train at the proper level?* There haven't been many games in the last two or three years when I felt strong all the way through. And it frustrates me, because I've never worked harder in my life.

In the front five, I can't let my intensity drop. I need to be going as hard in the sixty-seventh minute, when we can break a team, as I am in minute one. Players like me don't have the ability to turn a game in an instant, like Keith Earls or Tommy Bowe. We can turn a game, maybe, by being relentless for eighty minutes. And I was conscious, going around the field against Saracens, that I wasn't doing my job the way I wanted. I was a little slower to get off the ground after a breakdown, I was hitting rucks higher and with less aggression.

It probably wasn't as clear to the untrained eye in the stand, but I knew on the field that I wasn't where I needed to be. And it's a terrible feeling to have, in the middle of a game. You want to move as hard as you can. You know where you need to go – and you need to be there *now* – but you just can't get there in time. So you end up chasing your tail. You don't make it into the right position for one phase, but you're on your way to it – which means you're almost out of play for the next phase as well. And so for those few seconds of the game your team is effectively playing with fourteen men.

When you're fit and strong, you tell yourself that when it's all on the line you'll be talking so much that the guys around you will be gaining confidence from you. You're going around the pitch thinking: *I'm going to be the one who gets us a turnover here.* That's the confidence that true fitness and sharpness bring you. That's where Vunipola had got himself on Saturday and it's why he was by far the best player on the pitch.

A good few Munster supporters were gathered by the tunnel as we were walking off. I was in my own world at that stage, and I kept looking straight ahead, down the tunnel. I was embarrassed about our performance – and mine. I didn't want to make eye contact with anyone, even though I was vaguely aware that people were clapping us off the pitch, really generously – obviously diehards.

Back in Limerick that night, a few of us went for a drink at the Black Swan, near my house in Annacotty, and people were coming over and being extremely nice, decent, positive. In a lot of ways it's bad that our supporters don't expect as much from us these days.

I got a lovely letter from a supporter called Michael this morning, inside a card which said, 'I attended Mass for you today.' It made me smile, seeing that. Right now I know I've got to dig in. I've been here before and I know what it takes to get out of it.

I obviously take defeats badly but I can't walk around the

place with my head down. Inside, I'm in a bit of turmoil. The fairytale of winning another European Cup with Munster isn't going to happen but I still have to keep working at it and train as hard as I can.

For three or four days after a defeat as bad as Saturday's, everything seems worse than it is. By Wednesday I was telling myself I'd just had a bad day, but that I did some good things as well. I came around. I just got on with it.

We play Sale on Sunday, and if we put in a good performance I'll probably feel different. People could ask me about retiring a week from now and I might have a completely different answer.

Tuesday, 27 January 2015

Sale sent over a second team. They ran out of puff after half-time and we didn't, but I was happy that we stuck to the task and beat them by a really good score, 65–10. It was great to get the win but we can't kid ourselves that it was anything other than a second team – and a Sale second team. Their first team lost every other game in the pool.

We still have the Pro 12 title to play for, and if we can get all our best players on the pitch after the Six Nations we should have as good a chance as any team in the league.

Toulon have been in touch, talking about a contract for two seasons, until 2017. I don't know if I have that in me. A week ago I would have said definitely not, but I'll see how it goes. It would be a great move for the family and, rugby-wise, I wouldn't be back in a situation where I'm constantly fighting to drive standards. I'd be expected to bring certain things, but not that. They have world-class players everywhere.

They want me to make my mind up and sign fairly soon,

but I'm not in a position to do that. I'll probably know where I am after the Six Nations. If I'm playing well and feeling good in the games, I may take a look at it.

Tuesday, 3 February 2015

Captaincy has always been difficult to enjoy, but I probably find it easier in Irish camp than I have done in the past, because of how the coaches run things. Eoin Reddan isn't in the squad at the moment and Johnny Sexton is out for another week with concussion, so we have a fairly quiet group. There are a lot of guys who are concentrating on getting themselves right. Nothing wrong with that, but at the same time you need players driving things on and holding people accountable too.

The icing on the cake will be when the team can drive itself. I thought Leinster had that under Joe in 2012, when they beat Ulster in the Heineken Cup final. The leadership in their group was obvious, and we're missing a little bit of that with Ireland at the moment. I'm trying to bring it out and hopefully it will come. It's not something Joe is pushing for. It's not something that can be forced. But it will make us a better team.

Right now we just need a bit more assurance about where we are, but you never really know until you take to the field. We'll have a better idea after the weekend in Rome.

Tuesday, 10 February 2015

I was rooming with Earlsy in Rome. He's an easy roomie, but I still had to work hard at staying relaxed. I didn't head off for walks with my headphones on, I didn't force-feed myself with carbs, or measure the amount of water I drank, and I felt less sluggish because of it. I just did what came naturally. I made sure I spent time with relaxed guys and good friends like Sean O'Brien and Sean Cronin. I went to Rala's room. I read my book, *I Am Pilgrim*. It was still tough, but it was better than it had been.

It wasn't a great performance by us, but we pulled away after a slow start. I didn't feel bad out there. I was going quite hard right to the end.

Federico Pucciariello, our former prop at Munster, rang me today. He's good friends with Diego Domínguez, who's taking over as head coach of Toulon. Freddie said: 'Diego just wants to let you know that the club would love to have you there after the World Cup. He thinks you could play for another three years.'

Three years! I'd be nearly thirty-nine when I finished! It's nice that he has such faith in me, but I don't think I'll be going to Toulon for three years – I'm fairly sure of that.

Wednesday, 11 February 2015

Training had a whole different dynamic this morning. We spoke with the coaches yesterday about demanding more from us. Joe was on top of everyone and the opposition put the starting fifteen under savage pressure – match pressure. That's going to happen when guys feel they have a crack at getting in the team, if they train well. And Joe encourages that.

I absolutely love those sessions when we're all on edge, coaches and players, approaching a training session with the same intensity as a match. The coaches were right in the thick of it. They knew exactly what they wanted from everyone, all of the time. There were no grey areas, and no hiding place if you didn't do it the way the coaches wanted.

Joe won't mince his words, but he'll always soften them later. You're never going to walk into the team room and find him scowling. He might come over when you're looking at training on the computer, and he'll crack a joke and explain where you went wrong.

'How many three-point games have you been involved in? That play – done right – could win it for us on Saturday.'

The plays in rugby have got much more demanding and intricate. If a player is new to our set-up, you could scratch the surface of his understanding and find he knows *what* he's supposed to be doing at a certain point in the move, but he doesn't really know *why*. For Joe, that means he's not going to do his own small job in the process as well as he could. So he keeps going after that lack of clarity, whenever he sees it. He *makes* people understand, in a very skilful way.

Johnny wasn't around for the Italy game last week, but he's fit again now. Today was the first time we've been held to really high standards since we came together for the Six Nations, and we didn't train well. Anyone watching us would have thought we're going to lose to France by fifty points, but I felt a lot better after it. The intensity was much closer to what France will bring and we found out more about ourselves.

When training isn't so demanding, you don't know where you really stand and you can sleepwalk into the match. Training as close as possible to match intensity provides the information you need. What's real is what's actually done, and Robbie Henshaw impresses me more every day I see him. He's a brilliant player and an unbelievably hard worker. I love it when class players are workhorses as well. He has the potential to be incredible and his partnership with Jared Payne looks really strong.

Johnny's presence is incredibly reassuring. The out-half has to take a lot of responsibility and, like Rog before him, Johnny plays a massively selfless role in what we do. He encourages, criticizes and demands more from everyone on every play. He's hard on people, but it makes us so much better. At the end of training he was smashing into guys, trying to counter-ruck in a non-contact session. It is so encouraging when your out-half is on the edge like that. Everyone else can follow.

It's very rare I'd feel sure before a game that we were going to win – even rarer when it's against France. But I'm confident we will put in a performance.

Tuesday, 17 February 2015

I was playing international rugby for seven years before I was on a winning team against France, so any time we beat them feels great. We got the battle we expected and we put up a dogged performance against a really powerful side. We weren't pumping ourselves up to be incredibly physical – we weren't really pumping ourselves up at all. Guys just focused on their jobs, the tiny roles within those jobs. Along with Joe, that attitude is driven by our fitness coach, Jason Cowman. He's a mindfulness fan. You don't worry about what's going to happen – you just focus on what's happening now. It has taken hold fairly well within the squad.

We have England next. They've had some flaky characters in their team since they won the World Cup in 2003, but there are none now. Chris Robshaw is a really honest, hard-working captain, and they're a very good side. They're hungry, disciplined, all about physical aggression. They'll try to run over us, so we need to stop that and put it to bed early.

It will probably come down to who can be a more clever team. And I think we can.

I'm enjoying the build-up to the games at the moment, insofar as I can. The coaching staff's philosophy of focusing on the processes is a really enjoyable way to prepare. I'm putting down good training weeks, moment by moment. I'm not getting too distracted by thoughts of what the game might bring.

Friday, 6 March 2015

England were a good team playing badly. I was surprised by how much they struggled to deal with simple kicks. And some of the penalties they gave away were poor. So they gave us a leg up, but it was a great opportunity for them to learn and they'll be better for it. With our kicking game, you can't have players who aren't confident under a high ball, and they didn't handle it. Wales will be different.

We made some big psychological statements early on. I'd say they expected supremacy in the scrum, because it's only a couple of months since Joe Marler put Mike Ross under a lot of pressure, playing for Harlequins against Leinster. It must have been a shock to them, a blow to their psyche – but we'd worked hard on it. Rossy held his own and Rory Best is such a powerful scrummager. Jack McGrath is a great young prop and we had Cian Healy coming off the bench, incredibly hungry – so we were comfortable.

We prepared specifically for their props, Marler and Dan Cole. Greg Feek, our scrum coach, has been a real pleasure to work with and has turned scrummaging into one of the most enjoyable parts of the week. We scrummage little and often, with a big emphasis on technique and video feedback.

He has unlocked so many gems for our scrum through poring over the videos. For the first time in my career the scrums are the first thing I like to watch after training.

I was really disappointed at how I felt at the end. I was absolutely wrecked. For some reason I seem to have gone backwards rather than forward since the Australia game. We don't have a game this weekend, so I've allowed myself to feel the bumps and the bruises and the tiredness. I couldn't imagine playing tomorrow or Sunday, but that's mostly psychological: if we had a game, I wouldn't let myself think that. It's not a conscious decision, it just happens. You start convincing yourself early in the week that you're fine, that you just need to do a couple of things during the week and you'll be good for the weekend. It's nice to let myself believe I'm tired.

Monday, 16 March 2015

When I was trying to relax on Friday, before the Wales game, a load of text messages were coming through on my phone, congratulating me on my hundredth Ireland cap. I was getting them all week and trying to reply to as many as I could. I was delighted to make the number, but it would have been better if nobody had known about it, and people hadn't been writing about me all week. That way, I could have taken a little quiet satisfaction out of it on my own. It's great to be one of those guys with a hundred caps, but in the context of the week and the championship it was irrelevant to me.

We had plenty of opportunities to beat Wales, but we didn't take them. There was no desolation in our dressing room afterwards, probably because we still have a chance at the championship and we know where we went wrong. We were really, really disappointed – but we move on.

364

We were 12–0 down very quickly. Wayne Barnes was tough on us. He said to me early on: 'Players cannot fall on the wrong side of the ruck.'

I said: 'What if they roll away really quickly and get back on the right side?'

He told me it was going to be a penalty regardless and so I passed that on to the team:

'He's being very strict on this. Keep the faith – because if we have the ball, we'll get the same penalties.' Then, after about twenty minutes, he just changed how he was reffing it. We created problems for ourselves and can't blame everything on the man in the middle, but it was very disappointing.

I had a good game in most of the visible things, but the turnover around the halfway line that led up to their try in the second half was my fault. The ball was free and I went to secure it, but Alun-Wyn Jones got in ahead of me and blew me off it.

We lost a five-metre exit lineout, and we also lost a five-metre drive-to-score lineout. We've been really good from close range in recent years, but Sam Warburton got up in the air and stole the ball. Five metres from their line, you need to be winning your lineout. Even if you win the ball in a crap position and fall in a heap on the ground, you have possession on their line. The bottom line is, it was my call and we lost it. We scored from a drive later on but it's still bugging me, four days later.

I know people have been saying I played well, but my part in the turnovers that led to their try and gave them momentum will be with me for the rest of the week. It's not that I'm giving myself a really hard time, but it's just gnawing away at me a little bit. I'd rather have taken those moments out of my game, and not made any line breaks, because they affected the outcome a lot more than the good things I did.

We have to rate the games for exertion, an assessment of how much they took out of us, and I have given the last two ten out of ten. I was so wrecked at the end of the Wales game it was unbelievable. It wasn't worse than the England game, though, so at least I feel like I'm getting better.

Wednesday, 18 March 2015

I looked at the Welsh game on my laptop again today, and for most of it I was thinking, *This is actually a really good performance.* Joe's meeting was tough, which I expected, but when I spoke to him about it yesterday he told me the game had given him more belief than he'd had before.

He said: 'I hope we will never go 12–0 down on the back of our own silly errors in a big game again. But what we did after that was pretty special.'

So that made me feel really good about Saturday at Murrayfield.

Friday, 27 March 2015

In Edinburgh, at the Balmoral Hotel on Princes Street, I had room 360 to myself. My bag stayed on the floor in the middle – I'm not particularly tidy, but I'm not untidy either.

The championship was likely to come down to points difference between ourselves, England and Wales. We had a number in our heads – we thought a fifteen-point win could be good enough for us – but I'm old-fashioned and I didn't want to get too hung up on the margins. On the Friday night, at the captain's run in Murrayfield, I told the forwards that if we wanted to rack up a score we'd have to take Scotland to a place they'd never been before, fitness-wise. To do that, we needed to produce our fittest game in an Irish jersey.

Before I spoke, I had a quick chat with Jamie Heaslip. He said: 'Discipline is going to be massive – it wasn't good last week. I've looked at my penalty a load of times – I can't be lying flat on my back tomorrow.'

Hearing that helped, because when a senior player is putting his hand up it makes it easier to make the same point to the less experienced guys. Four forwards gave away the penalties that put us 12–0 down.

I'd given away the first penalty myself, and it's still bugging me. That helped me make my point, when we huddled up, about being diligent and accurate against Scotland: 'When I make a tackle, I won't fall on the wrong side. Pete, you can't put your elbows on the ground when you're poaching. Jamie, you can't lie on your back when you're placing the ball. And, Jack, you can't fall on the wrong side either.'

On the morning of the game I felt very relaxed. My work was done early in the week. I was able to switch off. I was getting into a good place for these big games.

I've always got a notebook at the coaches' meetings. I'll write down a lot of the phrases they come out with. I've heard all the buzzwords before, but I still circle them and put an asterisk alongside them. Before I speak to the players myself, I pull out the notebook and look at the things I've underlined or circled, so that I can hammer them home in the dressing room and give the lads relevant information, instead of talking off the top of my head.

Nobody else spoke at Joe's meeting – the players knew our preparation had been good and there was nothing more to say.

I was looking forward to the creamed rice at the Balmoral, because it's been beautiful there before, but it was burnt. All

I could force in was pasta and a little bit of potato, so I felt hungry, walking back to my room. Emily and Paddy were there when I walked in – Lola is at home, being spoilt by Emily's parents, Pat and Keave. Paddy was in flying form, running around the room. When it was time for them to go, he said, 'Best of luck,' which I'm sure Emily coached him to come out with.

I always have a long, hot shower before I leave the room. In the past I've spent that time dreading the game, or going over my lineouts, or thinking about nothing at all, depending on where my head was at the time. On Saturday, as the water hit me, I was thinking about three rucks where I didn't do my job right against Wales and I was editing them in my head, fixing them, visualizing myself doing them exactly right.

I don't listen to music on the team bus. There was a time when I did, but it was just a phase, like almost everything else about my preparation over the years. I sit at the back, in the middle, where I can stretch my legs. There was a little bit of banter, nothing much, because the guys who are quiet on the bus need that preparation time. I was that way myself for most of my career. By then you're almost cramming for an exam, thinking about what you have to do, and telling yourself you're going to do it. Sometimes, before the biggest games, you think about your family and what it will mean to them if you win or lose.

The sun was high in the sky when I walked on to the field to check the wind before the coin toss. It was blowing a little, from left to right, and I wanted to play into it for the first half, with the sun on our backs. Greig Laidlaw won the toss but took the kick-off, so it worked out well. After the warm-up, Joe and Jamie spoke in the dressing room. We knew then that Wales had hammered Italy by forty-one points, so we needed to beat Scotland by at least twenty-one and then hope England didn't pass us on points difference later, against France.

'It doesn't change anything we do,' Joe said. 'We still try to break these guys down the same way and win the game the same way.'

Then we were into it.

In the fifth minute, I scored my first try for Ireland in almost nine years. We were hammering at their line and I forced myself to stay out of a few rucks. It's a part of my game I'd been examining over the last few months, because I'd been going to too many and not having enough impact. I knew I needed to be more effective when I was required, be it to carry or to shift bodies, so that was running through my mind early in the game as we went at them. I glanced at one or two and stayed back from them, and then suddenly the ball was sitting up right in front of me, three metres short. I only put it down on the line for a millisecond, but I knew I'd scored.

The second try, from Seanie, came from a lineout that Gert Smal gave us a while back. After that I was fairly confident that we'd get the points we needed if we didn't try to force it.

We were pretty muted when the whistle went – we'd set England a good target but we knew they were capable of opening up. England needed to win by twenty-six points to deny us the championship. I was watching the game with Devin Toner and Rob Kearney, and when France went 15–7 up I thought, *This is done and dusted.* Then the nightmare started unfolding. France were playing suicide rugby and at one stage I convinced myself it was gone, but when the whistle finally went England were six points short.

For a few seconds, I didn't feel anything. It was such a strange way to win it. I looked around and all the lads were hugging one another and high-fiving. There was eighties music playing when we went back down the tunnel to get the trophy and our supporters were lighting the place up with their mobile phones. It was my second time lifting the championship trophy as captain, and I felt a great sense of pride that we'd won it back to back: the first time Ireland had done that since the late 1940s.

In the function room, I had four bottles of Beck's before I realized it was non-alcoholic.

I was looking forward to the two days ahead: Sunday with my teammates and our families, slagging and joking and telling each other how we loved each other by the end of the night; then Monday night on a barstool at O'Shea's pub in Limerick, with my brothers and Dad beside me, and a few of the lads, drinking a few pints of Guinness and having the craic.

On Sunday night in Dublin 4 I was at the bar in The Bridge, alongside Simon Easterby. We were chatting, we had

pints in front of us and I was thinking, *This is perfect now.* The rest of the lads were in a cordoned-off area upstairs, but I was happy where I was, drinking with someone of my own vintage.

After a couple of hours I started feeling hungry, but when I stepped outside there were no fast-food places open. A cab came along and I hailed it. The driver took me to a chipper in Camden Street, where there were three nurses in the queue, getting themselves a burger before going on to Copper Face Jacks.

I ordered two burgers myself, and garlic chips with cheese. I had thought the only place you could get them was the Chicken Hut in Limerick, but they were beautiful.

One of the nurses told me she was from Killarney. I said: 'Me and my wife like the Europe Hotel. It's one of the nicest places I've ever stayed.'

'Well,' she said, 'I wouldn't be a fan of it myself, now.'

I asked her why. I was ready to take her on.

'Killarney has the best B&Bs in the country,' she said. 'If I was visiting, I'd be trying to find myself a nice cosy place, where the owner looks after you like a friend.'

'That's actually a good point,' I said, and then they headed off to Coppers.

When I got back to Limerick, at lunchtime on Monday, I was able to relax and enjoy it more. The way I see it, there are three teams coming out of the Six Nations feeling very good about themselves before the World Cup: Ireland, Wales and England. Maybe England will feel it most, because they know they were a few metres from winning it and they've definitely got more in them. Their second half against Wales and their game against France were big performances.

We're in a great place too, but we have to be very careful. We can't afford to get ahead of ourselves. And we can't afford to lose any of our best players to injuries.

I was beginning to lose the faith over my fitness, but over the past few weeks things have started coming together for me. For at least a year I felt like I wasn't getting the returns for the work I was putting in, but I'm definitely playing better now and the body feels good.

It's amazing how up-and-down sport is. Two months ago, on the plane coming back from the Saracens game, I was trying to figure out how I could retire before the World Cup. Today I heard that I've been voted Six Nations Player of the Tournament. It's all so fickle, professional sport. If France had conceded a try late on, I wouldn't be getting anything like the praise that I've had this week, and yet I'd have done nothing differently.

Earlier on Sunday, in the giddiness of it all, I started thinking I had it in me to carry on for another while in France. I even asked Eanna Falvey, our doctor, who probably knows my body better than anyone: 'Physically, do you think I could do it?'

'A hundred per cent,' he told me.

Then Diego Domínguez rang me during the week and said: 'I understand that you are trying to make a decision. But I just wanted to make sure you know that we would really love to have you.'

I'm friendly with Toulon's S&C guy, Paul Stridgeon, from the Lions, and I know he'd be great to work with. When you're going on thirty-six, having someone in the set-up who understands what your body needs is a massive plus.

I told Diego I still wasn't sure and that if he needed to get his recruitment done, he should get on and do it, because I'm not going to rush into anything.

'We will wait for you,' he said.

So we'll see.

24

There's a scene in Andre Agassi's book, *Open*, that has stuck
with me. He was hobbling through a hotel lobby, a day after
beating Marcos Baghdatis in five sets at the US Open. He
was thirty-six and he'd been playing pro tennis for twenty
years. His back was banjaxed. He needed cortisone shots
to keep going. His father – who had been obsessed with
making him the world's best tennis player since he was a
small child – appeared from out of nowhere and grabbed
his arm.

'Quit,' he said. 'Just quit. Go home. You did it. It's over.'

I was with Dad yesterday and I thought of that passage on
the way home in the car. He was nothing like Agassi's father
when I was young, but we've been on my sporting journey
together since I was six. I think he'd be very happy if I retired

after the World Cup, but he won't say it. If I play on in France, I know he'll support my decision. He'll come to as many of my games as he possibly can, with Mam, and they'll probably say a few prayers that nothing bad happens to me.

I've only played once since the Six Nations, at Edinburgh two weeks ago. It was a poor enough game and I didn't play particularly well. It was really wet, and when we mauled them early in the first half it was like a knife going through butter. Straight away I was thinking, *We're just going to hammer this all night.*

We had thirteen lineouts and we drove eleven of them. We were quite poor when we played but we gave away very few penalties and we mauled them to death. We scored five tries and three came from mauls.

At one stage we mauled them and won a penalty. There was no advantage so we kicked it down the field and mauled them again off the lineout. The ref gave us another penalty, but this time he played advantage. We did nothing with it, so when he went back for the penalty we kicked it into the corner and mauled them over the line. Beautiful rugby!

For me, that should go down as try of the season for us. We were out there looking for the best and easiest way to win the game. And we found it.

Probably more than any other part of the game, mauling is a big team effort. Someone can play the most important role without being visible or touching the ball. I might have hatched the plan myself or, if Axel has come up with something, me and one or two of the lads will drive the detail. The challenge is trying to make players' roles easy to follow and execute. If the detail takes up too much brain space, the chances of us executing it with the aggression required are slim.

Mauling is old school, but ever since my Young Munster

days it's been a part of the game I love. If someone does something wrong in training, the guys driving the plan have to correct them and stay on top of them. And really, I don't want to do that. I don't want to have to tell a player three times in a row that he hasn't got it right, but that's my job. I'll annoy people – I'm sure sometimes I'll even annoy the coaches – because I won't let a guy do it wrong.

My satisfaction comes when it works out in the game, and we deliver on all of the detail that I might have had to clash with someone over during the week.

Monday, 11 May 2015

I think I will go to France. There's nothing agreed with Toulon, but I've a good idea of what they'll be offering. It's good money, not massive by any means, but the decision has never been about that.

I've found it unbelievably difficult, trying to decide. Even though I was leaning towards it after the Six Nations, my head was full of doubts and questions.

Would I be ruining my reputation if it didn't work out?

What if the way I played in the Six Nations was a flash in the pan?

What if I go there and they decide I'm not big enough?

Imagine if they didn't pick me.

What if they didn't have enough second-rows – and I got wheeled out every week?

What if Paddy doesn't settle?

Are we wrong to be taking him away from everything he knows?

I've told Toulon I'm not going to do anything until Munster's season is over, because it's too close to the run-in now. We have a chance of winning the Pro 12 and it wouldn't feel right to do anything until June. I don't want to mess up my relationship with Munster. Once I decided that and they agreed to wait, I had peace of mind.

Axel and the other Munster coaches have known for a while that I won't be playing next year. There's a part of me that feels guilty about that, because it has been a tough enough first year for them – even though things have started coming together over the last couple of months.

Joe wanted me to see out the last year of my IRFU contract and go for three Six Nations titles in a row. He was adamant that he wanted me to keep going and it's a great goal to have – will Ireland ever get a chance to do something like that again? But my mind was made up on international retirement a good while ago and I've been very at ease with the decision. He was pretty disappointed when I told him, which was a great compliment to get.

Wednesday, 27 May 2015

Yesterday, an elderly lady came to training and gave me a watch, the kind you put in a waistcoat pocket. She said she was from Thomondgate, which is literally a stone's throw from Thomond Park. She had got the watch engraved: *Thanks for the memories.* It was an incredibly nice moment and I couldn't have been more touched.

I played my last home game for Munster on Saturday, against Ospreys in the Pro 12 semi-final. I didn't make any announcement about it – I didn't even tell the lads. A couple of them knew, but mostly I kept it to myself. I didn't want a load of texts coming through. I wanted to enjoy it in my own way, to have that nice feeling you get when you're alone with a good book in a coffee shop and the world is going on around you. I wanted to be able to look back on a normal week, so that the memory of it was my own version of events, not other people's.

I didn't do a whole lot on Monday as I was quite sore from the weekend's game. I missed weights and did them on my own in the gym on Tuesday afternoon after rugby. I was hoping I'd have the place to myself, and I did. I put some music on and reflected a little. It was just nice to be working hard in a Munster environment, having a few moments to myself, knowing what was coming.

I told Earlsy on the Thursday morning before the game. We were heading to Cork together for training. The conversation lasted no more than a couple of minutes, and then we switched the radio on. I'm a Newstalk man, he's more Spin South West. When you're very comfortable in somebody's company, as I am with Earlsy, you often don't need to talk. We must have listened for forty-five minutes without saying a single word.

After training, we gave Dave Kilcoyne a lift home and it was like having a journalist in the back seat, armed with a notebook full of questions.

He's some character, Killer. We also call him Mr Desmond Cash. As with most nicknames, I haven't a clue where it comes from.

Because I'd let Earlsy know earlier in the day, I told Killer it was going to be my last home game. Later that night I called Peter O'Mahony, but they were the only three I said it to.

In the car, Killer was joking about trying to change my mind.

'Ah, you can't do it, Big Red!'

'One more year, Rouge! Come on!'

Then came the questions, literally non-stop all the way back to Limerick. I couldn't stop laughing, because apart from the fact that Killer is hilarious it was such a contrast to the silent journey down.

'What's the most important thing to have as a rugby player?'

'In my position, probably fitness.'

'Are you fitter now than when you were twenty-five?'

'No.'

'Surely you are.'

'I'm trying to be – but I don't think I'm going to get there.'

'Why not?'

'Because I'm old! And I've had a lot of injuries.'

'Have you always had an agent?'

'No.'

'What did you do when you didn't?'

'I didn't really need one when I was starting out.'

For an hour and a half, he never ran out of steam.

'Who's the best S&C coach you ever had?'

'Who were the fittest forwards you ever played against?'

'What are your plans for the future?'

'Where'd you get those sunglasses? I must get a pair for the holidays.'

'I must show you the job I did on my back garden, Paulie – it's like Marbella out there.'

When we got back to Limerick, I went to our gym at UL again. I thought I'd have the place to myself but when I walked in I was delighted to see Duncan Casey, J. J. Hanrahan and Ronan O'Mahony doing some sneaky extras. Their work ethic made me feel good.

The Ospreys game was close, 21–18, but we made the final. The three tries we scored were absolutely top-drawer. It was the best we've played all year, except for about seven bad errors which nearly let them back in. But I was so happy at the end – it was the best feeling I've had with Munster since the Harlequins game two years ago. I'd hate to imagine what losing would have felt like, because it was bad enough thinking – for a minute – that we'd lost it. They went over our line right at the end, but Nigel Owens thought he saw a knock-on and he called for the video. It was good refereeing – a lot of them wouldn't have been as sharp.

When we walked towards the middle of the field to applaud the crowd, I could sense the lads were pulling back, but I still gave a bit of a wave. I wasn't thinking, *This is it. This is goodbye.* I don't know if the supporters were thinking it, when they saw me do that. I suppose a lot were, but in that moment it was all about the win for me, and thanking them for getting behind us during the season.

Every now and then, over the last few years, I imagined what it would be like to play my last game at Thomond Park. I never wanted any fanfare over it, but I thought it would be nice to be taken off with a couple of minutes left, with the crowd knowing it was the last time for me. I'd give them a wave, they'd give me a clap. That was all I wanted it to be, but for that to happen you have to put up with so much hassle during the week, and in the end I was happy with how it worked out and that week will be a great, simple memory for me.

The stadium wasn't as full as it would have been a few years ago, but there was still a good crowd. If Munster had publicized it as my last game, it would have been a different week for me. It was a semi-final and we got the crowd we got. They were genuine Munster fans. They were going to be there whether it was my last game or not.

Walking back towards the tunnel, I was conscious of keeping my emotions in check. I knew if I started thinking about it being my last time wearing the jersey on home ground, I could have ended up in tears in front of thousands of people.

It only really hit me when I saw the lads were giving me a guard of honour. It was becoming real then; it wasn't my little secret any more. I could hear the supporters shouting my name as I walked under the stand, but I didn't look up because I was starting to lose it.

Some of the lads not in the twenty-three were in the dressing room when I walked in. I high-fived a few of them and sat in my place, under number five. I don't have any particular feelings of sentimentality towards our dressing room, I suppose because I've changed in so many places with Munster over the years. The old dressing room at Thomond Park was less fancy and there wasn't room for the subs to get changed there, but as a physical space I don't think it will stand out any more or any less in my memory. What I'll remember is being within the same four walls as the friends I made at Munster, especially on the best days, when we were the only ones who really understood what it had taken for us to win.

Usually, when I walk back into the dressing room after we've won, we will have the craic and feed off the buzz that winning gives us. On Saturday, the lads who were there must have seen that I needed a minute to myself. I started taking my jersey off straight away and when it was over my head the tears came. I wasn't thinking anything, sitting there, but I was feeling something. Sadness and happiness, I suppose, that it was over. I felt so privileged to have played here for so long.

I was fine by the time the rest of the lads came in. I threw my jersey into the middle and then we formed a circle to sing our song, 'Stand Up and Fight', as we always do after a big win. They called me into the centre of the circle to start us off, and I knew there was no point in arguing with the mob.

After a few seconds, I went back to where I'd been standing. I loved getting that feeling again, of being surrounded by friends, knowing that we had delivered.

Thursday, 30 July 2015

The Pro 12 final, against Glasgow, was the biggest disappointment of my Munster career. There aren't many games I'd like to have back, because time heals and you move on, but I wish I could play that one again. I'd love to be back on the field, just before it started, so that I could empty the tank in the first five minutes and set myself up for a big game.

Glasgow played well and we didn't perform. We just didn't have it. I didn't do a lot myself, I didn't step up – which still bugs me, two months later. When we won Heineken Cups, we had a full team out every time. We were very lucky from an injury point of view. For that final, three of our best players were missing – Peter O'Mahony, Tommy O'Donnell and Conor Murray. They were a massive loss, because each of them brings a huge amount to our game.

I felt very low after it – I didn't want to talk about it to anyone. It was the same feeling of despondency I had after the 2005 Lions tour, only worse, because it took longer to shake off. It would have been easier to deal with it if I could have trained really hard the following week, and had another game to play at the end of it. Knowing that I'd never play again for Munster – and that I'd gone out on such a low

note – was really, really tough to take. The worst of it was the lack of intensity we'd shown, and I blamed myself for not setting a better example.

I went on holiday with Emily and the kids, a cruise, but I wasn't myself for those two weeks. I'd always wanted to go on a cruise, but the food wasn't great and the gym wasn't up to much either, so I couldn't really get the frustration out of my system like I'd done before. While on holiday we'd been on our laptops, looking for nice places to live in Toulon, close to the sea, but even that didn't excite me. When we got home, I reconciled myself to it and moved on. I know I will look back at some brilliant memories, and whatever frustration I experienced along the way will fade to nothing.

I don't think I was fooling myself that we had it in us to win trophies these last few years. We just needed to be better at everything we could control. We definitely improved as the season went on. We were first or second in the league for the fewest penalties given away, but we needed to be first by a long way, and first in the other things that win games.

I'd like to think there have been players on our team who have benefited from me caring about them and staying on top of them. I didn't always do it in the right way, but I always thought it was in their best interests, as well as the team's. Whatever I did, I did it for the right reasons.

I hope I gave a good example to the younger lads of what's required. The beauty of team sport is that if we want to stand on the podium to lift the trophy, we have to help other people. And we need to care about them. It's the only way to be successful in a team environment, unless you've got the money to sign the very best players in the world.

Being much older than most of the guys in the team was such a different experience to the way I started out, but I loved it. I cared about those players. The enjoyment I got from spending time with them, training with them and playing with them was special.

I'd love to see them lifting a trophy and shaking off the burden of trying to follow past Munster teams. To be in the stand with Paddy, watching them win something big and creating something of their own, would give me every bit as much satisfaction as if I was down on the pitch myself.

25

Tuesday, 15 September 2015

We leave at four o'clock tomorrow for England and the World Cup. Things are good. The results in our last two warm-up games were disappointing, but we'll be better for them. We were missing tackles and making poor defensive decisions. We gave away fifteen penalties against Wales – and we never give teams that kind of access into games. We just can't take for granted all the things we've been good at, or forget how hard we had to work at them to reach that standard in the first place.

One of the reasons we won the championship two years in a row is that we don't give away stupid penalties. The work of our ball carriers on the ground and our rucking is a massive part of our game. So a big part of my job during the tournament will be to help make sure that everyone turns up in the games with the behaviours that look after the strengths in our game.

It can be very technical in our training camp, and we needed those matches to bring us back to reality. The coaches need games: they give them something to go after, and that's when our improvement rockets. Joe wants us to see the problems before they unfold. He says you can't solve a problem while it's happening right in front of you, so you solve it before it happens. He's trying to sharpen our brains all the time.

So I'm not worried. I'd like us to have been better, but we had nearly fifty guys in camp at different stages, and now that it's a smaller group I'm fairly sure things will be corrected.

Joe has been relaxed enough about the mistakes. I'm sure they've frustrated him, but he hasn't shown it. He's putting a big emphasis on discipline and the particular rules he thinks refs will be going after.

Success for us would be playing to our potential. I'd like to make the semi-final, and see what happens from there. Having said that, I'd be devastated if we made the semi-final and played poorly in it.

The preparation has been different from the last World Cup. We haven't trained as hard. That's wrong, actually – it's more that we haven't trained as *long*. It's been about training with intensity for shorter periods.

We've been doing some excellent sessions that have challenged our fitness in exiting from our own 22. When I can barely breathe, I've got to sprint across the pitch and try to win a five-metre lineout, then execute a whole other play. There's a lot of trust in Jason Cowman's input into our conditioning, so I feel very relaxed. The next-job, moment-by-moment mentality helps, too.

I played sixty-six minutes in the last warm-up game, against England, and found the first half really hard. In the second half, I felt a lot stronger. I'd love to have stayed on the pitch, because I'd have a better idea of where I am physically.

At Twickenham, Donnacha Ryan recorded a speed score of 8.75 metres per second. I have gone better than him over longer distances this pre-season, but my fastest speed in the game was seven metres per second. That meant he was 25 per cent faster and more explosive over a short distance. Often, in rugby, you've only got a split second to generate speed and power. A ruck unfolds in front of your face or under your feet and you've got to hit it hard and fast.

The difference between us might have been a little exaggerated, because Donnacha got a chance to really open up and sprint hard, and I didn't. But it made me wish I had that gas, and I wondered what kind of impact I might have on a game if I was travelling at 8.75 metres per second. Ten years ago, before we all had GPS devices in our jerseys, was I as fast as that? I wish I knew!

When you see another second-row putting up a stat like that, it brings you closer to your own sporting mortality. I was never especially fast, but when I was younger I was faster than most second-rows. Now I'm probably average at best. I looked at Iain Henderson's scores too – he has real gas.

Monday, 21 September 2015

We're staying at St George's Park in Staffordshire, the home of English football. It's an amazing facility and everything about it is great, apart from the photograph of Peter Shilton above my bed in the room me and Earlsy are sharing.

We played our first game of the tournament on Saturday, against Canada. I'm not sure where we stand after it, because they didn't put us under much pressure, but we were happy enough with how it went. It was a hard game, fitness-wise, because the ball was in play a lot. But that will only help us later on. I finished the game strongly and really feel I could be on the cusp of some good form. Midweek, I'm having a lot of ups and downs in terms of how I feel, physically. Some days my back is achy and I feel incredibly old; others, it's like I'm in my twenties again.

Friday, 25 September 2015

I brought some books with me, but I've sent them all home. I was reading Matt Cooper's biography of Tony O'Reilly, but it wasn't performing the function I needed it to at a World Cup. I need a book that switches off my brain, so I got the Tube in to Covent Garden in London today, spent a nice day on my own and bought *The Fist of God*, by Frederick Forsyth.

Wednesday, 30 September 2015

We play Italy on Saturday, and we need to put in a proper performance. I'm a little bit concerned that we haven't produced one since the end of the Six Nations.

I've set myself a goal for the game – four impacts, whether that's strong carries or big tackles. They may not be blatant standout moments to the guy watching on TV, but I'll know if I've made them or not.

I've got a notebook here that I started writing in years ago, after I began doing visualization with Caroline Currid. I read it over today and tried to see myself cleaning out rucks and getting off the defensive line hard and fast. I finally feel like I'm in the kind of shape where I can focus on playing well – and not on getting into the physical condition to play well.

Thursday, 8 October 2015

Last week, against Italy, was a solid game for me. I carried hard and straight, I did a lot of things really well. I had three impacts – one short of what I wanted. A big stat these days is high-speed metres. I might cover between five and seven kilometres in a game, but most of that won't be at a serious pace. On Sunday I think I was the only forward who covered more than one kilometre at high speed. It's rare that I top that stat, so it has given me a good buzz. I felt very good in the game and it was nice to have that confirmed after it, to get some evidence backing up the positive feeling I had about how I'd played and felt on the pitch.

We still haven't performed to our potential, or anything close to it, but we have a lot of guys who I think are ready to play well now. This weekend, I expect massive physicality from France. I expect them to be more disciplined than they've been. They gave us a serious leg-up when we beat them in the last two Six Nations, and I don't think that will happen again unless we put them under serious pressure. They prepare a lot better for World Cups, as it's the only time that they really get to spend a long block together, and I think they will be a far better team than we've played in the last two years. That means we'll have to be better ourselves – more accurate with the ball and more disciplined.

Against Italy, there were too many errors again, penalties we shouldn't have conceded, fourteen dropped balls. But on

Tuesday we trained with our best intensity in months and I'm beginning to feel good.

At this stage we need to own what we are doing. We can't expect to be spoonfed by Joe and the coaches. If we're doing things to stay on the right side of the staff, we're doing them for the wrong reasons. We need to have a deep understanding of the direction we're being given. Then we can put it into play because we know it and own it. That is coming. I can feel it.

We spoke about setting the physical tone and forcing France to respond. It can't be the other way round. We have to add the Irish passion and emotion to our technical and tactical knowledge. Sometimes it can be hard to balance one with the other. Too much emotion, and the technical side can suffer, and vice versa.

I felt we were in a great place to strike the balance. Johnny spoke about getting off the line. It's great when someone who has so many other roles to concentrate on is pushing that physical side of the game. It's an indication that the technical preparations are done. Now we need to get ready physically. When Johnny speaks, people listen. In many ways, he makes us a better team than we are.

Today, we trained hard again. We trained well. So I think we'll be ready.

Thursday, 15 October 2015, 3.30 p.m.

I'm getting the operation on my hamstring at half-six, and the nurse is coming around again in a while to shave the back of my leg, which should be interesting. I've just filled in the form asking what I want to eat later, after the surgery. I ticked a chicken salad sandwich, with ice cream. I don't think

I'm going to be able to eat that, though. I just want toast, with butter and jam – toast is nice after an operation – but it's not listed on the form. I'm not even going to bother arguing or discussing it with them. I'll just tell them I'd like toast when I wake up.

When I was in the medical room with Peter, watching the second half of the France game – seeing us pulling away from them – I wasn't thinking about my tournament being over. I haven't felt any emotion about the end of my Ireland career. Not yet, anyway. I've been injured enough times to have learned that you've got no choice but to accept your fate.

Earlsy has been looking after me; dressing me in the morning, getting my food, putting me to bed. It's been a bit of craic and I'm glad I'm spending my last few days in the Ireland camp rooming with him.

I'm not sure what's going to happen now – after this, I mean. I'll be thirty-six in five days' time. A big part of me is saying that I've had nearly fifteen years of being a rugby player and that it's enough. But I just haven't figured it out yet, I haven't decided how to handle it. I'm trying to let it come to me, rather than go looking for the answers. So I'll wait to see what the surgeon says tomorrow. I'll know more then. All I know now is that I've got a tendon that's ripped off the bone. I'm not aware of what the technical term for that is. I'm sure I'll hear it.

I don't really know how long the injury will keep me out for, or whether I'll be able to come back at all. People are telling me it could be four months, six months, eight months – it all depends. I'm down about it, but there's nothing I can do. It is what it is. It's life.

If I decide to play on, I know it's going to be very difficult, another mental battle. The prospect of rehabbing it at home, and having to answer the same questions every day, is pretty bleak. But I don't think it will be any easier if I do the rehab in Toulon. It will be hard to settle there, knowing that I'm being well paid for contributing nothing. So I just don't know, at the moment.

I was beginning to think that I could play really well down there. When you're confident and fit, eventually you hit a game where people keep running at you and the ball is always coming your way. You're so fit that you're there for every opportunity. And I just felt one of those games was around the corner for me. If it wasn't going to happen in the World Cup, I thought it might come with Toulon. I really felt I had finally got there, just about, and that it was only a matter of time before I proved it, out on the pitch. And now I'll never get to find out whether I'd won the battle or not.

But maybe half of it was being there in the first place.

Monday, 26 October 2015

The injury is called a complete hamstring avulsion – and I got the toast. I was lying on my side in the bed and I was able to butter it and put the jam on myself. Then I fell asleep again and when I woke up they told me the operation had been a success. The doctor asked if I had any questions, but I wasn't in the form for asking them. Normally, I'd plague him for detail, get a comeback date in my head and have a fixture list in front of me before he left the room. I didn't know what I wanted to do, retire or carry on, and any more questions depended on the answer to that one.

I got back into camp later that day. The lads were preparing for the quarter-final against Argentina, but I was far from the only guy who was going to be missing. In the end, we took the field without Johnny, Peter, Jared, Seanie and myself. All of us were big into driving the team in terms of line speed, and we didn't have enough of it on the day.

Argentina played out of their skins, but against Australia in the semi-final they were stopped by a really hard defence, and it made me think that a performance as good as the one we'd produced against France would have been enough to get us home. But that was just pointless speculation then, and now.

Since we got home, last week, I've been able to take the positive out of it. I finished with Munster in a final, albeit on a poor performance. My last game for Ireland was a great performance against France, even if the best of it came after I'd been carried off! Very few players ride off into the sunset with a trophy and at least I know I was giving it everything. I went down trying to be as good as I could be every day and that's enough for my peace of mind.

Sometimes, in the past, doing my best wasn't enough for me. I felt I needed to do more than my best, which isn't possible. I wish it hadn't taken me until almost the end of my career to realize that what matters is giving your best to the moment that you're in. I finally got to a point where I could walk in after a day's work and say to myself: *I can't get any better at rugby tonight – I can stop thinking about it.*

It's only when I look back on the second half of my career – the years of trying to get fit after injuries, of trying to figure a whole load of things out – that I can see it wasn't all about rugby for me. During those years I learned a lot about myself, about preparation, about what high performance actually is, about looking forward and not back, and being able to see different points of view. It took longer than it should have, but I've become better at giving myself a break.

Over the past week, I've had some internal conversations about whether I should retire. I don't feel frustrated any more about losing so much time to injuries, so I know I could walk away now without feeling any regret. The truth is I could have done that before the World Cup.

Whether I play on is not a decision that's based on an evaluation of the pros and cons, like a normal big choice in life. The yes and no of it lies within my head and my body. I find it hard to put my finger on the logic behind the answer, so it has come down to what I suppose is gut instinct. A large part of me is sick of coming back from injury. I really don't know how much I fancy that battle again.

At the same time, something at the back of my mind keeps telling me that if I don't at least try to have the experience in France with Emily, Paddy and Lola, I'll always regret it.

When I started answering my own questions –

Have I not done enough?

Why put myself through another long rehab?

What if I don't get back to 100 per cent?

– I felt I did have enough done in my career to be happy with it. I decided that even if I only get back 90 per cent of the fitness I had in the first half against France, I can live with that. As long as I'm giving 100 per cent during the week and in the games, it will be enough. I can just enjoy the rugby and the new experience for my family, happy that I'm doing my best.

Epilogue

Towards the end of January, while out to dinner with Emily, I said it to her: 'I don't think I'm going to get back.'

I'd been thinking it for a couple of weeks, but until I acted on those thoughts they weren't real. I fought them off, until that night. But once the words were out of my mouth, it was done.

I worked hard to rehab the hamstring, but I never got the feeling that it was coming right. Sometimes it felt a little better in the mornings, but often it was the same. After almost four months I still wasn't close to being back to running, and I had to face up to the fact that it was one injury too many. Down the line I'll be fine to play five-a-side soccer with friends, but high-end professional rugby is different.

When I told Dad I was retiring, he said he was disappointed for me, but I sensed that he was mostly relieved, even happy.

'Have you told Toulon?' he asked.

'Not yet,' I said. 'I've only just decided.'

'I think you should go down there and tell them in person.'

He had said the same when I told him I wanted to give up swimming, more than twenty years ago.

It's eight months since the injury now and I feel fine – not perfect, because there are still some niggles now and then, but pretty good.

The idea of going to a gym and doing the same exercises

as everyone else, when I've spent years training hard for professional sport, doesn't really appeal right now. I'll find a solution, though. My body is still adjusting to life after rugby and I always knew it was going to need maintenance to keep the aches and pains at bay.

The thing about a career in team sport is that you learn all these lessons – you become a better person, a better trainer, tactically and mentally on a different level to when you started in the game – but that all coincides with your body going the other way, until it gives in. I'm glad now that I called it when I did. Getting out then meant I left the game in good physical shape.

I first rehabbed the injury in Munster, where the lads were dealing with a whole new series of challenges. They were struggling and I didn't have any part to play in putting things right, so I had to stay disconnected and I found it awkward and difficult to be there. I imagine they felt the same way, seeing me around the place.

Watching some of those games, when things were going badly for the lads, I often felt stressed and nervous. I knew how desperate they were to be successful and how hard they were working to put it right. Sometimes it was like I was feeling their pressure in my own stomach. When you're out of it and things are bad, you can despair a little bit. I suppose that's what you do when you're a fan and the team isn't winning. And that's what I am now: a Munster fan.

Being around the place wasn't doing them, or me, any good so I took myself out of the Munster environment and rehabbed in Dublin. I found a very good physio, Enda King, and we put in four intensive weeks. Even though it didn't work out, I wish I'd met Enda when I was in my mid-twenties, because I think he'd have saved me from myself. At times, during my career, I'd be getting treated by a physio in one room, then walking out the door into the gym and probably doing the wrong things for my body. I have realized that strength development is also about injury prevention, bullet-proofing your body. It was another lesson that came too late.

I have a little trepidation about whether I'll find something that will give me anything like the fulfilment I've got from playing rugby. It's easy, as a player, to offer opinions on how it should be done. To actually put a plan in place and make it work is a thousand times harder. I'll be doing a little bit with the Munster academy in the new season. I have some knowledge that can be imparted fairly easily to a group of young players. After that, we'll see.

What I loved most about rugby was competing, and the pressure it put on people in so many different ways. I loved being part of a sport in which the out-half might touch the ball seventy times in a game and the tighthead never, but the prop could still be man of the match. I think I could grow to love any sport if it offered me a high level of competition, but I'm not sure there are any with the same values as rugby. Shaking hands after the game no matter what had happened, clapping each other off, beers in the dressing room and endless stories – the game has changed a lot, but those old-school traditions were precious to me and they continue.

Some of the friends I made during my time as a player are ones I might not have any contact with for two or three years at a time, but I don't need to be in touch with them often to know we earned each other's trust and have a relationship that will last a lifetime. So even though I might not talk to some of them very often, when I do meet them I'm almost giddy. Those friendships, more than any trophy, are the most important thing that came out of my career.

When I look back on my time as a player, I sometimes

think that I could have done more, but mostly I'm happy with it.

I made mistakes. I always trained and worked hard, but towards the end I realized I could have been more clever a lot earlier in how I went about it. I didn't always have the discipline the team needed from me and I could be difficult with coaches, but I was always trying to do the right thing.

People ask me if I miss the game. I wouldn't say I don't miss it, but I was ready to finish and I don't feel any void. I don't pine for the training ground or the big games. I don't look at the lads playing and think, 'I'd love to be there.' When I watched Ireland win in South Africa for the first time, I never felt any jealousy, because my time was done. I wasn't forced to retire at twenty-eight, like Felix Jones and Ian Dowling, Barry Murphy and Luke Fitzgerald. Things will always happen that remind me of how good it was to win with my team, but I enjoy looking to the future.

A few months after the 2009 Lions tour, I read a book by John Wooden, the American basketball coach. There was a line that resonated with me then, and I got a pen and underlined it.

> Success is peace of mind which is a direct result of self-satisfaction in knowing you made the effort to become the best of which you are capable.

I always had that somewhere at the back of my mind, but it took a long time for it to sink in. It took years.

Until relatively recently, if you'd asked me what success was, my answer would have been: 'Winning a trophy at the end of the year.' There was a time when I started every season for Munster thinking it would be a failure if we didn't finish it with the Heineken Cup in our hands. I loved it when we won things, and I'm very proud of my achievements with

every team I was part of; but eventually I started to appreciate that success is about more than medals.

I had my chance. I had my time. I did it as well as I could. I think I trained even harder when I finally realized that all you can ever do is your best at something. If you're trying hard to make your best better, and your team better, then that's success. And that's enough.

Acknowledgements

Paul O'Connell

Thanks to everyone who gave up their time in the production of this book. Thanks to Brendan and Michael of Penguin Ireland for their patience, help and guidance. Special thanks to Alan English for his effort, commitment and passion for the job. Sorry my body held out so long, Alan. Enjoy the golf!

Alan English

Spending so much time in Paul's company during the writing of this book was thoroughly enjoyable from start to finish. One of the most pleasing aspects of the process was that some of the best achievements in his career came near the end of it. Neither of us had imagined, when we made a start towards the end of 2009, that he would still be playing six years later.

There were times when injury threatened to force his retirement before it eventually took its toll, particularly the back injury that resulted in an operation – his second back surgery – on the last day of 2012. Because I had privileged access to him, I was very much aware of how big a challenge it was for him to battle his way back from that operation, at thirty-three, in time for Munster's Heineken Cup quarter-final against Harlequins. For that reason, his man-of-the-match performance, just over three months after the surgery, is my own favourite memory from his playing days. He was an inspiration that day, but I will remember it not so much for what he did on the pitch, but for what it took for him to be there in the first place.

He felt he didn't deserve to be singled out as the best individual in that game, when younger Munster players had stepped up in a big way, and I never once saw a man-of-the-match award in his house, or any kind of medal or jersey from his career. For me, and I'm sure many others, he often judged his own performances too harshly, but he always viewed them in the context of what he had brought to the team.

Many thanks, Paul, for trusting me to help tell your story. We got there in the end.

I'm grateful to the O'Connell family for their help and kindness along the way, particularly Paul's wife Emily, his parents Michael and Shelagh, and his brothers Justin and Marcus. Shelagh's brother, Bob Quilty, has amassed an extraordinary collection of scrapbooks detailing Paul's career, which I drew on in the early stages.

I've always enjoyed working with Michael McLoughlin and Brendan Barrington at Penguin Ireland, but never more so than during this book's long gestation period.

I'm grateful to my brother Tom and my good friend David Walsh for being great sounding boards along the way. Thanks also to my sister Sinead, who fought – and won – a battle of her own as this book was being completed.

Finding the time to write books when you've got a proper job to do as well would be impossible without a massively supportive family. Love and many thanks once again to Anne, Holly, Aisling and Jack, and to my parents, Tom and Anne.

Photography Credits

Photos not listed below are courtesy of the author.

Page vi: James Crombie/Inpho
Page 46: *Limerick Leader*
Page 49: *Limerick Leader*
Page 66: Billy Stickland/Inpho
Page 81: Inpho
Page 97: Billy Stickland/Inpho
Page 99: Billy Stickland/Inpho
Page 104: Patrick Bolger/Inpho
Page 116: Anthony Phelps/Inpho
Page 126: Morgan Treacy/Inpho
Page 131: Lorraine O'Sullivan/Inpho
Page 136: Billy Stickland/Inpho
Page 138: Dan Sheridan/Inpho
Page 143: Billy Stickland/Inpho
Page 158: Dan Sheridan/Inpho
Page 160: Morgan Treacy/Inpho
Page 172: Billy Stickland/Inpho
Page 174: James Crombie/Inpho
Page 179: Morgan Treacy/Inpho
Page 184: Billy Stickland/Inpho
Page 190: Dan Sheridan/Inpho
Page 198: Billy Stickland/Inpho
Page 228: Billy Stickland/Inpho
Page 245: Billy Stickland/Inpho
Page 248: Billy Stickland/Inpho

Index

The abbreviation POC stands for Paul O'Connell.

416